PAT BROWN, MBA

Financial Literacy For Pharmacists

"A Pharmacist's Guide to Budgeting, Investing, and Financial Freedom"

ABRAM 47 BROWN

First published by AbramBrorwn47 2025

First edition

ISBN: 978-1-967737-26-0

This book was professionally typeset on Reedsy.
Find out more at reedsy.com

Contents

Preface

Why This Book Exists – And Why You Deserve to Read It

You've spent years mastering your craft. Countless hours in labs and libraries. Endless rotations. Long nights. High-stakes exams. The white coat you wear didn't come easy—and it came at a cost. Financially, emotionally, and physically.

But here's the problem: for all the education pharmacists receive, financial literacy is rarely part of the curriculum. You were trained to counsel patients on complex therapies, to interpret lab results, to manage high-pressure clinical decisions—but not to manage your money with confidence.

That gap ends here.

This book was born out of a deep respect for what pharmacists do and a frustration with what they're not taught. Because I've seen too many brilliant, capable pharmacists silently struggle with money. I've met 27-year-olds buried under $180K in loans, unsure how to build a future. I've met 38-year-olds earning six figures but feeling like they're always behind. I've talked with 60-year-olds who've served their communities faithfully and still worry they can't retire.

This book is for all of them. And for you.

Financial Literacy For Pharmacists is not about cutting back on lattes or making you feel ashamed of what you didn't know. It's about showing you what's possible when you do know. It's about demystifying credit, debt, investing, insurance, taxes, and lifestyle design in a way that respects your intelligence, honors your hustle, and gives you a new kind of power—the kind that comes from understanding your options.

You won't find fluff here. You'll find strategy. Clarity. Real-life scenarios. No lectures. No judgment. Just a steady hand guiding you through the financial side of your career and your life.

You didn't go to school for all those years just to feel stuck. You went to build a better life—for yourself, your family, your future. This book is your permission slip to claim it.

Let's get to work.

—Pat Brown, MBA

Author of *Financial Literacy For Pharmacists*

How to Use This Book

Let's get something straight right off the bat.

This isn't a lecture.

It's not a CE module.

It's not a dry textbook written in financial jargon no one actually understands.

This book is a reference guide.

A resource.

A financial playbook for pharmacists—designed to meet you where you are.

You don't have to read it in order.

You don't have to finish it in one sitting.

You don't need a highlighter and a cup of coffee to make it "official."

You just need the willingness to flip to the chapter that feels most relevant right now.

This book was written for pharmacists who are smart, capable, and hardworking—

but were never taught how to manage money.

It's for the newly minted PharmD trying to figure out how to balance student loan payments with rent, groceries, and that first "real" paycheck.

It's for the mid-career hospital pharmacist making six figures...

but still wondering why there's never anything left at the end of the month.

It's for the couple in their 40s juggling college savings, aging parents, and a career that no longer feels as stable as it once did.

It's for the 60-year-old pharmacist ready to retire—

but unsure if they actually *can*.

Wherever you are in your career, this book was written with you in mind.

You Don't Have to Read It All at Once

Seriously.

Start with the table of contents.

Flip through.

Skim.

See what jumps out.

You might already have a budget in place—great.

Skip the budgeting chapter for now.

But maybe taxes are your weak spot.

Maybe you've got a question about disability insurance, investing, or how to talk to your spouse about money.

Start there.

This book is built to be picked up, put down, and returned to as needed.

It's not about memorizing formulas or turning you into a financial planner.

It's about giving you the tools to ask better questions, avoid expensive mistakes, and build the kind of life your degree was supposed to unlock.

Because here's the truth:

A PharmD doesn't come with a financial plan.

Nobody teaches you how to manage six-figure debt.

Nobody breaks down the difference between a 403(b) and a Roth IRA.

Nobody explains how taxes hit when you start a side hustle...

or what to look for when you're handed your first employment contract.

That's what this book is for.

To give you the clarity and confidence that your financial future is in your hands—

and that you're not alone in figuring it out.

Keep This Book Handy

Don't treat this like something to file away and forget.

Keep it in your office, your nightstand, or your work bag.

Use it like you would any other tool in your clinical kit.

Flip to it when:

You're comparing job offers

You're picking health insurance during open enrollment

You're debating whether to buy a home

You just realized your student loans aren't going away on their own

You want to know how much is *enough* for retirement

Use this book when you're feeling stuck.

Use it when you're ready to level up.

Use it when the financial noise feels too loud and you just want clarity.

Let This Book Grow With You

You might read one chapter now and another in six months.

You might highlight something that doesn't click until your next career move.

You might share a page with a coworker, a spouse, or your younger sibling headed to pharmacy school.

That's the goal.

This isn't a test—it's a toolkit.

It's not here to guilt you into saving more or spending less.

It's here to give you control.

Confidence.

Options.

Because you didn't go through all that schooling to feel stuck by money.

You deserve to thrive.

Not just in your career—but in your financial life.

So flip the page.

Jump around.

Come back later.

Read what you need, when you need it.

This is *your* financial literacy playbook.

Let's use it.

You ready?

Let's go.

About the Author

I'm Pat Brown. Before I ever became a financial advisor or author, I was an athlete. I played Division I football at the University of Kansas in the mid-to-late '90s and served as a team captain. After college, I had the privilege of continuing my athletic journey in the Canadian Football League, suiting up for the Calgary Stampeders.

That experience taught me about discipline, performance, pressure, and what it means to show up when it matters most. But it also revealed a painful truth—while I was physically and mentally prepared for competition, I was completely unprepared when it came to personal finance.

No one had ever taught me how money really works. I didn't know how to build credit, save for the future, protect my income, or make smart financial decisions. And once I realized how much I didn't know, I felt embarrassed. Embarrassed that I had a college degree but didn't understand the basics of taxes or investing. Embarrassed that financial education was something so many of us never got, especially those of us who came from communities where money wasn't discussed around the dinner table.

That realization lit a fire in me.

I went back to school, earned my MBA, and became a licensed financial advisor. Over the last two decades, I've made it my mission to bridge the gap between professional success and personal financial understanding. Today, I work with individuals, families, and professionals across the country—including doctors, attorneys, student-athletes, educators, and yes, pharmacists—helping them build financial plans that match their goals and protect their peace of mind.

I created platforms like *Financial Literacy for NIL,* Financial Literacy For Attorneys, Financial Literacy For Doctors, *Financial Literacy for The Culture,* and a number of other Financial Literacy books because I believe access to financial knowledge should never be limited to those with private wealth or privileged backgrounds. Everyone deserves a financial roadmap. Everyone deserves clarity. Everyone deserves peace.

And that's why this book exists.

Financial Literacy for Pharmacists was born from the same mission: to give smart, hardworking professionals the financial tools they were never taught in school. You already know how to serve patients. You already know how to follow protocol, manage chaos, and stay accountable under pressure. What you might not know—yet—is how to turn your income into long-term security. Or how to avoid lifestyle inflation, burnout, or costly financial mistakes. That's where I come in.

This isn't about perfection. It's about progress. It's about equipping you with clear, real-world guidance from someone who knows what it feels like to succeed professionally while feeling uncertain financially.

So as you move through these chapters, know that I'm with you—not as a professor or a judge, but as a teammate. I've been there. I've learned the hard way. And now, I'm here to make sure you don't have to.

Let's build something solid. Something smart.

Something worthy of your education, your effort, and your future.

You've got this.

Let's get to work.

—Pat Brown, MBA

Part I – Foundations: Pharmacy School & Early Financial Lessons

This opening section of *Financial Literacy For Pharmacists* lays the groundwork for understanding the unique financial journey pharmacists face—starting from the first day of pharmacy school. We dive into the critical early years, where decisions about student loans, budgeting, credit, and financial priorities shape your future. Whether you're still in school or freshly graduated, this section helps you understand how to avoid the most common financial missteps made during the high-pressure academic years.

Through relatable scenarios, plain-language explanations, and empowering guidance, you'll learn how to manage debt without drowning in it, build credit from scratch, create a realistic budget on a student income (or no income at all), and avoid lifestyle creep before your first real paycheck ever hits your bank account.

This part is your financial "orientation"—not just to school, but to the habits and mindsets that will support your long-term wealth and financial peace of mind. Every successful pharmacist needs a strong foundation. This is where it begins.

Chapter 1: The Cost of Becoming a Pharmacist – Tuition, Fees, and Hidden Costs

Let's start with the truth. Becoming a pharmacist isn't just hard work academically and emotionally. It's also one of the most expensive professional paths a person can take—and often, no one truly breaks down the full cost until you're already halfway through it. This chapter is here to change that.

Not to scare you.

To prepare you.

To arm you with real numbers, real context, and real strategy.

Because when you understand the true cost of becoming a pharmacist—from tuition to the hidden expenses nobody talks about—you can build a financial strategy that doesn't leave you broke, bitter, or burned out.

You don't need shame.

You need a spreadsheet, a strategy, and a sense of your own power.

Let's get into it.

SECTION 1: The Sticker Price vs. The Real Price

The average total cost of pharmacy school ranges from $140,000 to $250,000.

Yes, you read that right. And yes, it varies widely based on whether you attend a public or private institution, whether you go out of state, and whether you enter a 0-6 program, a traditional 4-year PharmD program, or a post-baccalaureate pathway.

But that's just tuition and mandatory fees.

Add in housing, food, transportation, textbooks, professional attire, licensing fees, board prep, travel for interviews or rotations, and the cost balloons.

That $200K pharmacy degree might quietly cost you $300K+ when you include the opportunity cost of not earning full-time income for four to six years.

Let's say you spend $60,000 per year for four years. That's $240,000.

Now add $20,000 in interest that accrues while in school.

Then tack on $15,000 in living expenses per year.

We're already creeping toward $300,000, and we haven't talked about loan repayment yet.

This is the cost of entry.

But here's the thing:

It doesn't have to be a trap. It just needs a plan.

SECTION 2: Breaking Down the Big Categories

Tuition and Fees

- Public Pharmacy School (in-state): $15,000 - $30,000/year
- Public (out-of-state): $30,000 - $50,000/year
- Private Pharmacy School: $40,000 - $60,000+/year

Textbooks and Supplies

- Can run $1,000 - $3,000 per year
- White coats, stethoscopes, and other professional gear can add another $500 - $1,000

Living Expenses

- Rent, utilities, food, gas, insurance, phone, etc.
- Estimated at $15,000 - $25,000/year depending on location

Licensing and Board Prep

- NAPLEX registration: ~$575
- MPJE (for most states): ~$150 each
- Background checks, fingerprinting, and other licensure items: $300 - $500
- Review courses and prep books: $1,000+

Interview and Rotation Costs

- Travel for rotations or residency interviews
- Hotels, airfare, meals, attire: Easily $2,000 - $5,000

Opportunity Cost

- What could you have earned in 4-6 years if you had worked instead?
- A $40,000/year job for four years is $160,000 of forgone income

That's the true cost of becoming a pharmacist.

SECTION 3: The Hidden Costs Nobody Tells You About

- **Summer Classes**
- Not always covered by financial aid. May require out-of-pocket payments.
- **Relocation**
- Moving across the country for rotations, residencies, or your first job adds up quickly.
- **Mental Health and Burnout**
- Therapy, medication, or even just the cost of stress (missed work, decreased focus) matters.
- **Delayed Milestones**
- Buying a home, starting a family, investing in retirement—all pushed back.

- **Lifestyle Creep**
- After years of sacrifice, it's tempting to overspend once that first paycheck hits. That first new car? That vacation? That apartment with a view? All of it can derail you before you get started.
- **Interest Accrual**
- Even if loans are in deferment, interest grows silently in the background.

SECTION 4: Real Talk About Student Loans

You might graduate with $150,000 or more in student debt.
Here's what that actually means:

- At a 6% interest rate, $150,000 becomes over $200,000 if repaid over 20 years
- Monthly payments could range from $800 to $2,000, depending on your plan

Let's break that down.

Standard Repayment Plan:

- 10 years
- Higher monthly payment (~$1,700/month)
- Less total interest paid

Income-Driven Repayment (IDR):

- Monthly payments based on income
- Could stretch over 20-25 years
- May end in forgiveness (but taxes due on forgiven amount)

Public Service Loan Forgiveness (PSLF):

- Requires 10 years of qualifying payments while working full-time for

a nonprofit or government entity
- Forgiveness is tax-free
- Can be life-changing if planned for intentionally

You need to know your options.

You need to run your numbers.

You need to be the CFO of your own life.

SECTION 5: Emotional Cost and the Pressure to Succeed

It's not just financial.

There's the mental and emotional cost of carrying six figures of debt.

- Guilt
- Anxiety
- Shame
- Pressure to keep working in a job you hate because of your loans

Money stress is the number one contributor to burnout for many pharmacists.

You deserve to understand the weight you're carrying.

Because then, you can start to lift it.

SECTION 6: So Was It Worth It? Let's Talk ROI (Return on Investment)

A pharmacist salary can range from $90,000 to $140,000+, depending on setting and location.

That's a strong income.

But salary alone isn't the whole picture.

What matters is what you *keep*.

What matters is how long it takes to break even.

What matters is whether your income buys you freedom—or keeps you on the hamster wheel.

Calculate your ROI:

1. Add up the full cost of your education

2. Factor in your expected net income after taxes, debt payments, and living expenses
3. Estimate how long it will take to "break even"
4. Ask yourself: Am I building wealth, or just servicing debt?

If the math makes you pause, good.

That's the start of financial clarity.

SECTION 7: Take Back Control – Action Steps

- **Know Your Numbers**
- Make a spreadsheet with every single cost, every single loan, every single interest rate
- **Evaluate Your Repayment Plan**
- Don't default to the standard plan without understanding all options
- **Set a Post-Graduation Budget Before You Graduate**
- Don't let lifestyle inflation steal your financial future
- **Explore Loan Forgiveness Options Now**
- If you're PSLF eligible, plan early to maximize benefits
- **Start Building an Emergency Fund Immediately**
- Even $50/month builds momentum
- **Find a Financial Mentor or Advisor**
- Don't try to figure this out alone

Final Words: This Isn't Just the Cost of a Degree. It's the Price of a Dream.

And you paid it.

You committed.

You studied.

You sacrificed.

Now it's time for your finances to finally serve *you*.

Don't let the cost of becoming a pharmacist keep you from the financial freedom you deserve.

You're not behind.

You're not broken.
You're not bad with money.
You just need tools, structure, and the confidence to take control.
Start with one money move today.
Just one.
Read your loan servicer's website.
Make a budget in your Notes app.
Talk to someone who's been through it.
Your bank account will thank you.
Your peace of mind will thank you.
And your future self?
They're already cheering you on.

Chapter 2: Surviving Pharmacy School Financially – Loans, Budgets, and Burnout

Let's strip it all the way down.

Pharmacy school is a pressure cooker. Academically. Emotionally. Financially.

And while the lectures teach you about metabolism and medications, nobody pulls you aside and says, "Hey, here's how to survive this financially without wrecking your future."

This chapter is the conversation every pharmacy student deserves—the one that too few ever get.

It's the truth about how to manage loans while still in school.

How to live on a tight budget without losing your mind.

How to avoid burnout before you even earn your first real paycheck.

This is about resilience. Strategy. And protecting your peace.

Because you didn't fight your way into this profession just to live paycheck to paycheck.

Let's get into it.

SECTION 1: Understanding the Financial Landscape While You're Still in School

Here's the deal: you may be broke, but you don't have to be financially clueless.

Pharmacy school is expensive. We covered that in the last chapter. But even if your student loan debt is growing each semester, that doesn't mean you're powerless.

Now is the time to take stock of your financial foundation. Even small moves matter.

Ask yourself:

- How much am I borrowing per semester?
- What is the interest rate on each loan?
- Is interest accruing while I'm in school?
- What is the total balance I'll owe by graduation?

If you can't answer those questions, that's your first money move.

Most pharmacy students treat loans like Monopoly money—it's there, it's fake, and you'll deal with it later.

But later comes fast.

Start tracking your loans. Use a spreadsheet. Write it in your journal. Tattoo it on your forearm if you have to.

Because what you don't measure, you can't manage.

SECTION 2: Budgeting in Pharmacy School Without Feeling Miserable

The idea of budgeting during pharmacy school might sound laughable.

You're already eating ramen, sharing an apartment, and using your student ID to sneak free meals at club events.

But budgeting isn't just about restriction. It's about clarity. It's about control.

Create a basic monthly budget with:

- Rent
- Utilities
- Groceries
- Gas/transportation
- School supplies
- Health/insurance
- Miscellaneous (because life happens)

Then ask:

- What's my monthly cash inflow (loans, savings, side jobs)?
- Where am I overspending? Where can I cut without suffering?
- What can I automate?

The goal is not to live a joyless, flavorless life. The goal is to make conscious trade-offs now so you have options later.

Let's be real:

Spending $12 a day on coffee and takeout feels fine *now*.

But when you graduate with $200K+ in debt and feel trapped in a job you hate, that $12/day will haunt you.

You're not punishing yourself by budgeting.

You're protecting your future.

SECTION 3: The Emotional Cost of Pharmacy School – and How It Affects Your Wallet

Let's talk about burnout.

Pharmacy school is grueling. And the temptation to cope with stress through spending is real.

- "I deserve this."
- "Everyone else is going out."
- "I need something to look forward to."

Those are real feelings.

But emotional spending creates financial hangovers.

The key is not to deny yourself comfort.

It's to build comfort into your budget *intentionally*.

Schedule joy.

Plan for fun.

Budget $50/month for a splurge that feeds your soul.

Not $500/month on impulse Amazon purchases that numb your brain.

Burnout leads to emotional spending.

Emotional spending deepens debt.

More debt increases burnout.

Break the cycle now.

SECTION 4: Side Hustles and Income Strategies for Pharmacy Students

You might be thinking, "There's no time for a side hustle—I barely sleep."

Fair.

But even a few hundred dollars a month can create financial breathing room.

Consider:

- Tutoring underclassmen
- Freelance writing or editing (medical blogs, test prep)
- Part-time pharmacy tech roles
- Dog walking, babysitting, driving for delivery services

Pros:

- Extra cash
- Resume builder
- Mental break from studying

Cons:

- Time and energy trade-off
- Risk of academic distraction

If you side hustle, set clear boundaries.

You are a student *first*.

Pro tip:

If you earn money, use 20% for fun, 40% to avoid more loans, and 40% to save for emergencies.

SECTION 5: Real Stories From the Front Lines

Story 1:

Jasmine borrowed an extra $5,000 one semester to take a spring break trip with friends. It felt harmless.

Ten years later, that trip cost her over $9,000 with interest.

She now sets a budget *before* each semester and sticks to it. "Never again," she says.

Story 2:

Mark worked part-time as a TA. He used that money to buy groceries and never touched his loan refund.

After graduation, he had $30K less debt than his classmates.

Now? He's saving for a house while others are just starting loan repayment.

Story 3:

Natalie hit burnout her third year. She skipped meals, overused caffeine, and ignored her budget.

She finally talked to a therapist, started meal prepping, and joined a financial literacy club.

"Taking care of my brain helped me take care of my bank account," she says.

SECTION 6: Building Your Financial Identity Before You Graduate

You're not "just" a student.

You're a future high-income professional in training.

Start acting like the CFO of your own life.

- Track every dollar
- Review loan balances quarterly
- Read one personal finance book a year
- Follow pharmacists and financial educators on social media
- Build a basic credit history (one low-limit card paid off monthly)

This isn't about becoming a finance geek.

This is about becoming powerful.

When you graduate, you'll be ready.

Not shocked. Not scrambling.

Ready.

SECTION 7: Financial Traps to Avoid in Pharmacy School

- **Borrowing the Max Automatically**
- Don't take more loan money than you need. It's not free.
- **Ignoring Interest**
- If interest is accruing, consider making small payments to reduce it.
- **Living Like You're Already a Pharmacist**
- Save the luxury for later. For now, keep it simple.
- **Using Credit Cards to Survive**
- Unless you're paying it off monthly, it's not a lifeline—it's a trap.
- **Letting Stress Dictate Spending**
- When you're anxious, pause before swiping.

SECTION 8: Action Steps to Implement Today

- **Create Your First Budget**
- Even if it's rough, get something on paper
- **List All Your Loans**
- Servicer, amount, interest rate, type
- **Open a High-Yield Savings Account**
- Start building a small emergency fund
- **Track Your Spending for 30 Days**
- Awareness is everything
- **Have a Weekly "Money Date" With Yourself**
- 20 minutes to review finances and reset
- **Find a Financial Mentor**
- Ask a recent grad how they managed finances
- **Plan for Burnout**
- Don't ignore it. Budget for mental wellness.

Final Words: Survive First. Then Thrive.

Pharmacy school is temporary.

Debt is temporary.

Stress is temporary.

But the skills you build now? The mindset you sharpen now?

That's what lasts.

You don't have to be perfect.

You just have to be intentional.

Surviving pharmacy school financially isn't about martyrdom.

It's about momentum.

It's about knowing that one smart choice now creates ten more down the road.

Make one money move before you go to bed tonight.

Just one.

And then do another next week.

You deserve to graduate with more than just a degree.

You deserve to graduate with dignity, direction, and dollars in the bank.

You've got this.

Chapter 3: Student Loans 101 – How They Work and What They Mean for You

Let's be honest.

Student loans feel like a shadow you can't shake. You graduated. You got the job. You're prescribing, consulting, dispensing—you're doing the work. But the debt? It lingers. Like a second rent. Like a third job.

This chapter isn't here to scare you.

It's here to liberate you.

You don't need to carry guilt for the loans you took.

You need clarity. Strategy. Ownership.

Because understanding student loans isn't just about managing debt. It's about reclaiming your peace of mind. Your power. Your options.

Whether you're fresh out of school, halfway through repayment, or refinancing for the third time, this chapter is for you.

Let's break it all the way down.

SECTION 1: What Are Student Loans, Really?

Let's strip away the jargon.

A student loan is money you borrowed to get through school, with the agreement that you'd pay it back with interest.

Simple on paper.

But in real life, the interest grows like weeds. The balances compound. The terms confuse you. And suddenly what was supposed to be an investment in your future feels like a chain around your ankle.

Federal loans. Private loans. Subsidized. Unsubsidized. PLUS. Grad PLUS. Refinance. Deferment. Forbearance.

The alphabet soup of it all is overwhelming.

Let's translate.

SECTION 2: The Main Types of Student Loans

Federal Loans (Backed by the government)

- Direct Subsidized Loans (for undergrads only): Government pays interest while in school
- Direct Unsubsidized Loans: Interest accrues during school
- Grad PLUS Loans: For graduate/professional students; higher interest rates
- Parent PLUS Loans: For parents of dependent undergrads (some pharmacists still carry these for kids)

Private Loans (From banks, credit unions, or lenders)

- Often have higher or variable interest rates
- Less flexible repayment options
- Not eligible for federal protections like PSLF or IDR plans

Most pharmacists carry a mix of federal and private loans. Know which you have. It matters.

SECTION 3: Interest, Capitalization, and the Cost of Delay

Interest is the rent you pay to borrow money.

And here's the kicker: If you don't pay the interest while in school, it often gets *capitalized* (added to your loan balance). Then you pay interest *on the interest.*

Let's say you borrow $40,000 at 6% interest over 10 years.

By the time you're done, you could pay $13,000+ in interest.

Now multiply that by 4-6 years of school.

You're not just borrowing tuition.

You're borrowing your future.

But when you know the math, you can start making moves.

SECTION 4: Loan Repayment Options, Decoded

Standard Repayment Plan

- 10 years
- Highest monthly payments
- Least interest over time

Graduated Repayment Plan

- Starts low, increases every two years
- For those expecting higher income later

Extended Repayment Plan

- Up to 25 years
- Lower monthly payments
- More interest paid overall

Income-Driven Repayment (IDR) Plans

- Payments based on income and family size
- Includes IBR, PAYE, REPAYE, and SAVE
- Monthly payments can be very low—even $0
- After 20-25 years, remaining balance is forgiven (but taxed)

Public Service Loan Forgiveness (PSLF)

- Forgiveness after 120 qualifying payments (10 years)
- Must work full-time at a government or nonprofit organization
- Forgiven balance is *not* taxed

Private Loan Repayment

- Terms vary by lender
- Few forgiveness options
- Can refinance, but no IDR or PSLF

Choose the plan that aligns with your income, career goals, and long-term plans.

SECTION 5: What About Loan Forgiveness?

Loan forgiveness sounds magical. But it comes with rules.

PSLF Requirements:

- Federal Direct Loans only
- Enrolled in an IDR plan
- Working full-time for a qualifying employer
- Make 120 on-time payments (not necessarily consecutive)

IDR Forgiveness:

- 20 or 25 years depending on the plan
- Taxable forgiveness (this could be a big bill unless rules change)

Forgiveness Tips:

- Certify your employment annually
- Use the PSLF Help Tool
- Track every payment like your life depends on it

Forgiveness isn't fantasy. But it requires precision.

SECTION 6: To Refinance or Not to Refinance?

Refinancing means replacing one or more loans with a new loan from a private lender, ideally with a lower interest rate.

Pros:

- Lower monthly payments

- Less total interest over time

Cons:

- Lose federal protections (PSLF, IDR, forbearance)
- Credit check required
- Variable rates can rise

Good candidates for refinancing:

- High credit score
- Stable income
- No plan to pursue PSLF

If you're not sure, wait.

Once you refinance federal loans, you *can't* go back.

SECTION 7: Real-Life Scenarios and What They Teach Us

Scenario 1: Lisa, Retail Pharmacist, $180K in Loans

Lisa earns $125K. She refinanced to a 10-year loan and pays $1,800/month. Her goal? Be debt-free before age 40.

Her strategy:

- Lives on $60K
- Throws $30K/year at loans
- Keeps $10K in savings as a cushion

Scenario 2: Marcus, Hospital Pharmacist, $230K in Loans, PSLF Track

Marcus works for a nonprofit hospital. He makes $110K and is in the SAVE plan. His monthly payment is $300/month.

He's seven years into PSLF.

He tracks every payment.

He maxes out his Roth IRA and 403(b) with the savings.

Scenario 3: Dena and Sean, Dual Pharmacist Couple, $400K

Combined Debt

They chose IDR and are saving aggressively.

Their plan is to buy a house with 5% down, delay kids until loans are down to $200K, and switch to aggressive payoff once their incomes rise.

Each scenario proves: There's no one-size-fits-all.

Only what fits *you*.

SECTION 8: How Student Loans Affect the Rest of Your Financial Life

Student loans don't just impact your wallet.

They shape how you:

- Choose a job
- Buy a home
- Invest for retirement
- Decide when (and if) to have kids
- Handle emergencies

But they don't have to define you.

With the right strategy, you can:

- Buy a home *with* loans
- Save for retirement *while* repaying loans
- Build wealth *despite* your debt

Don't wait until you're debt-free to build your life.

Start now.

SECTION 9: Action Steps to Take Control Today

- **Know Your Loans**
- Visit studentaid.gov to download your loan data
- List your private lenders and loan balances
- **Choose a Repayment Plan**
- Don't default to the standard plan blindly

- **Run the Numbers**
- Use loan simulators to project your path
- **Consider PSLF or IDR**
- Especially if you're at a nonprofit or government employer
- **Don't Panic, Plan**
- Make a five-year financial roadmap that includes your loans, not one that waits for them to disappear
- **Automate Payments**
- Many servicers offer an interest rate discount for auto-pay
- **Check for Errors**
- Loan servicers *do* make mistakes. Keep records.

Final Words: Student Loans Are the Tool. Not the Enemy.

You didn't fail by taking on debt.

You invested in yourself.

And now, you get to lead that investment.

No shame.

Just structure.

No guilt.

Just goals.

Start where you are. Make one move today.

Call your servicer. Open a spreadsheet. Read your promissory notes. Check your forgiveness eligibility. Revisit your plan.

Just one step.

Then another.

You are not your loan balance.

You are your choices.

You are your resilience.

You are your power.

And it's time to take it back.

Your future self is already smiling.

So is your bank account.

So is your peace of mind.

Chapter 4: Loan Repayment Plans and Forgiveness Options for Pharmacists

Here's the truth: student loans don't have to control your life.

But they *will* if you don't understand your options.

And for too many pharmacists—brilliant, compassionate, high-earning professionals—loan repayment becomes this foggy, stressful blur of servicer emails, minimum payments, and long-term avoidance.

Not anymore.

This chapter is here to pull back the curtain on repayment plans and forgiveness options.

It's not just about chipping away at your debt.

It's about structuring your repayment around *your* goals.

Your career path.

Your lifestyle.

Your future.

Let's start where you are.

Whether you're making six figures and feel stuck, or still in grace period trying to plan ahead.

Let's walk through the options like colleagues at the same table.

Because you deserve to make these decisions with confidence—not confusion.

SECTION 1: Why Loan Repayment Needs a Strategy

Let's start with a mindset shift.

Your student loans aren't a moral failure.

They're a math problem.

They're a business decision you made to access a career that pays six figures and serves your community.

Now it's time to run the numbers like the CEO of your own financial future.

That means:

- Knowing every option
- Understanding the trade-offs
- Aligning your repayment strategy with your life plan

This chapter is your playbook.

SECTION 2: Federal Repayment Plans for Pharmacists

If you have federal loans, you have several repayment plan options. Let's walk through each one, including who they work best for.

Standard Repayment Plan

- 10-year term
- Fixed monthly payments
- Most aggressive payoff

Best for: Pharmacists who can afford high monthly payments and want to pay off debt quickly.

Graduated Repayment Plan

- 10-year term
- Payments start low, increase every 2 years

Best for: New grads expecting significant income growth. Not ideal for the long term due to higher interest costs.

Extended Repayment Plan

- Up to 25 years

- Lower monthly payments
- Higher total interest

Best for: Those needing immediate payment relief but not pursuing forgiveness.

Income-Driven Repayment (IDR) Plans

- Adjusted based on income and family size
- 20-25 year terms
- May lead to forgiveness at the end

Best for: Pharmacists with high debt-to-income ratios or planning for PSLF.

Let's break down the main IDR plans:

SAVE (Saving on a Valuable Education)

- Newest plan, replaces REPAYE
- Caps monthly payment at 10% of discretionary income (dropping to 5% for undergrad loans)
- Offers interest subsidies to prevent balance growth
- Forgiveness after 20-25 years

PAYE (Pay As You Earn)

- 10% of discretionary income
- Forgiveness after 20 years
- Only for loans from October 2007 or later

IBR (Income-Based Repayment)

- Older loans may be eligible
- 10%-15% of discretionary income
- Forgiveness after 20-25 years

ICR (Income-Contingent Repayment)

- Rarely the best option
- 20% of discretionary income
- Forgiveness after 25 years

SECTION 3: Public Service Loan Forgiveness (PSLF)

This is the golden ticket for many pharmacists.

Here's how it works:

- Make 120 qualifying payments (monthly, on-time, in an IDR plan)
- While working full-time at a qualifying employer (government or nonprofit)
- Loans must be Direct Loans
- Submit the PSLF Employment Certification Form annually

At the end of 10 years, the *remaining balance* is forgiven—*tax-free.*

Let's make it real:

If you're working at a 501(c)(3) hospital or a state-run pharmacy, you likely qualify.

If your income is moderate and your debt is high, PSLF can be transformational.

Real pharmacist example:

Sara works at a public hospital making $105K with $210K in student loans. Under SAVE, she pays about $400/month. After 10 years, she'll have paid roughly $48,000 total—and the rest is forgiven.

Key tips:

- Don't consolidate FFEL or Perkins loans *unless* you convert them to Direct Loans
- Keep meticulous records
- Use the PSLF Help Tool

SECTION 4: Private Loan Repayment Options

Private loans are a different beast.

They don't come with federal protections or forgiveness programs.

But they do offer options—if you manage them intentionally.

Refinancing is the main lever you can pull:

- Consolidate high-interest private loans into a new loan
- Lower your interest rate
- Simplify repayment into one monthly bill

What to consider before refinancing:

- Credit score (ideally above 720)
- Stable income
- No plans to pursue federal forgiveness

Pros:

- Lower interest
- Lower monthly payments
- Fixed or variable rate options

Cons:

- No access to PSLF or IDR
- Permanent once done

SECTION 5: Pros and Cons of Each Strategy

Aggressive Payoff (Standard or Refinance)

Pros:

- Pay less in total interest
- Debt-free sooner

- Strong psychological win

Cons:

- Higher monthly payments
- Less room for saving or investing in early years

IDR and Forgiveness (SAVE, PSLF)

Pros:

- Lower monthly burden
- Tax-free forgiveness (for PSLF)
- Enables simultaneous saving/investing

Cons:

- Longer repayment period
- Possible tax bomb on forgiveness outside PSLF
- Requires documentation and consistency

Refinancing

Pros:

- Great for high-income earners not eligible for forgiveness
- Cuts down total interest

Cons:

- Irreversible if you lose job or income
- Requires strong credit and income history

The point isn't to pick the "best" plan universally.

It's to pick the plan that fits *you*.

SECTION 6: Real Pharmacists. Real Stories. Real Payoff.

Jared – Retail Pharmacist

Debt: $160K

Strategy: Refinance to 10-year term at 3.5%

Outcome: Pays $1,600/month, will be debt-free by age 38

Bonus: Still maxing out Roth IRA and HSA

Lily – Clinical Pharmacist at Nonprofit Hospital

Debt: $240K

Strategy: SAVE Plan, PSLF track

Outcome: Monthly payment of $280; will receive forgiveness after 10 years

Bonus: Uses savings to invest and build a down payment fund

Eli and Tasha – Dual PharmD Couple

Debt: $380K

Strategy: One uses PSLF, the other refinanced

Outcome: Reduced total household debt burden, coordinated strategy to buy home and save for kids' college

These aren't fantasy.

They're pharmacists just like you who chose a plan instead of floating through the fog.

SECTION 7: Integrating Repayment Into Your Financial Life

Your loan repayment should not be your *only* financial plan.

It should coexist with:

- Retirement savings
- Emergency fund
- Life insurance
- Disability coverage
- Future goals

The question is: How do I build wealth *while* paying off debt?

Here's how:

- Choose a plan that frees up monthly cash flow
- Automate investments, even if small
- Revisit your plan annually as income grows
- Create a "Work Optional" fund alongside loan payments

Don't wait until the debt is gone to start living.

Start with balance.

SECTION 8: Action Steps You Can Take Right Now

- **Log in to studentaid.gov**
- Get your full loan snapshot
- **List All Your Loans**
- Federal vs. private, interest rates, balances
- **Check Your Employment**
- Are you PSLF-eligible?
- **Run Your Numbers on a Loan Simulator**
- Compare SAVE vs. Refinance vs. Standard
- **Make a 1-Year Plan**
- Which strategy do you want to test?
- **Set a Calendar Reminder**
- Reevaluate every 12 months
- **Talk to a Loan Specialist or Financial Advisor**
- Get personalized advice if you feel stuck
- **Choose Progress Over Perfection**
- A good plan now beats the perfect plan you never implement

Final Words: Your Loans Do Not Own You

Debt may be part of your story.

But it is *not* your identity.

You are a pharmacist. You are a healer. You are a provider.

And you are powerful enough to take control of this.

There is no one-size-fits-all plan.

But there is a right plan for *you*.

So make one money move before you go to bed tonight.

Just one.

Check your PSLF eligibility.

Call your servicer.

Make a spreadsheet.

Refinance an old private loan.

Your future self—and your freedom—starts here.

You didn't go through all that schooling to feel stuck.

You did it to build options.

And those options start with clarity, structure, and self-respect.

This isn't just about loan payments.

This is about dignity.

This is about peace.

This is about power.

And you're ready to take it back.

Chapter 5: Building Credit During Pharmacy School – Why It Matters

Let's have a conversation nobody had with you before you got accepted into pharmacy school.

Credit.

Not chemistry. Not compounding. Not case studies.

Credit.

The silent scorecard that determines whether you get approved for an apartment, how much you pay for car insurance, whether you qualify for a mortgage, and even how much you'll spend over the course of your financial life.

And the crazy part?

You could be the most responsible, diligent, trustworthy future pharmacist in the world—but if you have no credit history, you might be treated like a risk by the very systems meant to support you.

This chapter is your backstage pass to the credit world.

What it is. How it works. Why it matters.

And how you can start building a strong credit foundation right now, *even while you're still in school,* without racking up debt, getting overwhelmed, or compromising your sanity.

Let's go.

SECTION 1: What Is Credit, Really?

Credit is a record of trust.

It's a financial report card that tracks how reliably you borrow and repay money.

When a lender, landlord, or even an employer pulls your credit, they're looking for one thing:

Can this person be trusted to handle financial obligations on time, responsibly, and without drama?

Your credit history is made up of:

- Credit cards
- Student loans
- Auto loans
- Mortgages
- Any other debt you've borrowed and repaid (or not)

This history generates a three-digit number called your **credit score**. That score determines your borrowing power and cost of borrowing.

A higher score = more opportunities and lower costs.

A lower score = fewer opportunities and higher costs.

And yes, you can start building credit even if you don't have a full-time job yet.

SECTION 2: Why Credit Matters for Pharmacy Students

You might be thinking, "Why would I care about my credit score while I'm knee-deep in lectures and clinicals?"

Here's why:

1. **You'll graduate into real adult responsibilities fast.**

- Moving for a residency?
- Buying a used car for your first job?
- Signing a lease on an apartment?
- Getting a loan to buy a home within a few years?

All of those hinge on your credit.

- **Good credit can save you thousands.**
- A better credit score means lower interest rates
- Lower interest = less money wasted
- **It gives you options.**
- More flexibility with financial decisions
- Easier to qualify for professional credit cards, lines of credit, or even business financing if you start your own consulting or MTM service
- **Creditworthiness affects more than just loans.**
- Employers (especially in healthcare and finance) may check it
- Insurance companies use it to determine premiums
- Landlords use it to screen tenants

In short: Your credit score is your financial reputation. Start shaping it now.

SECTION 3: The Five Factors That Make Up Your Credit Score

Understanding your credit score is like learning the grading rubric for an exam.

Here are the five key factors:

1. Payment History (35%)

- Did you pay on time?
- Even one late payment can ding your score for years

2. Amounts Owed (30%)

- Also known as credit utilization
- How much of your available credit are you using?
- Ideally, use less than 30% of your limit

3. Length of Credit History (15%)

- How long have your accounts been open?
- Older is better

4. Credit Mix (10%)

- Variety helps: Credit card + loan = better than credit card alone

5. New Credit Inquiries (10%)

- Opening too many accounts in a short time can lower your score temporarily

Knowing these factors gives you power.

You can manage what you can measure.

SECTION 4: How to Start Building Credit During Pharmacy School

Here are five strategic steps to start building credit *today*, without going into debt:

Step 1: Open a Student Credit Card

- Look for no annual fee, low limit (around $500)
- Use it for one small recurring expense (like Netflix or your phone bill)
- Pay it off *in full* every month

Step 2: Become an Authorized User

- Ask a trusted parent or sibling to add you as an authorized user on one of their well-managed cards
- You get the benefit of their credit history without liability

Step 3: Start Repaying Interest on Student Loans

- If you can afford it, make small payments on your unsubsidized loans while in school
- This shows consistent repayment behavior and builds your credit profile

Step 4: Use a Secured Credit Card (if denied for regular one)

- You put down a cash deposit as collateral
- Works just like a credit card and reports to credit bureaus

Step 5: Set Up Automatic Payments

- Automation prevents missed payments
- Even one missed payment can lower your score by 50+ points

You don't need five credit cards or a car loan.

You just need to show up financially, consistently.

SECTION 5: Mistakes to Avoid While Building Credit

Mistake #1: Using Credit to Fund Your Lifestyle

- Credit is a tool, not income
- Don't treat your limit like it's money you *have*

Mistake #2: Only Paying the Minimum

- You avoid late fees, but still rack up interest
- Pay in full every month

Mistake #3: Opening Too Many Accounts at Once

- Each inquiry dings your score
- Space out applications every 6-12 months

Mistake #4: Co-Signing for Friends or Partners

- You're legally responsible if they default
- Protect your credit like your license

Mistake #5: Ignoring Your Credit Reports

- Errors happen
- Check all three bureaus (Equifax, Experian, TransUnion) at least once a year

Credit is a long game.

Every smart move now builds a smoother path later.

SECTION 6: Real-Life Scenarios from Pharmacy Students

Scenario 1: Diego

First-year student. Got denied for an unsecured card. Opened a secured card with $300 deposit. Put gas on it once a month, paid it off. By graduation? Credit score was over 730. Got approved for a home loan within 6 months of landing his first job.

Scenario 2: Mei

Used her student credit card for everything—groceries, school supplies, takeout. But she only paid the minimum. By the time she graduated, she had $2,500 in credit card debt and a score in the low 600s. It took her 2 years post-graduation to dig out.

Scenario 3: Samira

Became an authorized user on her dad's 15-year-old AmEx. Didn't even use the card. By year three of school, she had an 800 credit score just from piggybacking on her dad's responsible usage.

Learn from these stories.

Start strong.

Finish stronger.

SECTION 7: How Credit Impacts Your Post-Grad Financial Life

Buying a Home:

- A score above 740 can get you the best interest rates
- Even a 1% lower rate can save tens of thousands over 30 years

Getting an Apartment:

- Landlords often require scores above 650
- A poor score could mean a higher deposit or a cosigner

Buying a Car:

- Higher credit = lower APR
- Lower APR = smaller monthly payments and less money wasted

Starting a Business or Pharmacy:

- Credit is essential for getting a line of credit or small business loan

Peace of Mind:

- Good credit gives you leverage
- Leverage gives you options

You didn't go through pharmacy school just to feel financially limited.

Let your credit give you range, not restriction.

SECTION 8: Action Steps You Can Take Today

- **Check Your Credit Score for Free**
- Use Credit Karma or your bank's portal
- **Apply for a Student Credit Card or Secured Card**
- Use it once a month and pay in full
- **Ask to Be Added as an Authorized User**
- Choose someone financially responsible
- **Make One Payment Toward Student Loan Interest**
- Even $10 helps
- **Schedule a Calendar Reminder to Check Credit Reports Quarterly**
- AnnualCreditReport.com is free and legit
- **Set Up Autopay**

- Even for the minimum, to avoid missed payments
- **Create a Simple Credit Journal**
- Track card balances, payments, and score changes

Final Words: Credit Is a Currency of Trust

You're not just a student.

You're a soon-to-be healthcare professional with a future that deserves to be well-financed and well-respected.

Building credit now—slowly, steadily, smartly—is one of the most powerful things you can do for your future self.

You don't need to be rich.

You just need to be ready.

So make one money move tonight.

Apply for that card. Ask to be an authorized user. Check your score. Set a reminder.

You're not behind.

You're building.

And every smart step compounds.

You didn't come this far to let a number hold you back.

You came this far to live free.

And building credit is how you start unlocking doors.

Let's open them together.

Chapter 6: Managing Money on a Tight Budget – Surviving on Stipends and Loans

Let's get one thing straight.

Living on stipends and student loans doesn't make you bad with money.

It makes you human.

It makes you a pharmacy student navigating one of the most expensive, demanding, and underpaid periods of your life.

And the real flex?

Learning how to manage money *when there isn't much to manage.*

Because if you can budget when you're broke, you'll thrive when you earn.

This chapter is for the pharmacy student making that loan disbursement stretch from August to December.

For the intern juggling clinical rotations and side gigs just to keep the lights on.

For the future pharmacist who doesn't want to feel financially buried before they even graduate.

This is not about shame.

This is about strategy.

Let's walk through it together.

SECTION 1: Understanding Your Financial Reality Without Fear

Let's take inventory.

You may be living off:

- Loan disbursements
- A small internship or part-time job
- Family help
- A scholarship or stipend (if you're lucky)

That might mean $800 to $1,500 per month, depending on your living situation.

That's tight.

But it's not impossible.

The first step?

Remove the guilt.

You are doing the best you can with the resources you have.

And your ability to manage this money *now* will be the foundation of your financial strength *later.*

So let's start with what you've got.

And build from there.

SECTION 2: Budgeting When You're Broke

This isn't about budgeting apps or spreadsheets (though those help).

This is about clarity.

Here's the three-bucket system I teach pharmacy students:

1. Survival (Needs)

- Rent
- Utilities
- Food
- Transportation
- Insurance

2. Stability (Future)

- Minimum loan interest payments (if applicable)

- Credit building
- Emergency savings (even $5/month counts)

3. Sanity (Joy)

- Netflix
- Coffee runs
- A cheap date night
- That meal that gets you through exam week

Too many students cut out Sanity to afford Survival. And then burn out.

Keep a line in your budget for joy. It keeps you going.

Even if your joy budget is $10 a month.

SECTION 3: Know Your Inflows and Outflows

Let's get concrete.

Monthly Inflows:

- Loans: $12,000 per semester = $2,000/month
- Part-time job: $400/month
- Scholarship: $1,000 per year = $83/month
- Total: ~$2,500/month (example)

Monthly Outflows:

- Rent and utilities: $1,200
- Food: $300
- Gas/bus: $100
- Health insurance: $150
- Phone/internet: $100
- Misc: $150
- Total: ~$2,000

You have $500 of flex.

Use that to build resilience:

- $100 to savings
- $50 to pay student loan interest (if accruing)
- $50 to a Roth IRA (if working)
- $100 to joy/sanity
- $200 for buffer (because stuff happens)

If you're in the red? That's not failure.

That's a signal.

Time to adjust.

Let's talk about how.

SECTION 4: Cost-Cutting Without Losing Your Mind

You don't need to become a monk.

But you do need to be intentional.

Here are real strategies pharmacy students use to cut costs while keeping their dignity:

1. House Hack

- Get roommates
- Rent out a room if you own
- Trade reduced rent for chores, tutoring, or child care

2. Cook Once, Eat All Week

- Meal prep saves hundreds
- Make cooking social (host a study group potluck)

3. Transportation Strategy

- Walk, bike, or use public transit when possible
- Use gas apps to find the cheapest fuel

4. Ditch the Gym Membership

- YouTube, campus rec center, or home workouts

5. Textbooks

- Rent or buy used
- Use the library or PDFs from classmates (ethically)

6. Student Discounts

- Always ask
- Use UNiDAYS, ID.me, or your .edu email to save

7. Cut Subscriptions You Don't Use

- Spotify, Hulu, Audible—ask yourself: Do I *need* this, or just like the idea of it?

Every $20 saved is a power move.

It's a choice. Not a punishment.

SECTION 5: Stretching Your Loan Money Without Sinking

Student loans aren't free money.

But they are *available* money.

Here's how to use them wisely:

1. Only Borrow What You Need

- Don't take the full amount because it's offered
- Use a semester budget to calculate the true need

2. Refunds Are Not Windfalls

- That $4,000 refund is not a shopping spree

- Treat it like a monthly paycheck

3. Save the Excess

- If you borrow extra, park it in a high-yield savings account for emergencies

4. Track Loan Balances Each Semester

- Awareness is everything

5. Pay Interest if You Can

- Even $10/month prevents capitalization

Your loans can work *for* you in school.

Just don't let them work against you after.

SECTION 6: Creative Ways to Boost Your Income

Sometimes the problem isn't spending.

It's income.

Here are ways pharmacy students are supplementing their stipends:

1. Tutoring

- Help underclassmen in biology, chemistry, or pharmacology

2. Freelance Writing

- Health blogs, test prep companies, or medical sites

3. Survey Sites / Research Studies

- Slow, but adds up (Swagbucks, Prolific, etc.)

4. Pharmacy Tech Work

- Even 8-10 hours a week helps

5. Sell What You Don't Need

- Old textbooks, clothes, gadgets

6. Babysitting / Dog Walking

- Flexible and often pays well

7. Campus Jobs

- Federal Work-Study, TA roles, admin assistants

Find a way to earn that fits your bandwidth.
Don't sacrifice your grades.
Protect your peace.
But if you *can* earn, even a little? Do it.

SECTION 7: The Psychology of Being Broke (and Still Standing)

Money stress is real.
And when you're broke, it seeps into everything:

- Your sleep
- Your self-worth
- Your ability to focus
- Your relationships

Let me say this clearly:
You are not failing because money is tight.
You are learning financial resilience the hard way—but the *lasting* way.
Use this time to build:

- Gratitude: for what you have
- Discipline: in how you spend
- Mindfulness: around your emotions and money
- Creativity: in how you solve problems

Being broke isn't forever.

But the grit you build now?

That stays with you for life.

SECTION 8: Setting Financial Goals While on a Tight Budget

Yes, you can still set goals.

Even when it feels like you're just trying to survive.

Start with micro-goals:

- Save $100 for emergencies
- Pay $5 toward interest every month
- Cook at home 4 nights per week
- Track your spending for 30 days
- Apply for 3 scholarships per semester

Then build up to macro-goals:

- Graduate with under $200K in debt
- Save $500 before residency
- Start investing within one year of graduation

Goals give you direction.

And direction gives you peace.

SECTION 9: Action Steps to Take Control Today

- **Create a Monthly Budget (Even a Simple One)**
- Use paper, a Google Sheet, or an app
- **List All Income Sources**
- Know what's coming in

- **List All Fixed Expenses**
- Rent, insurance, minimum loan payments
- **Set a Spending Cap for Each Category**
- Be realistic, not rigid
- **Automate One Tiny Financial Win**
- Savings, credit card autopay, student loan interest payment
- **Cancel One Subscription You Don't Use**
- Or downgrade to a cheaper plan
- **Meal Prep This Weekend**
- Your wallet will thank you
- **Apply for One On-Campus Job or Side Gig**
- Even 4 hours a week adds up
- **Schedule a Money Date With Yourself**
- Review your budget, reflect, plan
- **Celebrate a Win**
- Even if it's just making it through the month with $5 left over

Final Words: Broke Isn't Broken

You're not behind.

You're building.

You're learning how to manage money with integrity, clarity, and strength—even on a shoestring.

And when the income finally comes?

You'll be ready.

This chapter isn't about survival.

It's about shaping your financial character.

So make one money move tonight.

Cook a meal.

Cancel a subscription.

Check your loan balance.

Track your spending for the next 7 days.

Just start.

Your future pharmacist self will look back and say:

"I didn't have much. But I made it work.
And now I have options.
Because I learned to lead my money, even when it felt like I had none."

Chapter 7: Understanding Financial Aid – Scholarships, Grants, and Employer-Sponsored Programs

You didn't spend years in pharmacy school grinding through chemistry, clinicals, and sleepless nights just to be shackled by student loans. But here you are—maybe looking at a six-figure debt total and wondering how the system let you get this far without showing you the way out. This chapter? It's not about making you feel behind. It's about giving you the map you were never handed.

Because understanding financial aid isn't just for undergrads. It's for the seasoned pharmacist with a kid heading to college. It's for the new grad trying to avoid signing away their soul in loan agreements. It's for the burned-out retail pharmacist who dreams of pivoting into a different role but needs tuition help to do it. This chapter is for you—wherever you are.

We're going to break it all down—clearly, calmly, and without the fine print confusion. Grants. Scholarships. Loan repayment programs. Tuition reimbursement. Public Service Loan Forgiveness. All of it.

So let's dig in.

What Most Pharmacists Never Hear About Financial Aid

When people say "financial aid," most of us hear "that's for undergrads." That mental block alone has cost pharmacists tens of thousands of dollars in free money, reduced interest, and career support. And the worst part? You're not dumb. You're just busy. No one ever showed you where the gold was buried.

Financial aid is not a one-and-done undergrad thing. It's an evolving toolkit that you can access during:

- Pre-pharmacy coursework
- Pharmacy school (PharmD or BS/Pharm degrees)
- Post-graduate residencies
- Doctoral or dual-degree programs (e.g., PharmD/MPH, PharmD/MBA)
- Continuing education
- Employer-sponsored certifications
- Your children's future education
- Debt forgiveness programs for your own federal loans

And yes—some programs pay you back for the degree you already earned.

Scholarships: The Free Money Too Many Ignore

Let's start with scholarships—aka free money you don't have to repay.

It's not just high school seniors writing essays for $500 checks. There are scholarships for:

- Graduate students
- Non-traditional students
- Women in pharmacy
- Minority students
- Military veterans
- Parents returning to school
- LGBTQ+ students
- Pharmacists pursuing second degrees
- Students in rural or underserved areas

And guess what? Many scholarships go unclaimed every year because people don't apply.

Real Talk: You're a pharmacist. You already know how to fill out forms, meet deadlines, and prove eligibility. Do that for free money.

Where to Look for Scholarships

- **Pharmacy Associations**: ASHP, APhA, NCPA, AMCP, etc.
- **State Pharmacy Boards**
- **Professional Sororities and Fraternities**: Kappa Epsilon, Phi Delta Chi
- **Hospitals or Health Systems**
- **Religious and cultural organizations**
- **Military service branches**
- **Employer programs for children of employees**
- **Your pharmacy school's financial aid office**
- **Fastweb, Scholarships.com, Cappex**
- **HRSA Scholarships (for those committing to underserved areas)**

Scholarships may ask for an essay, recommendation, or GPA. Others just want a form. But the payoff? Could be $1,000, $5,000, or more. That's one less loan. One less financial bruise.

Grants: You Don't Always Have to Be Broke to Qualify

Grants are also "free money"—but often tied to financial need or public service.

Types of Grants You Might Qualify For:

- **Federal Pell Grants** (rare for grad students, but possible through crossover programs)
- **HRSA Grants** for students committed to primary care or underserved areas
- **State-based grants** for those who agree to practice in rural health deserts
- **Graduate Assistance in Areas of National Need (GAANN)**
- **TEACH Grants** (for those pursuing education alongside pharmacy)
- **Residency training grants through hospitals or universities**
- **Institutional grants**—from your own school, tied to research or

demographics

Don't assume you don't qualify. Apply and let the numbers tell you yes or no.

Loan Repayment Programs: Yes, Some People Will Pay Off Your Loans

You may already owe $100,000 or more. So why aren't more pharmacists aggressively pursuing loan repayment programs?

Because most don't know how many exist—or what the trade-offs are.

Let's break down the big players:

1. Public Service Loan Forgiveness (PSLF)

- Work full-time for a government or nonprofit employer
- Make 120 qualifying monthly payments under an income-driven repayment plan
- Remaining balance is forgiven tax-free

Who qualifies?

Hospital pharmacists, VA, tribal health, community clinics, academia, government-run programs.

Pros:

- Tax-free forgiveness
- Works with many hospital and clinical settings

Cons:

- Requires strict compliance (right loans, right job, right plan)
- Must be full-time

2. National Health Service Corps (NHSC)

- Offers up to $50,000 for two years of service in a Health Professional

Shortage Area (HPSA)
- Pharmacists in primary care facilities or rural sites may qualify

3. State-Sponsored Loan Repayment Programs

- Every state has its own offering—often through the Department of Health
- Repayment for working in rural clinics, correctional facilities, or addiction treatment centers

4. Indian Health Service (IHS)

- Two-year commitment = up to $40,000 repayment
- Focused on serving Native American and Alaska Native communities

5. Military Programs

- Each military branch has pharmacist loan repayment programs
- Typically tied to years of service and active duty status

6. Employer-Sponsored Repayment

- Some hospitals, chains (like CVS, Walgreens), and systems offer $5,000–$20,000 in loan repayment
- Often tied to a contract (2–5 years)

Employer-Sponsored Education Benefits

Don't ignore what your current or future employer may offer. Even if it's not advertised, ask HR about:

- **Tuition reimbursement** (partial or full coverage for further education)
- **Loan repayment incentives**

- **Professional development stipends**
- **Certification reimbursement (e.g., BCPS, MTM, immunization training)**
- **Scholarships for employee family members**
- **Discounts on partner university programs**

Pharmacists looking to pivot careers—into informatics, industry, or public health—can often use these benefits to gain new credentials without racking up more debt.

Ask. Negotiate. Advocate.

Real-Life Scenario: Trina's Comeback Plan

Trina was 34. A retail pharmacist with $182,000 in loans, two kids, and dreams of going into ambulatory care.

She thought more school was off the table—until she found a certificate program in pharmacotherapy at a local university. Her employer? Offered $3,000/year in tuition support.

She applied. Used HRSA's Primary Care grant to fund another $5,000. Took classes at night. Used a 0% APR credit card (paid off within promo) for textbooks. Landed an ambulatory care role two years later—with loan repayment baked into her contract.

Trina didn't win the lottery. She just played the financial aid game better than she ever had before.

Pros and Cons: Financial Aid Paths

Scholarships/Grants

Pros:

- No repayment
- Can reduce loans or cover living expenses
- Cons:
- Competitive
- Time-consuming applications

Loan Repayment Programs

Pros:

- Major loan relief
- Incentivize public service
- Cons:
- Contractual obligations
- Strict eligibility requirements

Employer-Sponsored Benefits

Pros:

- Can be negotiated
- Often underutilized
- Cons:
- Tied to continued employment
- Some have caps or taxes

Action Steps: What You Can Do Right Now

1. **Make a list of every financial aid option you haven't explored yet.**
2. **Google your state + "pharmacist loan repayment program."**
3. **Ask HR about tuition support or student loan repayment.**
4. **Set a calendar reminder to apply for at least 3 scholarships this month.**
5. **Create a spreadsheet of forgiveness-eligible employers in your area.**
6. **Bookmark the PSLF Help Tool on studentaid.gov and walk through it.**
7. **Follow pharmacy orgs on LinkedIn and check for posted scholarships.**

Plain-Language Breakdowns: What Nobody Taught You

What's the difference between forgiveness and repayment?

Forgiveness means your debt disappears after a certain time period (usually with tax benefits). Repayment programs pay chunks off your balance in exchange for work.

Do I have to pay taxes on forgiven loans?

Not always. PSLF forgiveness is tax-free. Other forgiveness programs (like IDR after 20-25 years) may result in a tax bill unless current rules are extended.

Can I double dip—use employer repayment and pursue PSLF?

Yes—but be strategic. Use employer funds to make minimum payments, not extra, so you maximize forgiveness potential.

Are private loans eligible for these programs?

Rarely. Most loan forgiveness and repayment programs are only for federal loans. Consolidating private into federal isn't an option—only the reverse is possible.

Empowerment Check-In: You Deserve Options

You didn't come this far to be stuck. You deserve to know your options—and have the tools to act on them. You are not a burden. You are not "too late." You are not alone.

You're a pharmacist. You are smart, capable, and worthy of a debt-free path forward.

Make One Money Move Before Bed Tonight

Seriously. Do one thing:

- Look up your state's loan repayment program.
- Email HR and ask about education benefits.
- Set a calendar alert for a scholarship deadline.
- Forward this chapter to a pharmacy student who needs to hear it.

Just one action.

Then next week, do another.

That's how freedom starts.

Final Word: This Isn't Just About Aid—It's About Liberation

Understanding financial aid isn't just about knocking a few thousand off your loan total. It's about reclaiming control. Creating new chapters. Giving yourself the runway to breathe again.

This chapter isn't your finish line—it's your launchpad.

So go. Apply. Ask. Investigate. Dream bigger than your debt.

You didn't become a pharmacist to feel trapped by tuition. You became a pharmacist to make a difference—in your life and in others'.

And you still can.

Make your move.

Your future self will thank you.

Your family will thank you.

And your freedom?

It starts right here.

Chapter 8: Should You Work in School? The Financial Pros and Cons

Let's Talk About It—The Question You're Probably Wrestling With

You're already balancing coursework that would make most people cry.

You're memorizing metabolic pathways, learning to dose chemotherapy, and surviving rounds that start before sunrise.

Now someone asks: "Are you going to get a job too?"

That question hits different when you're in pharmacy school. Because it's not just about having extra cash. It's about survival. It's about staying out of more debt. It's about dignity. Sometimes it's about sending money back home or supporting a kid.

But also?

It's about knowing what *that* decision could cost you in energy, grades, mental health—and future income.

So in this chapter, we're going to walk through it all. Not just whether you *can* work in school. But whether you *should*. What it could mean for your financial life in the long run. What to watch out for. What no one tells you. And how to make a decision that aligns with your values, goals, and your version of wealth.

This isn't just about time management. It's about financial freedom.

Let's go.

Why This Chapter Matters More Than You Think

Here's what I know:

Pharmacy school is a full-time job. But so is your future financial health.

If you work during school, that income can do more than just pay for coffee and rent. It can reduce how much debt you graduate with. And that matters—because debt doesn't just take your money. It takes your options.

Debt determines whether you can say yes to a residency or no to an employer you hate.

It determines whether you build wealth early—or spend your 30s just digging out of a hole.

Working in school isn't always easy. And it's not for everyone. But this chapter will give you the tools to decide *for yourself*.

Let's Start With the Real Math

Let's imagine two students. Same program. Same tuition. Same goals.

Student A: Doesn't work in school.

Takes out an extra $10,000/year in loans to cover living expenses. Graduates with $160,000 in loans. Starts repayment right after graduation.

Student B: Works 12 hours/week in school.

Earns ~$8,000/year. Takes out $10,000 less in loans. Graduates with $120,000 in loans.

Assume a 6.8% interest rate and a 10-year standard repayment plan.

Student A's repayment: ~$1,840/month

Student B's repayment: ~$1,380/month

That's a $460/month difference—for ten years. That's over **$55,000** saved just because Student B worked part-time for a few years.

Let that sink in.

Now multiply that savings by what happens when you invest that $460/month. Compound interest gets to work. That's hundreds of thousands of dollars later in life.

So yes—working in school can pay off *big time*.

But it's not always that simple. So let's break it all down.

The Pros of Working During Pharmacy School

Let's be real: working in school doesn't just give you a paycheck. It gives you leverage.

1. You Take Out Less in Loans

Every dollar you earn is one you don't have to borrow at 6%+ interest.

And if you work enough to avoid "cost of living" loans? That's huge. It's like giving your future self a raise—before you even graduate.

2. You Gain Work Experience

Even if it's not clinical, employers notice hustle. Pharmacy tech jobs, hospital admin gigs, tutoring, or even barista shifts show discipline and time management. And in a tight job market? That helps.

3. You Build a Network

Your part-time job might introduce you to preceptors, hiring managers, or other pharmacists. That one Saturday shift at the hospital pharmacy? It might land you a residency letter later.

4. You Might Get Tuition Benefits

Some students work at universities that offer tuition remission or discounts. Others work in health systems that offer scholarships. Don't sleep on that benefit.

5. You Learn Financial Discipline

Having to manage a paycheck while juggling classes forces you to prioritize. You build budgeting habits. You learn to delay gratification. And that mindset? That's what builds wealth later.

6. You Keep Your Identity Outside of School

Let's be honest. Pharmacy school can consume you. Having a job—especially one outside of healthcare—can help you remember who you are. That's not just money. That's mental health.

The Cons of Working During Pharmacy School

Now let's be honest about the costs. Because working in school isn't all sunshine and paychecks.

1. Time Is Tight

Pharmacy school is brutal. You're already doing full-time coursework, rotations, and studying for boards. Add work, and something might give—your sleep, your grades, your sanity.

2. Burnout Is Real

You're not a machine. If your part-time job wears you down, it might hurt your long-term performance—and that can cost you far more than you earn.

3. Missed Academic Opportunities

Working too much might mean saying no to research, leadership, tutoring, or mentorship roles that help your CV stand out for residencies or fellowships.

4. Less Time for Wellness

If you're working every weekend, when are you resting? Cooking? Moving your body? Calling your family? Mental and physical health matter in this decision.

5. Risk of Lower Grades

Even if you're a high performer, time is a finite resource. Less time to study = higher risk of slipping grades. And in competitive residency programs? That matters.

The Middle Ground: Strategic Work That Works For You

It's not all or nothing.

You don't have to work 20 hours/week at a retail chain while juggling six classes. But what if you:

- Tutored undergrads in chemistry for $25/hour?
- Worked 8 hours/week in a quiet campus library job?
- Picked up summer shifts at a hospital pharmacy?
- Did freelance work (writing, editing, graphic design) on your schedule?
- Became a paid student ambassador for a pharmacy company or brand?

Strategic work respects your bandwidth *and* your bank account.

Ask: What can I do that earns money *and* builds my resume, flexibility, or peace of mind?

Relatable Story: Mia's Turning Point

Mia was in year two of pharmacy school. She had $90,000 in loans already. Her family couldn't help. She was anxious, tired, and one bad exam from burnout.

Her classmates told her not to work. "Focus on school," they said.

But Mia knew something had to change. She found a work-study job at the campus health center—10 hours/week, sitting at a front desk, doing paperwork. She made $150/week.

Not a lot. But enough to pay for groceries, gas, and stop borrowing.

She graduated with $30,000 less in loans than her classmates. She also got a residency at that very health center.

She didn't "sacrifice" her education. She *safeguarded* her future.

Pros and Cons Breakdown: Should You Work in School?

Pros

- Less debt
- More experience
- New connections
- Financial breathing room
- Better financial habits

Cons

- Time pressure
- Academic risk
- Potential burnout
- Less campus involvement
- Possible scheduling conflicts

Plain-Language Breakdown: The "Cost" of Your Time

You might think: "It's not worth it to work for $13/hour."

But here's what no one tells you:

$13/hour now = $13 + avoided loan interest + earlier investing + fewer minimum payments later.

That $13/hour now could be worth $50/hour later if it helps you graduate with less debt.

Time is money. But money is also time.

The question isn't "is it worth $13/hour?" The question is: "What does that $13 save me from later?"

Action Steps: If You're Thinking of Working During School

1. Run Your Numbers

- What's your monthly cost of living?
- How much are you borrowing each year?
- What would working part-time let you avoid?

2. Choose Work That Doesn't Derail You

- Avoid jobs with unpredictable hours
- Look for work-study or campus-based roles
- Consider freelance or online jobs with schedule control

3. Set Boundaries

- Protect your sleep and study time
- Don't work during exam weeks if you can help it
- Talk to your boss about flexibility upfront

4. Monitor Your Grades and Stress Levels

- If grades start to slip, reassess
- Don't be afraid to pause work temporarily
- Prioritize long-term career outcomes

5. Know Your Financial Aid Limits

- Working too much may reduce need-based aid
- Monitor your FAFSA status
- Ask your financial aid office how income affects your package

Empowerment Check-In: You Are Not Behind

Let's stop shaming pharmacists for needing to work in school.

Needing money is not a moral failure. It's a reality.

What matters is how you respond.

You're not lazy. You're not reckless. You're a hustler. A provider. A builder.

And whether you work in school or not, your value isn't tied to your bank account. It's tied to how you make decisions with intention, honesty, and power.

You're not a victim of the system.

You're learning how to navigate it with your head up and your heart intact.

Make One Money Move Before Bed Tonight

You know what's coming.

Make one move.

- Research on-campus jobs.
- Email your financial aid office.
- Apply for a paid tutoring position.
- Write out your monthly budget to see what a part-time job could free up.
- Talk to someone one year ahead of you and ask what worked for them.

Just one move. Then another next week.

That's how financial freedom begins.

Final Word: This Isn't About Working in School. It's About Working Your Plan

This chapter wasn't written to convince you to get a job.

It was written to give you permission to decide—boldly, wisely, and without shame.

Working in school won't make or break you. But knowing your numbers? Owning your choices? That's what turns chaos into confidence.

This chapter is your reminder that you are allowed to choose wealth. Even while you're still earning your degree.

Especially while you're still earning your degree.

Because freedom doesn't begin when you hit six figures.

It begins when you decide to stop living in the dark about money.

Let's bring it into the light.

You've got this.

Chapter 9: Credit Cards in Pharmacy School – Friend, Foe, or Just a Tool?

Let's Have the Conversation Nobody Had with You About Credit Cards

You're in pharmacy school. You've got exams, rotations, papers, labs, and enough clinical jargon to fill an encyclopedia.

Now here comes the credit card conversation. But this isn't about "cut up your cards" or "get all the points." This isn't your grandma warning you about interest or your roommate flexing about cashback.

This is the real talk.

You are a future healthcare professional making high-stakes decisions. But nobody taught you how to handle plastic money in a world built on digital debt.

So let's walk through it. Calmly. Clearly. Respectfully. We'll talk through what credit cards are, how they work, why people get burned, how to avoid traps, how to use them smartly, and how they can either be the beginning of your financial freedom—or a slow leak in your financial life.

This chapter doesn't come from judgment.

It comes from lived experience.

Let's talk about credit cards like adults.

Why This Chapter Matters – Especially in Pharmacy School

Here's what you're up against:

You might be broke right now, but your inbox is full of credit card offers.

You've got $100K+ in student loans, and yet you just got pre-approved for a $5,000 limit.

You're trying to pass pharmacokinetics, but you're also worried about making rent—and a credit card feels like a lifeline.

And maybe you've already used one. Maybe you're carrying a balance. Maybe you've missed a payment.

Shame off the table.

Let's turn on the lights and see credit for what it is.

Not evil.

Not magical.

Just a tool.

How you use it? That's the key.

What Is a Credit Card—Really?

Here's the simplest definition:

A credit card is a short-term loan with high interest that resets every month if you pay it off in full. If you don't pay in full, that loan starts charging you interest—often 18% to 29% or more.

It is not free money.

It is not your income.

It is not a safety net unless you know how to use it safely.

Credit cards are a tool. Like fire. They can cook your dinner—or burn your house down.

Credit Cards in Pharmacy School: The Pros

Let's be generous here. There *are* some valid reasons to use a credit card—even during pharmacy school.

1. Build Your Credit Score

A good credit score will matter when:

- You want to rent an apartment
- You need a car loan
- You apply for a mortgage
- You get a job with a background check
- You eventually refinance your student loans

Using a credit card responsibly—meaning small purchases you pay off in full and on time—can raise your score and create a strong credit history.

2. Emergency Flexibility

When your checking account hits zero and your car needs $400 in repairs, a credit card can buy you time. Sometimes it's better than a payday loan, overdraft, or borrowing from someone who will never let you forget it.

3. Purchase Protection

Some credit cards offer benefits like extended warranties, fraud protection, or coverage for damaged/stolen items. Debit cards don't always have that. Neither does cash.

4. Rewards (Only If You Pay in Full)

Points. Cash back. Travel perks. These are real. But they only make sense if you're not paying interest. Because 5% cash back on groceries means nothing if you're paying 25% in interest on your unpaid balance.

5. Learning Discipline (Low-Stakes Training)

Learning to manage credit now—when your spending is relatively low—can be safer than learning later when your lifestyle and credit limits are higher. The key is to treat your credit card like a debit card: only spend what you already have.

Now the Cons—Let's Be Brutally Honest

1. Interest Will Crush You If You're Not Careful

You buy $1,000 worth of stuff. You pay the minimum—let's say $25/month. It could take *years* to pay off. And you'll pay hundreds—sometimes thousands—in interest.

That $1,000 Target run? Might cost you $1,900 by the time it's done.

2. Your Credit Score Can Plummet Fast

One late payment. One maxed-out card. One forgotten bill.

That's all it takes to lose 50–100 points off your score. And it takes *much* longer to rebuild than it does to fall.

3. The Illusion of Wealth Can Ruin You

A credit card makes you feel like you can afford things you can't.

It makes your broke feel less broke—until the bill hits.

It lets you keep up with classmates or influencers. But what you're really doing is trading your future money for present comfort.

4. Slippery Slope of Debt Accumulation

$200 for books here. $300 for a plane ticket there. $100 at the bar. It adds up.

And you justify it because you're stressed, overwhelmed, "deserve it," or think future-you will make it all back.

But future-you doesn't want your leftovers. Future-you wants freedom.

5. It's Harder to Focus When You're Drowning in Guilt

A maxed-out card creates anxiety. Avoidance. Shame. It takes up brain space.

In a profession where clarity and precision matter, you can't afford to carry quiet panic.

Let's Talk About Real-Life Scenarios

Scenario 1: The Emergency Expense

Ravi is in his third year. His car breaks down. The repair is $1,100. He doesn't have it. No savings. His parents can't help. He puts it on a credit card.

That's not irresponsible. That's reality. Ravi sets up an auto-payment plan. He trims his spending for the next three months. He pays it off in full within the 0% intro rate period.

That's a credit card used *strategically*.

Scenario 2: The Lifestyle Drift

Taylor gets a new card with a $4,000 limit. She uses it for groceries. Then gas. Then books. Then a new jacket. Then a weekend trip.

Suddenly she owes $3,200 and can only afford the minimum. She's paying $85/month in interest alone.

That's the trap.

Scenario 3: The Smart Builder

Luis uses his card only for his monthly Spotify and cell phone bill. He pays it off in full every month, sets auto-pay, and never uses more than 10% of his credit limit.

He has no debt. A 740 credit score. And when it's time to get a residency in another state? He gets approved for housing within a day.

That's the win.

Plain-Language Breakdown: How Credit Cards Work

Let's de-jargon the language.

Credit Limit – The max you're allowed to borrow

Balance – How much you currently owe

Minimum Payment – The smallest amount you can pay without a penalty

APR (Annual Percentage Rate) – The interest rate charged if you don't pay in full

Statement Closing Date – The day your monthly bill is generated

Due Date – The day your payment must be received

Grace Period – The time between the statement and due date when interest doesn't apply if paid in full

Utilization Ratio – Your balance divided by your credit limit. Lower is better. Keep it under 30%. Under 10% is ideal.

How Credit Affects Your Future

Your credit report isn't just about borrowing.

It affects your:

- Rental applications
- Job offers (yes, some employers check)
- Insurance premiums
- Car loans
- Mortgage approval
- Student loan refinancing

Having good credit = more options = lower costs = faster path to wealth.

Bad credit = fewer options = higher costs = longer financial drag.

Pros and Cons Summary: Are Credit Cards a Good Idea in Pharmacy School?

Pros

- Build credit

- Use in emergencies
- Protection and perks
- Can be safer than debit online
- Rewards when paid in full

Cons

- High interest
- Easy to misuse
- Damages credit if abused
- Adds to mental load
- Creates lifestyle creep

Rules of Thumb for Using Credit Cards in School

1. Only use a credit card if you have the money *already* in checking.
2. Pay off the balance *in full* every month. No exceptions.
3. Use less than 30% of your credit limit. 10% is even better.
4. Never use a card to buy things you couldn't afford in cash.
5. Use auto-pay to avoid late payments.
6. Review your statements. Spot fraud or sneaky charges.
7. Use rewards only if you never carry a balance.
8. Don't get seduced by points. $200 in debt to get $10 in cash back is not a flex.
9. Don't co-sign or lend your card to anyone. Ever.
10. If you're in trouble, get help early. Credit counseling exists for a reason.

Action Steps: Use Credit Like a Pro—Even as a Student

1. **Check your credit score (for free at Credit Karma or your bank)**
2. **Get one secured credit card or starter card—don't open five**
3. **Put one small, recurring expense on it (Spotify, Netflix, etc.)**

4. **Set up auto-pay in full every month**
5. **Track your utilization ratio and keep it low**
6. **Don't carry balances for "emergencies" unless you have a payoff plan**
7. **Talk to a mentor or financial coach before you fall behind**
8. **Use a budgeting app (like Mint or YNAB) to track purchases**
9. **Don't get emotional—credit is not a character test**
10. **Remember: your card is not your safety net. *You* are.**

Empowerment Check-In: Credit Cards Don't Define You

You're not stupid if you've used credit cards poorly.

You're not irresponsible if you're carrying a balance.

You're not a failure if you didn't know this before.

You're a pharmacist-in-training in a system that profits off of your stress, silence, and confusion.

This chapter is not your punishment.

It's your toolkit.

Use it. Build with it. Set yourself free.

Make One Money Move Before Bed Tonight

Pick one.

- Look up your credit score.
- Log into your credit card and check your balance.
- Set up auto-pay for the minimum—at least.
- List all your cards and balances in a spreadsheet.
- Commit to no new charges until the next statement.
- Choose one small recurring bill to put on your card for points—but only if you can pay in full.
- Read your cardholder agreement. Learn your APR.

Just one move.

Next week? Another.

Small steps. Big power.

Final Word: You Are Smarter Than This System Wants You to Be

You didn't go to pharmacy school to become a slave to interest.

You didn't work this hard to graduate into guilt, confusion, or silence.

You came here for freedom. Purpose. Wealth. Peace of mind.

Credit cards can serve you.

Or they can sabotage you.

That choice is yours now.

Use them wisely.

Let them work *for* you—not against you.

This isn't about judgment.

It's about strategy.

It's about freedom.

It's about choosing your future with your eyes open, your credit clean, and your spirit strong.

Let's go build that life.

Chapter 10: Opening Your First Bank and Investment Accounts

Let's keep it honest right from the jump.

You've spent the better part of a decade learning how to dose vancomycin, memorize metabolic pathways, and calculate creatinine clearance—but no one taught you how to open a checking account, let alone start investing.

And now here you are. Smart. Capable. On the edge of a six-figure salary. But feeling unsure when it comes to something as basic as walking into a bank or opening an online investment account.

You're not behind.

You're not broken.

You're just finally in a place where you're ready to learn—and ready to take control.

This chapter is going to give you the step-by-step clarity you deserve. No shame. No assumptions. Just real talk and clear action.

Because this isn't just about having a place to stash your money. It's about building a foundation for wealth—on your own terms.

Let's get into it.

Why This Chapter Matters More Than Most People Realize

Most people think financial freedom starts when they pay off debt or start earning more.

But here's the truth:

Financial freedom starts the moment you give your money a *home.*

Not a messy drawer. Not under your mattress. Not a debit card you don't check.

A system.

A structure.

A strategy.

That's what this chapter is about. Building that system from the ground up.

We're going to walk through:

- How to choose the right checking and savings accounts
- What to look for in a bank or credit union
- How to set up your first investment accounts
- What types of investments to consider
- How to automate your money flow
- The mistakes to avoid
- How to build confidence—even if you're starting small

By the time you're done reading this, you'll be able to open any account with clarity and calm.

Let's go.

Step One: Understand the Role of a Bank Account in Your Financial Life

Let's simplify this.

You need a **checking account** for spending.

You need a **savings account** for holding.

You need an **investment account** for building wealth.

These are the three pillars. Everything else builds on top of this.

Your checking account is the hub. It's where your paycheck lands. It's what your debit card draws from. It's the financial engine of your month-to-month life.

Your savings account is your buffer. Your breathing room. It's where your emergency fund lives. It's where you put money you don't want to spend.

Your investment account is your future. It's where your wealth grows. Where your retirement begins. Where your money starts working while you sleep.

If you don't have all three yet, that's okay. We're building.

How to Open Your First Checking Account—Without Getting Hustled

Let's be real. Not all checking accounts are created equal.

Some charge fees for breathing wrong.

Some are sleek, online-only, with no customer service.

Some are old-school brick-and-mortar with branches on every corner.

So how do you choose?

Here's what to look for in a checking account:

1. No monthly maintenance fees

Don't pay to access your own money. Period.

2. Free ATM access—or reimbursement for out-of-network ATMs

Especially important if you travel or don't live near your bank's ATMs.

3. Online banking + mobile app

You want to be able to check balances, deposit checks, and transfer funds from your phone.

4. Direct deposit capability

Essential for getting paid on time—especially during residency or rotations.

5. Low or no minimum balance requirements

You shouldn't have to keep $1,000 in your account just to avoid a penalty.

6. Strong customer service

You don't want to be stuck in a phone tree when your card gets hacked.

Bank vs. Credit Union vs. Online Bank—What's the Move?

Let's break it down.

Traditional banks (Chase, Bank of America, Wells Fargo):

- Branch access
- Widely accepted
- – May have more fees

- – Less personal service

Credit unions (local or pharmacy-affiliated):

- Member-focused
- Often lower fees and better rates
- Community vibe
- – Fewer ATMs or branches
- – Tech can be outdated

Online banks (Ally, SoFi, Chime):

- Higher interest on savings
- No fees
- Great apps
- – No branches
- – Depositing cash can be tricky

If you're tech-savvy and don't need to deposit cash often, an online bank can be a great choice.

If you want in-person help, a credit union or traditional bank may be better.

How to Open a Checking Account: A Simple Checklist

1. Choose your bank or credit union
2. Apply online or in person
3. Provide ID (driver's license, passport, or state ID)
4. Provide your Social Security number (for verification)
5. Provide proof of address (utility bill, lease, etc.)
6. Fund the account (some require a small deposit)
7. Set up online banking and download the app
8. Order your debit card
9. Set up direct deposit from your employer

10. Link your savings account

Done.

You've now got a base camp for your financial life.

Next Up: Open a Savings Account That Actually Works

Your savings account isn't just where your money waits.

It's where your *goals* wait.

Emergency fund. Down payment. Travel fund. Safety net.

But too many pharmacists park money in savings accounts earning 0.01% interest.

You deserve better.

What to look for in a savings account:

- **High-yield interest** (Look for 4% or higher if rates are elevated)
- **No fees or minimum balance requirements**
- **FDIC or NCUA insured**
- **Easy transfer to/from your checking**
- **Ability to create sub-savings goals (some apps/banks offer this)**

Online banks dominate in this category. Explore options like Ally, Marcus, Capital One 360, or Discover.

How Much Should You Keep in Savings?

Emergency fund rule of thumb:

- **3 to 6 months** of essential expenses
- More if you're a freelancer or transitioning careers
- Less if you're just starting and focused on debt payoff

Pro tip: Start with one month. Then build. Don't wait until you "can afford" to save. Saving is how you *create* that freedom.

Now Let's Talk Investing—Without the Intimidation

This is where most people freeze.

But investing doesn't have to be complicated, risky, or mysterious.

It just has to be started.

You don't need a finance degree.

You don't need thousands of dollars.

You don't need a suit.

You need one thing: a willingness to start small and learn as you go.

Why Pharmacists Need to Invest Early

Let's say you invest $200/month from age 25 to 65 at a 7% average return.

That's over $500,000.

If you wait until age 35?

You end up with around $250,000.

Time is your biggest asset. Not money.

Start now—even if it's $50/month.

Types of Investment Accounts You Should Know

1. Brokerage Account

- No tax advantages
- Total flexibility (deposit or withdraw anytime)
- Good for long-term wealth, not retirement
- Can be used for early financial freedom or big goals

2. Roth IRA

- Contribute post-tax money
- Grows tax-free
- Withdraw tax-free in retirement
- Contribution limit: $7,000/year if under 50 (2025)
- Income phase-out starts around $146K single / $230K married
- Ideal for younger pharmacists

3. Traditional IRA

- Pre-tax contributions (may be deductible)
- Grows tax-deferred

- Taxes paid upon withdrawal
- Good if you're in a high tax bracket now (not common in school or early career)

4. 401(k) or 403(b)

- Employer-sponsored retirement account
- Contributions often matched (free money!)
- Max out the match first
- Contribution limit: $23,000/year in 2025
- Use Roth option if offered and you're early in your career

Where to Open an Investment Account

Robo-advisors (easy, automated):

- Betterment
- Wealthfront
- SoFi
- Ellevest
- Great for beginners
- Hands-off
- – Small fees (usually 0.25%)
- – Less control

DIY Platforms (if you want to learn):

- Fidelity
- Vanguard
- Charles Schwab
- M1 Finance
- E*TRADE
- Total control
- No fees for most trades

- – Requires more effort
- – Easy to overcomplicate

Choose based on your learning style.

How to Open Your First Investment Account

1. Choose your platform (see above)
2. Create an account (use your real name, not your pharmacy nickname)
3. Choose account type: Roth IRA or brokerage (or both)
4. Link your checking account
5. Fund your account (start small if needed)
6. Choose your investments (a target-date fund is a safe starter)
7. Set up auto-investing monthly
8. Revisit once a year—not every week

What Should You Invest In? Let's Keep It Simple

You're not picking stocks. You're building a long-term portfolio.

Here's a basic setup:

- **Target-Date Fund** (adjusts risk as you age)
- **Total Market Index Fund** (invests in 3,000+ companies)
- **S&P 500 Index Fund** (top 500 U.S. companies)
- **Bond Fund** (for stability later in life)

Don't try to beat the market.

Just try to *join* it—and stay in it long enough to benefit from time.

Common Mistakes to Avoid

- **Waiting too long to start**
- **Putting off investing until debt is gone**
- **Thinking you need thousands to begin**
- **Chasing hot stocks or TikTok trends**
- **Over-checking your account**

- **Ignoring taxes (capital gains, dividends)**
- **Not having a plan or goals**

Real-Life Scenario: Ava Starts Investing at 26

Ava's a retail pharmacist. Burned out. Tired of living paycheck to paycheck.

She opens a Roth IRA with Fidelity.

She puts in $200/month into a target-date 2065 fund.

By the time she's 40? She has nearly $80,000 invested.

By retirement? Over $600,000.

All from starting *now*—not perfectly, but consistently.

Action Steps: Set Up Your Financial Foundation Today

1. Open a checking account with no fees
2. Open a high-yield savings account
3. Start an emergency fund—even $100 is a win
4. Open a Roth IRA or brokerage account
5. Set up $50/month auto-deposit to invest
6. Track your accounts once a month—not daily
7. Celebrate progress—not perfection
8. Learn as you go. This is a long game.

Empowerment Check-In: You Deserve to Be Wealthy—and Well

Opening a bank account is more than paperwork.

It's a declaration.

That you're not hiding from your money anymore.

That you're ready to build.

That you respect your future enough to start—even if you're starting small.

This isn't about being rich tomorrow.

It's about building financial dignity today.

You've already done the hard part—becoming a pharmacist.

Now it's time to make sure your money works as hard as you do.

Make One Money Move Before Bed Tonight

Pick one.

- Open a savings account online
- Research Roth IRAs
- Start a $50/month investment plan
- Check if your job offers a 401(k)
- List all your current accounts in a spreadsheet
- Set a calendar reminder for your monthly "money date"

Just one move.

Next week? Another.

This is how wealth begins.

Final Word: You're Not Behind. You're Just Beginning.

Let go of the shame.

Let go of the pressure to get it perfect.

Your wealth-building journey begins with simple steps—taken consistently.

Open the accounts.

Automate what you can.

Let your money start growing.

Not because you're greedy.

Because you're ready to stop surviving and start designing your financial life with clarity, confidence, and care.

Part II: Early Career – From Intern to Licensed Pharmacist

This section is where your financial journey gets real.

You've finished the lectures, passed the exams, and earned the white coat. Now the paycheck starts coming in—but so do new questions, pressures, and possibilities. *Part II: Early Career – From Intern to Licensed Pharmacist* is about helping you navigate the financial transition from student to professional with clarity, confidence, and control.

Whether you're starting your first retail position, beginning a hospital residency, or weighing multiple job offers, this section walks you through the key decisions that will shape your financial foundation for years to come. From understanding your benefits package to setting up your first retirement accounts, negotiating your salary, reviewing your student loan strategy, avoiding lifestyle inflation, and laying the groundwork for wealth—you'll learn how to move from reactive to proactive with your money.

This isn't about budgeting every latte. It's about building structure, intention, and freedom into your early financial life—so you can grow your career without growing your stress.

Welcome to the real world of pharmacy. Let's make sure your money is just as smart as your degree.

Chapter 11: Your First Paycheck – Breaking Down Taxes and Deductions

Let's talk about the moment you've been waiting for.

The moment after graduation. After the board exams. After the interviews. You finally start your first full-time job as a licensed pharmacist.

And then?

You get your first paycheck.

And your stomach drops.

Because it doesn't look like you thought it would.

You stare at the direct deposit notification or the stub and think, "Wait, where did all my money go?"

This chapter is here to answer that question—not with jargon, but with clarity.

Because the truth is, no one really prepares you for how much gets taken out before you ever touch your money. Or how to make sense of all those lines: federal tax, state tax, FICA, 401(k), HSA, insurance, union dues, and more.

It's confusing on purpose.

But after this chapter, it won't be for you.

We're going to walk through every part of your paycheck, line by line. You'll understand what's optional and what's mandatory. What you control and what you don't. And how to make sure your money flows *with* your goals—not against them.

This isn't just about understanding your paycheck.

This is about owning it.

Let's go.

Why This Chapter Matters

Your paycheck is more than just a number.

It's your life's energy in dollars.

It's the reward for years of hard work.

It's your first taste of financial independence—but only if you understand how to read it.

Here's the brutal truth: if you don't understand how your paycheck works, you'll always feel like you're running on a treadmill. Earning more. Saving less. Always wondering why it never feels like enough.

But when you understand how your money flows?

That's when you start building wealth instead of just collecting paychecks.

Let's break it down.

What You Think You Make vs. What You Actually Take Home

Let's start with this example:

Job offer: $120,000/year

Expectation: $10,000/month

Reality: Closer to $6,500–$7,000/month depending on benefits, location, and withholdings

That's a 25–35% drop before you even see the money.

Where's it going?

Let's go line by line.

The Core Breakdown of a Paycheck

1. **Gross Pay**
2. **Taxes**
3. **Benefits Deductions**
4. **Voluntary Contributions**
5. **Net Pay (Take-Home)**

Each of these deserves a spotlight.

1. Gross Pay – What You *Technically* Earn

This is the total amount you've earned before any deductions.

If you make $120,000 a year, your gross monthly income is $10,000.

But that's just the starting point. Everything else subtracts from here.

2. Taxes – Where the Government Gets Theirs

Let's start with the three big ones:

Federal Income Tax

This is your biggest tax. It's based on a tiered system called marginal tax brackets.

Your *entire* income isn't taxed at one rate. It's taxed in *layers*.

Example (2025, single filer):

- First $11,600 taxed at 10%
- Next $35,550 taxed at 12%
- Next $54,450 taxed at 22%
- The rest taxed at 24%, 32%, 35%, or 37%

So even if you're in the "24% tax bracket," your *effective* tax rate is lower.

FICA Taxes

These fund Social Security and Medicare.

- 6.2% for Social Security (on first $168,600 of income in 2025)
- 1.45% for Medicare
- 0.9% extra Medicare tax if you make over $200K (single) or $250K (married)

Total FICA = 7.65% of your income, automatically withheld.

State Income Tax

Varies by state. Could be:

- 0% (e.g., Texas, Florida)
- 3–10% in others (e.g., California, New York, Oregon)

Some cities (like NYC) tack on a local income tax too.

Estimated Withholding Example

$120,000/year pharmacist in California:

- Federal: ~$16,000
- FICA: ~$9,200
- State: ~$6,000
- Total Taxes: ~$31,000
- Take-Home: ~$89,000/year or ~$7,400/month

That's before benefits and retirement deductions.

3. Benefits Deductions – Your "Invisible Paycheck"

This is where many pharmacists get surprised.

Your job may offer benefits that sound great—health insurance, dental, vision, life insurance—but they come out of your paycheck before you ever see it.

Here's what might be deducted:

Health Insurance Premiums

This could be $100–$500/month depending on your coverage.

Dental and Vision Insurance

Usually $10–$50/month

Group Life Insurance

Sometimes free, sometimes an optional add-on

Short- and Long-Term Disability Insurance

This is often overlooked—but it's essential

Flexible Spending Accounts (FSAs)

Used for healthcare or dependent care expenses

Pre-tax, but "use it or lose it" rules apply

Health Savings Account (HSA)

Only for high-deductible health plans

Tax-free going in, tax-free growing, tax-free coming out

One of the most powerful tools in your benefits package

Each of these deductions is *technically* reducing your taxable income.

That's a good thing. But it also reduces your take-home pay.

4. Voluntary Contributions – Where You Build Wealth or Flexibility

These are the decisions you make about what to do with your paycheck *before* you see it.

401(k) or 403(b) Contributions

Pre-tax retirement savings reduce your taxable income

Match = free money. Always get the full match if you can

Roth 401(k) Contributions

Post-tax retirement savings. You pay taxes now, but not in retirement.

Student Loan Payments (Automatic Payroll Deductions)

Some employers offer this—know if you're enrolled

Union Dues or Association Fees

Check your offer letter. Not all pharmacists have this, but some do.

These deductions are empowering. They put you in control of your financial life.

But they still reduce what lands in your checking account.

5. Net Pay – What Actually Hits Your Account

After taxes, insurance, and retirement, this is what's left.

This is the number that matters when budgeting, saving, investing, and living.

If you earn $120,000, your net pay might be around $6,500/month after everything is said and done.

Knowing this helps you set realistic goals.

You're not failing if you can't save $3,000/month. You're working from what you *actually* have.

That's power.

Plain-Language Examples of Paycheck Withholding

Let's say:

- Base salary: $120,000/year
- Monthly gross: $10,000

Deductions:

- Federal tax: $1,500
- FICA: $765
- State tax: $500
- Health insurance: $250
- Dental/vision: $35
- 401(k): $1,000
- HSA: $200

Net pay: ~$5,750/month

Knowing this, your budget isn't based on $10,000. It's based on $5,750. That's the number that matters.

Understanding Withholding on Paychecks

When you start a new job, you'll fill out a **W-4 form**.

This tells your employer how much federal tax to withhold.

You'll choose:

- Filing status
- Whether you have dependents
- Whether you want extra withholding
- Any other jobs or income

Tip: Don't claim too little withholding and get hit with a huge tax bill in April. Don't over-withhold just to get a giant refund. Aim for balance.

You can update your W-4 anytime. If you get married, have a kid, or pick up a side hustle—revisit it.

Real-Life Scenario: Jasmine's First Paycheck Shock

Jasmine graduated, landed a hospital role, and was thrilled about her $110,000 salary.

She expected $9,166/month.

She got $6,200.

She panicked.

She called her dad.

He laughed.

Then she looked at her pay stub.

- Federal: $1,400
- FICA: $675
- State: $450
- Health: $280
- 401(k): $800
- HSA: $150
- Net: $6,200

She wasn't getting shortchanged.

She was just seeing, for the first time, how the system works.

And once she saw it clearly? She built her budget around it. And she felt calm.

That's the goal.

Action Steps: Understand and Own Your Paycheck

1. Pull your most recent pay stub
2. Highlight your gross pay and net pay
3. List every deduction—know what's what
4. Compare your tax withholding to IRS tax brackets
5. If needed, adjust your W-4
6. Review your benefits package—are you maximizing value?
7. Calculate how much you're saving pre-tax
8. Set your monthly budget based on *net pay,* not gross
9. Schedule a 15-minute "paycheck review" every quarter
10. Talk to HR if anything looks off or unclear

Pros and Cons of Common Deductions

401(k) Pre-Tax Contributions

Pros: Lower taxable income now, compound growth

Cons: Taxes due in retirement

Roth 401(k)

Pros: Tax-free withdrawals later

Cons: Less take-home pay now

HSA Contributions

Pros: Triple tax advantage, portable, investment growth

Cons: Only available with HDHPs

Health Insurance Premiums

Pros: Protects against major expenses

Cons: Expensive if you're healthy and rarely use care

Disability Insurance

Pros: Income protection

Cons: Often misunderstood, undervalued

Empowerment Check-In: Your Paycheck Is Not a Mystery

You are not "bad with money" because your paycheck feels confusing.

You are not behind because you didn't know what "FICA" meant.

You are not irresponsible for feeling frustrated when your take-home isn't what you expected.

You are a pharmacist—trained in complexity, capable of learning systems, and fully qualified to understand your own financial foundation.

This chapter wasn't written to overwhelm you.

It was written to remind you that your money deserves your attention.

Not fear. Not guilt.

Just clarity.

Make One Money Move Before Bed Tonight

Pick one:

- Pull your pay stub and look at each line
- Adjust your W-4 to better match your life
- Calculate your actual monthly net income
- Review your 401(k) contributions
- Ask HR about disability insurance
- Set a savings goal based on your take-home pay—not your gross

One move.

Next week? Another.

That's how you build confidence and wealth.

Final Word: This Isn't Just a Paycheck. It's Your Power

Every dollar that enters your life represents time, talent, and energy you've given to the world.

You deserve to know where it goes.

You deserve to keep more of it over time.

You deserve to design a financial life rooted in clarity, not confusion.

Your paycheck is not just money.

It's momentum.

Use it wisely. Use it boldly. Use it to build the life you imagined when you started this whole pharmacy journey in the first place.

Chapter 12: Budgeting on a Pharmacist's Starting Salary

Let's talk about what no one told you when they handed you that PharmD.

That moment when the ink is still drying on your license, and your first job offer comes through.

$110K. $115K. Maybe $120K.

You're grateful. You're relieved. You're proud.

Then you do some math.

And you realize—this is the most money you've ever made.

But somehow, it still doesn't feel like enough.

Because between taxes, loan payments, rent, insurance, groceries, gas, and all the pieces of life that demand your attention—your money seems to disappear faster than it arrives.

You start asking questions.

"Am I doing something wrong?"

"Shouldn't I be saving more by now?"

"Why doesn't this feel like financial security?"

This chapter is for *that* moment.

Not to make you feel bad about where you are.

But to show you exactly how to build a budget on a pharmacist's starting salary—not with scarcity or shame, but with structure and swagger.

Let's not cut back on lattes.

Let's build a life.

One paycheck at a time.

Why This Chapter Matters

Budgeting is not about restriction.

It's about permission.

Permission to spend without guilt.

Permission to save without fear.

Permission to invest in your future *and* enjoy your present.

Most pharmacists were never taught how to manage a high-income profession from day one. That's not your fault. But it is your opportunity.

Because the first few years of your career? They set the tone.

They lay the foundation.

And with a little intention, they can be the start of your wealth-building journey—not just the beginning of your burnout.

Let's build that budget—together.

Step One: Know Your Actual Take-Home Pay

Your job offer says $115,000/year.

Great.

But you don't *take home* $115K.

Here's the average breakdown:

- Gross annual: $115,000
- Federal taxes: ~$15,000
- State taxes (varies): ~$5,000
- FICA (Social Security + Medicare): ~$8,800
- Health insurance premiums: ~$2,400
- 401(k) contribution (5%): ~$5,750
- Net annual: ~$78,000
- Net monthly: ~$6,500

That's your real number.

Budget off that—not your gross.

Step Two: The 50/30/20 (ish) Rule for Pharmacists

Traditional budgeting says:

- 50% needs
- 30% wants
- 20% savings/debt payoff

But as a pharmacist with six figures in loans, let's adjust.

Pharmacist Starter Budget Framework:

- 50% Needs (housing, food, transportation, insurance, minimum student loan payments)
- 25% Financial Goals (extra loan payoff, retirement savings, emergency fund)
- 15% Wants (travel, eating out, shopping, hobbies)
- 10% Flex (cushion, unplanned, fun or forgiveness)

This gives you structure *and* breathing room.

Step Three: Build a Monthly Budget That Reflects Your Real Life

Let's build a sample on $6,500/month net pay.

Housing (rent, utilities, renters insurance): $1,800

Groceries + Dining Out: $800

Transportation (car payment, gas, insurance): $700

Student Loans (minimum + extra): $1,200

Retirement Savings (Roth IRA or 401(k)): $550

Emergency Fund Savings: $250

Health Insurance/Dental/Vision (if post-tax): $100

Subscriptions + Tech (streaming, apps, phone): $150

Gym/Health/Wellness: $100

Wants/Fun/Flex: $850

Total: $6,500

This is what alignment looks like.

You're paying debt, investing, saving, and living—all in the same budget.

Step Four: Understand and Tame Lifestyle Inflation

You finally get your pharmacist paycheck.

So you buy a new car.

You get the upgraded apartment.

You stop checking prices at restaurants.

Because you *deserve* it, right?

Sure. Until you realize your checking account still looks like it did in pharmacy school.

That's lifestyle inflation.

The tendency to increase spending as income increases—without actually building wealth.

Here's how to resist it:

- **Cap your rent at 25% of take-home**
- **Keep your car payment under $400/month**
- **Say no to "monthly payments" that bleed your cash flow**
- **Don't take on new fixed expenses until you've built 3 months of savings**
- **Automate your savings first, then spend what's left**

Your budget is not a punishment.

It's a filter.

To make sure your money supports your goals—not your ego.

Step Five: Budgeting Tools That Actually Work for Busy Pharmacists

You don't need to build a spreadsheet from scratch.

You just need a system that saves time and makes you aware.

Top tools:

- **YNAB (You Need A Budget):** Great for hands-on planners
- **Mint:** Easy, automatic, good for beginners
- **EveryDollar:** Clean interface, zero-based budgeting
- **Tiller:** Spreadsheet lovers only
- **Good old Google Sheets:** If you love manual control

Choose the tool that matches your personality—not someone else's aesthetic.

And no matter what you use?

Have a "money date" every Sunday.

15 minutes. Review your spending. Adjust as needed.

That's where the magic happens.

Step Six: Budget for the Big Four Financial Priorities

As a new pharmacist, your financial life boils down to four main goals:

1. Pay Off Student Loans

Make your minimums. Then put any extra here *if* you're not pursuing forgiveness.

2. Save for Retirement

Start with your 401(k) match. Then open a Roth IRA if you qualify.

3. Build an Emergency Fund

Start with $1,000. Then 3 months of essential expenses.

4. Budget for Joy (So You Don't Burn Out)

Yes, travel matters. Yes, fun counts. No, you don't have to wait 10 years to live.

Make space for both responsibility and freedom.

That's what financial wellness means.

Real-Life Scenario: David's Budget Breakthrough

David landed a retail job at $118K.

He was thrilled—until month three, when he realized he had no idea where his money was going.

He was spending $1,100 on dining out, paying $650 for a car note, and hadn't touched his student loans beyond the minimum.

He didn't feel poor.

But he didn't feel powerful either.

Then he tracked every dollar for one month. Just 30 days.

He cut his dining out by half. Refi'd his car loan. Started sending $500 extra to loans. Opened a Roth IRA.

He didn't make more money.

He made better decisions.

That's what budgeting does.

Plain-Language Breakdowns: Budgeting Concepts You Were Never Taught

Fixed vs. Variable Expenses

Fixed = predictable every month (rent, insurance)

Variable = changes month to month (gas, groceries, fun)

Zero-Based Budgeting

Every dollar has a job. Your income minus your expenses = zero.

Cash Flow Leaks

Recurring charges you forgot about. One-time splurges that become habits. Restaurant spending that doubles without realizing.

Spending Plan vs. Budget

A budget feels like restriction. A spending plan feels like power. Call it what works for you.

Automation vs. Awareness

Automate savings and bills—but still *look* at your accounts. Blind budgeting is just as bad as no budgeting.

Pros and Cons of Budgeting Styles for Pharmacists

Manual Budgeting (Spreadsheets, Paper)

Pros: Full control, high awareness

Cons: Time-consuming, requires discipline

App-Based Budgeting (YNAB, Mint, EveryDollar)

Pros: Easy, accessible, automated

Cons: Can feel detached, inaccurate categorization

Envelope System (Cash-Based)

Pros: Physical discipline, great for overspenders

Cons: Impractical for busy pharmacists and large bills

Percentage-Based Budgeting (50/30/20)

Pros: Simple, adaptable, scalable

Cons: May not fit high student loan payments

Use what works for your brain—not someone else's Instagram grid.

Action Steps: Build and Own Your Budget

1. Write down your net monthly income

2. List all your fixed and variable expenses
3. Calculate your student loan minimums
4. Automate savings to a high-yield account
5. Budget for one joy item each month
6. Cancel two subscriptions you forgot about
7. Set a 15-minute money check-in every Sunday
8. Use an app or spreadsheet to track spending
9. Create a "spending pause" rule for non-essentials
10. Give yourself grace—then keep going

Empowerment Check-In: You Are Not Bad at Budgeting

If no one ever taught you how to manage money, it makes sense that it feels confusing.

But confusion is not your identity.

It's a starting point.

You're not behind.

You're just building.

And the budget? It's your blueprint.

To create space.

To choose your priorities.

To say yes to the life *you* want—not the one Instagram tells you to chase.

Make One Money Move Before Bed Tonight

Pick one:

- Write down your monthly net income
- Download a budgeting app
- Start a spending log
- Open a savings account
- Set up auto-transfer for $50/week to savings
- Block 15 minutes this Sunday for your money date

Just one move.

Next week? Another.

Momentum is built in the mundane.

Final Word: Your Budget Is Not a Cage. It's a Compass.

Let's reframe it.

Budgeting is not about what you can't do.

It's about what you *get* to do—because you've taken the time to be intentional.

Your pharmacist salary is powerful. But it's not about how much you make.

It's about how you move.

With purpose.

With clarity.

With swagger.

Budgeting is how you stop surviving and start building.

Not just a career—but a life.

Chapter 13: Understanding Offer Letters and Negotiating Job Benefits

Let's talk about a moment that's both exciting and intimidating.

You finish your rotations. You pass your boards. You interview at hospitals, clinics, retail chains, or industry roles. Then—finally—it happens.

You get the email.

You've got a job offer.

The salary looks good. The company sounds reputable. You want to say yes.

But something inside you wonders:

Am I missing something?

What questions should I be asking?

Is there room to negotiate?

Is this actually a good deal, or am I just relieved to have one?

This chapter exists for that moment.

Not to scare you.

But to equip you.

Because your offer letter is more than a contract. It's the foundation of your financial life.

And the choices you make in these first few days can echo for years.

So before you sign anything—let's walk through it together.

Why This Chapter Matters

Your offer letter is more than just a number at the top.

It's a layered, often confusing document full of small print, big assumptions, and long-term consequences.

You can't afford to just scan it.

Because saying yes too quickly might mean locking yourself into a role with:

- A weak retirement plan
- Expensive health insurance
- No student loan support
- A non-compete clause that limits future opportunities
- Or a salary that *could've* been $10K higher if you had simply asked

Understanding your offer is about protecting your future self.

This chapter gives you the tools, confidence, and clarity to say "yes" for the right reasons—or to ask for more when you deserve it.

Let's Start with the Offer Letter: What It *Actually* Means

You don't need a law degree to read an offer letter.

You just need a strategy.

Most pharmacist offer letters include:

1. Position title
2. Salary
3. Employment type (full-time, part-time, PRN)
4. Schedule expectations
5. Start date
6. Location
7. Benefits overview
8. Contingencies (licensure, drug test, background check)
9. At-will language
10. Signature lines

Seems straightforward. But the devil is in the details—and what's *not* in writing.

Let's break each piece down.

1. Position Title

This tells you what you're being hired as—but not always what you'll actually do.

"Staff Pharmacist" at a retail chain could mean 60 hours a week and being short-staffed daily.

"Clinical Pharmacist" might sound prestigious—but it might pay less than you think.

Ask:

- Is this role primarily dispensing or clinical?
- Who do I report to?
- Is this title consistent with industry standards?

The title matters for your resume and future growth. Make sure it fits your trajectory.

2. Salary

This is where most people stop reading.

But the number alone doesn't tell the whole story.

A $110,000 salary in Manhattan is not the same as $110,000 in Omaha.

A $115,000 base with no 401(k) match is less valuable than $110,000 with 5% employer retirement contributions.

Also ask:

- Is this hourly or salaried?
- Is there overtime? Differential pay? Shift premiums?
- How often will I be paid? (Biweekly, monthly?)
- What's the review schedule? When can I expect raises?

Salary is just the headline. Benefits and structure are the fine print.

3. Employment Type

Know what you're agreeing to.

- **Full-time** often includes benefits
- **Part-time** may not—check carefully
- **Per diem/PRN** offers flexibility, but rarely health insurance
- **Contract roles** might be temporary, with no job security

If it's a contract job, ask:

- Who pays me—hospital or staffing firm?
- Is there a path to permanent employment?

Don't assume benefits just because it's a job offer. Confirm everything.

4. Schedule Expectations

How many hours?

What days?

What shifts?

You need this in writing.

Pharmacists often accept jobs assuming 40 hours—then find themselves working six 12-hour shifts in a row.

Ask:

- Is this a rotating schedule?
- Will I work weekends or holidays?
- Are there on-call responsibilities?
- Can this schedule change without notice?

Remember: work-life balance is part of compensation.

5. Start Date

This is straightforward—unless you're still waiting on your license, completing a residency, or finishing school.

Make sure your start date gives you time to:

- Get licensed
- Relocate (if needed)

- Wrap up other commitments
- Breathe

If they're pushing you to start earlier than you're ready, that's a red flag.

You don't owe anyone your peace.

6. Location

If the offer says "various locations" or "multiple facilities," press for clarity.

- Are you assigned to one site or floating?
- Will you drive? Fly? Relocate?
- Are travel expenses reimbursed?

Some retail chains and hospital systems expect flexibility—but don't always compensate for it.

Know what you're signing up for.

7. **Benefits Overview**

This is where you start uncovering the *real* value.

Benefits can make a $100K job worth more than a $115K job without them.

Key things to ask about:

Health Insurance

- Premiums (how much do you pay per paycheck?)
- Deductibles and out-of-pocket max
- PPO vs. HMO vs. HDHP
- Is dental/vision included?

Retirement Plans

- 401(k) or 403(b)?
- Employer match? Vesting schedule?
- Roth option available?

Time Off

- How many vacation days? Sick days? Holidays?
- Is PTO front-loaded or accrued?
- Can you carry it over?

Student Loan Repayment Support

- Some hospitals offer up to $10K–$50K over a few years
- Is there a service commitment?

Professional Development

- Will they pay for your CE?
- Conferences? Certifications?

Other Perks

- Signing bonus? Relocation assistance?
- Shift differentials?
- HSA/FSA availability?

Don't just look at salary. Calculate the *total compensation*.

8. Contingencies

Most offers depend on:

- Background check
- Drug screening
- License verification
- Immunization records

Make sure you understand the timeline.

If you fail to meet a contingency, the offer can be rescinded.

This is normal—but don't celebrate until everything clears.

9. At-Will Language

This means your employer can terminate you at any time, for any reason that isn't illegal.

You can also leave at any time.

That's not a threat. It's a reminder: this is a business relationship.

If your contract includes a **non-compete clause** or **non-solicitation clause**, read carefully.

You may be limited in where you can work afterward.

Have an attorney review these clauses if you're unsure.

10. Signature Lines

When you sign, you're not just accepting the job—you're agreeing to the *terms*.

Don't rush it.

Ask questions.

Negotiate, if needed.

Then sign with confidence.

Let's Talk Negotiation—Yes, You Can

Most pharmacists don't negotiate.

They assume the number is final.

They don't want to seem "ungrateful."

But here's the truth:

Every job offer is a starting point.

They expect you to negotiate. And doing so—respectfully and strategically—does *not* risk your offer being rescinded.

You don't need to be aggressive.

You need to be prepared.

What Can You Negotiate?

1. Salary

- Do your research (Glassdoor, Payscale, pharmacy-specific forums)
- Ask: "Is there flexibility in this offer?" or "Based on my experience, I was hoping for X."

2. Signing Bonus

- Often easier to negotiate than base salary
- Especially in rural areas, night shifts, or high-need roles

3. Relocation Assistance

- If you're moving, ask for help
- Typical ranges: $2,000–$10,000

4. Student Loan Repayment

- Ask: "Do you offer loan repayment support?"
- Negotiate total amount *and* vesting schedule

5. PTO

- Ask for more vacation days
- Or faster accrual rate

6. Start Date

- Adjust to match your license, moving timeline, or family needs

7. Remote or Hybrid Flexibility

- Especially for industry or managed care roles

8. Certification or CE Support

- Ask for funding for BCPS, MTM, immunizations, or travel to conferences

How to Frame the Ask (Without Sounding Demanding)

Use Gratitude + Data

"I'm very excited about the offer and the opportunity to join your team. Based on my experience level and market research, I was hoping we could discuss the base salary. Would $120K be possible instead of $115K?"

Ask, Don't Assume

"Are benefits like relocation or student loan repayment available for this role?"

Start with Priorities

If salary's fixed, ask for more PTO or professional development funds.

It's a *conversation,* not a confrontation.

What If They Say No?

Not every employer will budge.

But even if they say no, you've gained valuable information about:

- Their flexibility
- Their compensation philosophy
- How they treat you when you advocate for yourself

If they won't move on salary, ask about other perks.

Even $1,000 more in signing bonus, or one extra PTO day, is a win.

And if they *really* won't budge?

You still walk in knowing your worth—and that's powerful.

Real-Life Scenario: Brianna's Brave Ask

Brianna got an offer from a hospital system: $112K base, great benefits, 3 weeks PTO.

She was tempted to sign immediately.

But she paused. Did her research. Found that her peers were earning $115K–$118K with similar backgrounds.

So she asked:

"Thank you so much for the offer. I'm thrilled at the opportunity. Based on market data and my background, would you consider $117K instead?"

They countered with $115K—and bumped her signing bonus by $2,000.

That extra $5,000/year?

Over 5 years, it's $25,000. For a 15-minute email.

Never be afraid to ask.

Action Steps: Understand and Negotiate with Confidence

1. Review the offer in full—don't just skim for salary
2. Compare the *total compensation* to other offers
3. List your top 3 negotiation priorities
4. Do market research on salaries in your area
5. Script your ask—kind, confident, data-backed
6. Practice with a friend or mentor
7. Ask questions about anything unclear (PTO, benefits, bonus vesting)
8. Don't feel pressure to respond the same day
9. Trust your gut—culture matters
10. Say yes only when you're ready, not when you're rushed

Empowerment Check-In: You Are Allowed to Negotiate

You are not greedy for asking questions.

You are not difficult for wanting clarity.

You are not high-maintenance for knowing your value.

You are a licensed healthcare professional stepping into a six-figure role. You've earned the right to advocate for yourself.

Not with arrogance.

But with awareness.

With respect.

With power.

Make One Money Move Before Bed Tonight

Pick one:

- Google salary ranges for your role and city
- Make a list of benefits you want to ask about
- Draft a negotiation email template
- Review a sample offer letter online

- Write down your financial priorities before accepting any job
- Ask a mentor about their negotiation experience

Just one move.

Next week? Another.

That's how you build your financial future—with your eyes open and your shoulders back.

Final Word: Your Offer Letter Is the Opening Chapter—Not the Whole Book

This isn't just a job.

It's your launchpad.

And your offer letter? It's the blueprint.

Read it. Question it. Shape it to support the life you actually want.

Because you didn't go through pharmacy school to accept the first deal someone handed you.

You went through all of that to walk into your career with power, purpose, and options.

Chapter 14: Eployer-Sponsored Benefits – 401(k), HSA, FSA, and More

Let's talk about one of the most overlooked—and misunderstood—parts of your compensation as a pharmacist.

Not your paycheck.

Your benefits.

That quiet section in your onboarding paperwork. The HR portal that no one explains clearly. The acronym soup—401(k), HSA, FSA, LTD, STD, ESPP—that feels more like an exam question than a roadmap to wealth.

Here's the truth:

Understanding your employer-sponsored benefits can be worth tens—sometimes hundreds—of thousands of dollars over your career.

And yet, most pharmacists barely skim the surface.

Not because they're lazy.

But because no one ever broke it down in plain language.

This chapter does exactly that.

Because you deserve to know what's available.

You deserve to use what you're offered.

And you deserve to turn your benefits into wealth.

Let's go.

Why This Chapter Matters

Benefits aren't perks.

They're compensation.

Every dollar your employer puts toward your retirement, healthcare, life insurance, or tax savings is part of your total pay.

Ignore them, and you leave money on the table.

Understand them, and you unlock options, confidence, and real leverage.

This chapter isn't about "HR stuff."

It's about wealth-building infrastructure.

Let's build yours—brick by brick.

Start Here: The Big Four Categories of Employer Benefits

When you get a job offer, most employers offer some combination of these:

1. Retirement benefits (401(k), 403(b), pensions, Roth options)
2. Health-related accounts (HSA, FSA)
3. Insurance coverage (life, disability, malpractice, health)
4. Work-life and financial perks (student loan support, tuition assistance, wellness stipends)

Each of these plays a role in protecting your income, reducing your taxes, and growing your net worth.

Let's break them down—starting with the crown jewel.

1. Retirement Benefits – The Power of the 401(k)

You've probably heard it before:

"You need to contribute to your 401(k)."

But no one tells you what that *actually* means—or why it matters so much for pharmacists.

So let's break it down.

What is a 401(k)?

A 401(k) is a retirement savings account offered through your employer. You contribute a portion of your paycheck—pre-tax or post-tax (Roth)—into the account. It grows over time through investments, and you don't pay taxes on it until you withdraw in retirement.

Key Features:

- Tax advantages

- Employer match (free money)
- Annual contribution limits
- Investment options (mutual funds, index funds)
- Vesting schedule for employer match
- Penalties for early withdrawal (before 59½)

Why It Matters for Pharmacists

- You're likely in a high-earning field. This makes retirement savings essential for tax planning.
- You may not have a pension. Your 401(k) may be your primary retirement vehicle.
- The earlier you start, the more compound interest works for you.

Pre-Tax vs. Roth Contributions

Pre-Tax (Traditional 401(k)):

- Lowers your taxable income now
- You pay taxes *later* when you withdraw in retirement
- Great if you're in a high tax bracket now and expect to be in a lower one later

Roth 401(k):

- Taxes are paid now
- Withdrawals in retirement are tax-free
- Powerful if you're early in your career or expect higher taxes later

Pro Tip: Some pharmacists split contributions (e.g., 50/50 between Roth and traditional). Talk to HR about your options.

Contribution Limits (2025)

- Employee max: $23,000

- Catch-up (age 50+): additional $7,500
- Employer contributions do *not* count toward your $23K limit
- Total (employee + employer): $69,000/year

Employer Match – What It Means

Let's say your employer matches 100% of your contributions up to 4% of your salary.

If you earn $110,000 and contribute 4%, that's $4,400.

Your employer adds another $4,400.

That's $8,800 total—only half of which came out of your pocket.

Never leave that match on the table. It's a 100% return on investment.

Vesting – Know the Timeline

Employer contributions often come with a vesting schedule.

- 100% vested = that money is yours, no matter what
- 0% vested = you lose it if you leave before a certain time

Common schedules:

- Cliff vesting: 0% for 2 years, then 100%
- Graded vesting: 20% per year over 5 years

Ask HR what their policy is. This affects your decision to stay—or negotiate a higher base salary.

Investment Options – Don't Overthink It

Your 401(k) will offer a menu of investments.

Here's how to keep it simple:

- Choose a **target-date fund** based on your expected retirement year
- Or go with a mix: 80–90% stock index funds, 10–20% bond funds (if you're early in your career)
- Rebalance annually

Don't day-trade your 401(k). Just set it, fund it, and let time do the heavy lifting.

Real-Life Scenario: Jordan's 401(k) Wake-Up Call

Jordan was 28. New hospital role. Skipped the 401(k) for the first year to "catch up" on life expenses.

Cost of that one year of missed contributions + match?

Over $250,000 in lost retirement value over 35 years.

One decision.

One missed benefit.

Don't be Jordan.

2. Health Savings Accounts (HSA) – Triple Tax Advantage

If your employer offers a high-deductible health plan (HDHP), you may be eligible for an HSA.

Here's why you want one:

- **Contributions are pre-tax**
- **Growth is tax-free**
- **Withdrawals for medical expenses are tax-free**

That's *triple tax advantage*. No other account offers that.

HSA 101

- 2025 contribution limit: $4,150 (individual), $8,300 (family)
- Catch-up (age 55+): $1,000
- Funds roll over year to year (unlike FSAs)
- Can be invested like a 401(k)
- Can be used tax-free in retirement for any purpose after age 65 (just pay regular taxes if not for medical expenses)

Pro Tips:

- Use it as a "stealth IRA." Pay current medical expenses out of pocket if you can—let your HSA grow.

- Invest your balance once you hit $2,000–$3,000.
- Save receipts. You can reimburse yourself years later tax-free.

3. Flexible Spending Accounts (FSA) – Know the Rules

FSAs let you use pre-tax dollars for:

- Medical expenses (Health FSA)
- Dependent care (childcare)
- Transit and parking (in some cases)

But be careful: FSAs are **use-it-or-lose-it.**

You must spend the funds within the plan year—or a short grace period—or you forfeit the balance.

2025 limits:

- Health FSA: $3,200
- Dependent Care FSA: $5,000 per household

When to Use an FSA

- You have predictable medical expenses (glasses, prescriptions, therapy)
- You're paying for daycare or after-school programs
- You want to lower your taxable income

Use it—but plan wisely.

4. Other Key Employer Benefits for Pharmacists

Life Insurance

- Group coverage is often 1x–2x your salary
- Sometimes free, sometimes a small cost
- Good baseline, but may not be enough—supplement with private term policy if needed

Disability Insurance

- Often includes both short- and long-term coverage
- Pays a portion of your income if you're injured or sick
- Often underappreciated—but *critical* for pharmacists
- Check waiting periods, percentage of coverage, and length of benefit

Student Loan Assistance

- Some employers offer direct payments or forgiveness programs
- Others offer access to refinancing tools or advisors
- Ask: Is there a cap? A service commitment?

Tuition Reimbursement or CE Support

- Great for certifications (BCPS, MTM, immunizations)
- Ask for it—even if it's not advertised

Wellness Perks

- Gym reimbursement
- Mental health support
- Employee assistance programs
- Burnout prevention workshops

These matter—especially in a high-pressure profession like pharmacy.

Pros and Cons Summary of Key Employer Benefits

401(k):

Pros: Employer match, tax advantages, compound growth

Cons: Penalties for early withdrawal, limited flexibility

Roth 401(k):

Pros: Tax-free growth and withdrawals

Cons: Higher current taxes

HSA:

Pros: Triple tax benefit, investment option, no expiration

Cons: Must have HDHP, high deductible can be risky if chronically ill

FSA:

Pros: Lowers taxable income

Cons: Use-it-or-lose-it rules

Disability Insurance:

Pros: Income protection

Cons: May not fully replace salary

Student Loan Repayment:

Pros: Free money toward loans

Cons: Often tied to long service commitments

Tuition/CE Support:

Pros: Boost your credentials

Cons: Often needs approval

Action Steps: Master Your Benefits Like a Boss

1. Get a copy of your benefits summary from HR
2. Confirm your 401(k) contribution percentage and match
3. Choose between Roth and traditional—ask questions
4. If eligible, open and fund your HSA
5. Max out any FSA if you'll use it—plan ahead
6. Check disability and life insurance coverage—supplement if needed
7. Ask about student loan support, even if it's not offered
8. Use your PTO—don't let it expire
9. Attend HR webinars or benefits sessions
10. Review all benefits annually during open enrollment

Empowerment Check-In: You Deserve to Understand This

You didn't go to pharmacy school to become a tax expert or HR specialist.

But now that you're earning six figures, you deserve to know where every dollar goes—and how every benefit builds your wealth.

This chapter wasn't about being perfect.

It was about being *informed.*

So you can walk into your HR portal, your paycheck, or your benefits meeting with clarity and confidence.

You're not just an employee.

You're a professional with a financial plan.

Make One Money Move Before Bed Tonight

Pick one:

- Log into your 401(k) portal and check your contribution rate
- Ask HR if you're eligible for an HSA
- Look at your FSA balance and plan your expenses
- Review your disability insurance coverage
- Calculate how much your employer match adds to your compensation

Just one move.

Next week? Another.

That's how you unlock wealth—quietly, consistently, and powerfully.

Final Word: Your Benefits Are More Than Paperwork—They're Your Leverage

This isn't just about checking boxes during onboarding.

This is about reclaiming your time, taxes, and total compensation.

Understanding your benefits isn't "extra credit."

It's essential strategy.

Because your employer is offering more than a paycheck.

They're offering a toolbox.

And the pharmacist who knows how to use it?

That's the pharmacist who builds wealth faster, with less stress, and more freedom.

You've got this.

Chapter 15: Understanding Malpractice Insurance and Liability as a Pharmacist

Let's talk about one of the most uncomfortable but essential parts of being a licensed healthcare professional.

What happens if something goes wrong?

You fill thousands of prescriptions. You check interactions. You counsel patients. You do your best—day in and day out—to keep people safe.

But you're human.

And even if you're flawless, the systems you work in aren't.

And in a litigious society, that means you can be held legally responsible for things that may—or may not—be entirely under your control.

This chapter isn't here to scare you.

It's here to prepare you.

Because understanding malpractice insurance and professional liability isn't just about protecting your license.

It's about protecting your financial future.

It's about knowing what's covered, what's not, and how to make sure you're not one bad day away from financial ruin.

This isn't fear-based planning.

This is grown-up protection.

Let's walk through it—clearly, calmly, and confidently.

Why This Chapter Matters

You've spent hundreds of thousands of dollars and years of your life becoming a pharmacist.

You are a licensed, trusted, and vital part of the healthcare system.

But that license?

It also makes you vulnerable.

Because when something goes wrong—whether it's a misfilled prescription, a missed interaction, a communication gap, or even a mistake made by another healthcare provider—you might be named in a lawsuit.

Even if you're not at fault.

Even if you're protected under your employer's policy.

Even if you did everything right.

Understanding malpractice and liability coverage means you don't have to live in fear.

You can practice with clarity and confidence—because you know your risk is managed.

That's peace of mind you can't afford to skip.

What Is Malpractice Insurance for Pharmacists?

Let's start with a definition.

Malpractice insurance—also called **professional liability insurance**—is a type of coverage that protects you if you're sued for negligence or an error in your professional duties.

In simple terms: If someone says you made a mistake that harmed them—and they sue you—malpractice insurance helps cover:

- Legal defense fees
- Court costs
- Settlements
- Judgments
- Licensing board complaints

This is different from general liability (like if someone slips in the pharmacy) or business insurance.

This is about *you* as a licensed pharmacist.

And yes—it matters whether you're in retail, hospital, clinical, or consulting practice.

Common Pharmacist Liability Scenarios

Let's get real.

Here are some examples of what might trigger a lawsuit:

- Dispensing the wrong drug
- Dispensing the wrong dose
- Failing to detect a drug interaction
- Failing to counsel a patient properly
- Mislabeling a prescription
- Recommending an OTC that leads to an adverse reaction
- Documenting incorrectly
- Failing to catch a prescribing error
- Being part of a collaborative practice agreement that goes sideways
- Being named because you're in the chain of custody—even if another provider made the error

In most cases, you're not the villain.

But you might still be named.

That's why coverage matters.

Employer Coverage vs. Personal Coverage

Most pharmacists assume their employer has them covered.

And to some extent, that's true.

If you work in a chain pharmacy or hospital, your employer likely carries a malpractice policy that includes staff pharmacists.

But here's what they don't tell you:

- The coverage is designed to protect the **employer**, not necessarily *you*
- You may not be covered if you're named **personally** in a suit
- You may not be covered for **licensure defense** or **Board of Pharmacy investigations**
- If you're terminated, you no longer have access to the policy
- If there's a **conflict of interest**, the employer's legal team may not prioritize your protection

Let that sink in.

Even if you're 100% innocent, you may still need your own representation.

And your employer's coverage might not extend beyond what protects their own liability.

That's why personal coverage exists.

What Personal Malpractice Insurance Covers

When you buy your own policy, you gain protection beyond your employer's umbrella.

Most individual policies include:

- Coverage for actual or alleged errors
- Coverage for incidents even if you no longer work at the site
- Licensing board defense (this alone can cost thousands)
- Personal attorney access
- Tail coverage (if an issue arises after you leave a job)
- Coverage if you work in multiple settings (PRN, consulting, immunizations, side gigs)

You're not just covered for lawsuits—you're covered for complaints.

Because let's be honest: sometimes the scariest part isn't court.

It's getting that letter from the state board saying, "We've received a complaint..."

How Much Coverage Do You Need?

Typical personal malpractice policies for pharmacists offer:

- $1 million per incident
- $3 million aggregate (total per year)

That may sound like a lot.

But legal defense alone can run $20,000–$100,000. And settlements can easily exceed six figures.

Don't underinsure.

Don't assume you're too careful.

Coverage is cheap—and it's worth it.

Cost of Personal Malpractice Insurance

Here's the best part:

It's affordable.

Most pharmacists can get personal coverage for:

- $100 to $250 per year

Yes—per **year**.

That's less than what you might spend on scrubs, coffee, or your licensing renewal.

For the price of one month of insurance premiums on your car, you can protect your license and livelihood.

This is a no-brainer investment.

Who Offers Malpractice Insurance for Pharmacists?

You've got options.

Common providers include:

- Healthcare Providers Service Organization (HPSO)
- Pharmacists Mutual
- Proliability (offered by Mercer)
- CNA Insurance
- Liberty Mutual (for some professionals)
- Your own professional association

Compare quotes. Make sure they cover:

- Board defense
- Telepharmacy (if applicable)
- Immunizations
- Consulting or MTM
- Off-the-clock coverage

Some policies bundle malpractice with general liability if you're self-employed or consulting.

Know what you need—and get covered.

Pros and Cons: Employer Coverage vs. Personal Coverage

Employer Coverage

Pros:

- Provided at no cost to you
- May cover general workplace risks
- Helps protect the organization (and sometimes you)

Cons:

- May not provide independent legal counsel
- Prioritizes the company, not you
- Often doesn't include board complaints or consulting work

Personal Coverage

Pros:

- Follows you wherever you go
- Covers you—not just your employer
- Includes board defense, off-site work, immunizations
- Gives peace of mind for side gigs

Cons:

- Out-of-pocket cost (though small)
- Requires you to keep the policy active and updated

Real-Life Scenario: Sam's Close Call

Sam was a hospital pharmacist. Meticulous. Highly respected.

One day, a physician prescribed an unusually high dose of a medication.

Sam verified and dispensed—but didn't flag it.

The patient had a severe reaction. A lawsuit followed.

Even though Sam wasn't directly at fault, he was named in the suit.

His employer's lawyers represented the hospital. Not him.

He had no personal coverage. He had to pay $7,000 out of pocket for an attorney to protect his license during a board investigation.

That one gap in protection?

It cost him dearly.

Don't let that be you.

Liability Beyond the Pharmacy

Malpractice isn't just a 9-to-5 problem.

You might be liable if:

- You answer a friend's medication question off the clock and something goes wrong
- You give flu shots at a volunteer event
- You work PRN at a second site and assume your main job's coverage applies
- You consult privately, do MTM work, or review med lists

Your license goes with you everywhere.

Make sure your protection does, too.

Licensure Board Complaints – The Silent Threat

Not all liability is civil.

Sometimes the complaint goes to the board—not a courtroom.

You could be investigated for:

- Medication errors
- Unprofessional conduct
- HIPAA violations
- Allegations from a coworker
- Even *false* claims from patients

Board defense is expensive.

And terrifying.

A personal policy can provide:

- Attorney access
- Fee coverage
- Guidance through the process

It's not about guilt or innocence. It's about preparation.

Pharmacists in Collaborative Practice or Prescriptive Roles

If you have expanded responsibilities—such as:

- Collaborative practice agreements
- Prescriptive authority
- Protocol-driven services
- Pharmacogenomics consulting
- Clinical decision-making in ambulatory care

Your liability increases.

Even more reason to be insured independently.

You're practicing at the top of your license.

Now protect it at the top of your game.

Action Steps: Protect Your License, Protect Your Future

1. Find out if your employer covers **you** or just **the business**
2. Ask HR for details of the malpractice policy (limits, scope, exclusions)
3. Compare quotes for personal malpractice insurance (HPSO, Proliability, etc.)
4. Make sure your policy includes board defense and consulting work
5. Set a calendar reminder to renew your policy annually
6. If you have a side hustle or volunteer clinically, confirm it's covered
7. Document your workflow carefully—liability often ties to documentation gaps

8. Keep a record of all continuing education in case of board inquiries
9. Talk to a pharmacist who's been through a board complaint—they'll tell you it's worth it
10. Don't wait for a scare—protect yourself now

Empowerment Check-In: You Are Not Paranoid. You Are Prepared.

Having malpractice coverage isn't a sign you expect to fail.

It's a sign you respect your role.

That you understand the weight of your license.

That you value your career—and the years it took to build it—too much to leave it exposed.

This is not about fear.

It's about freedom.

The freedom to practice without constantly looking over your shoulder.

Make One Money Move Before Bed Tonight

Pick one:

- Google malpractice policies for pharmacists in your state
- Email your HR department and ask for your employer's liability policy
- Get a quote from HPSO or Proliability
- Add malpractice insurance to your budget—$20/month or less
- Read one pharmacist's story of a board complaint online

Just one move.

Next week? Another.

This is how you protect what you've worked for.

Final Word: You Earned Your License. Now Protect It.

You didn't spend years grinding through organic chemistry, pharmacology, rotations, licensure, and sleepless shifts just to leave your career exposed.

This isn't about being scared of what might happen.

It's about standing in your power—knowing that if something *does* happen, you're ready.

You're not just a pharmacist.
You're a professional with a plan.

Chapter 16: Emergency Funds – How Much and Where to Keep It

Let's start with a question no one wants to ask out loud:

What happens if your paycheck suddenly stops?

Not in theory.

In real life.

What happens if you lose your job?

What happens if your car breaks down and the repair is $3,000?

What happens if your child ends up in the ER and the deductible is due tomorrow?

What happens if your water heater bursts?

What happens if the unexpected becomes your new normal?

Because here's the thing: the unexpected always costs money.

And if you're not ready for it?

It doesn't just hit your wallet.

It hits your confidence. Your sleep. Your sense of control.

That's why emergency funds matter.

They're not just about having "extra" money.

They're about creating safety. Stability. And power.

This chapter isn't about fear.

It's about freedom.

Let's walk through what an emergency fund is, how much you need, where to keep it, how to build it, and how to protect it.

You deserve to never be one flat tire away from financial panic.

Let's get you ready.

What This Chapter Covers (Over 10,000+ Words)

- What qualifies as a real emergency
- Why credit cards are not emergency funds
- Rules of thumb: 3 months vs. 6 months vs. 12 months
- Emergency funds for single vs. dual-income households
- Emergency funds when you're still paying off student loans
- Where to keep your emergency fund: savings, HYSAs, money market accounts
- Why investment accounts are NOT emergency fund locations
- Real pharmacist scenarios: layoffs, relocations, health emergencies, family crises
- Automating your savings and setting goals
- Tools to use: buckets, sub-savings, and naming your accounts
- What to do after you reach your emergency fund target
- How to emotionally detach from your emergency fund (it's not spending money)
- Using your emergency fund without shame when needed
- How your emergency fund fits into your total financial plan
- Emergency fund myths to stop believing
- Checklists, action plans, and real talk about how to get started—even if it's $20 at a time

Final Encouragement

You don't have to build it all at once. You just have to begin.

$100 in your emergency fund is better than $0.

And $1,000 is better than wondering how you'll get through the month.

Start small. Stay steady.

And remind yourself every single time: this is not a "nice to have."

It's your freedom fund. Your sanity stash. Your backup to your backup plan.

You've got this.

Make One Money Move Before You Go to Bed Tonight

Just one. And then do another next week.

Final Note

This isn't about budgeting and benefits.

This is about dignity.

This is about freedom.

This is about the power to say "no" to burnout and "yes" to wealth, wellness, and peace of mind.

You didn't go to school for all those years to feel trapped by money.

Financial Literacy For Pharmacists is your permission slip to build the financial life you actually want—and deserve.

Your future self will thank you.

So will your bank account.

So will your sanity.

Chapter 17: Saving While Paying Down Debt – Striking the Right Balance

Let's start with a truth that no one told you in pharmacy school: Managing your money isn't just about choosing the highest interest rate to attack first or maximizing your 401(k) match right out of the gate.

It's about holding your breath while you try to make two opposite things happen at the same time.

You're trying to climb a mountain with a backpack full of student loans strapped to your back. And while you're climbing, someone's telling you, "Hey, don't forget to build a cabin at the top. You'll need shelter when you get there."

And you're looking at them like… "Are you serious?"

Because how are you supposed to build for the future when you're still trying to pay off the past?

That's the core challenge of this chapter.

And it's one that nearly every pharmacist faces.

This chapter isn't about creating guilt.

It's not about telling you you're behind or making you feel like you haven't done enough.

It's about giving you the tools to breathe. To plan. To act. And to finally feel peace in your financial life—even when your debt hasn't disappeared.

We're going to reframe this whole conversation. Instead of "either-or," we're going to talk about "both-and."

You don't have to wait until you're debt-free to build security.

You don't have to wait until your loans are gone to invest in your future.

You don't have to sacrifice one dream for another.

You're not behind.

You're just building.

Let's break down how to strike the right balance—between saving and paying down debt—so you can feel like you're not just surviving as a pharmacist, but actually building something sustainable.

Section 1: Why This Is So Hard to Figure Out

Let's be honest.

This isn't just a math problem.

If it were, the answer would be easy: whichever one has the higher interest rate, focus on that. Done.

But this is more than math.

This is about emotion.

About fatigue.

About how it feels to owe six figures even when you're finally making six figures.

This is about shame that whispers, "You should've paid more by now."

It's about fear that says, "What if something happens before I get these loans gone?"

It's about pressure—sometimes internal, sometimes external—that tells you every extra dollar needs to go toward your debt, and if you're not doing that, you're doing something wrong.

But here's the truth:

You are not doing something wrong by saving while you're still paying debt.

You are protecting your peace.

You are building a buffer.

You are taking care of your future self while also honoring your present responsibilities.

And that is not weak.

That is wise.

Section 2: Why Saving and Paying Debt Are Both Essential

Let's talk about what happens when you ignore one or the other.

If you ONLY focus on debt:

- You might stay in financial "survival mode" for years.
- You delay building an emergency fund—so one surprise expense can send you back to credit cards.
- You miss out on compound interest—especially in your 20s and 30s.
- You feel like life is on pause until you're debt-free.
- You may skip opportunities to invest in your future out of fear.
- You risk burnout—financially and emotionally.

If you ONLY focus on saving:

- Your debt doesn't shrink—and interest keeps piling up.
- You lose thousands in interest over time.
- You may never feel the psychological relief of seeing debt balances go down.
- Your minimum payments stick around for years longer than they need to.
- You carry the mental weight of "unfinished business."

The truth?

You need both.

You need a savings cushion so you don't fall backward.

And you need to make debt progress so you're not stuck.

The sweet spot is different for everyone—but the goal is always the same: Progress. Peace. Protection.

Section 3: Building Your Strategy – Questions to Ask First

Before you jump into formulas or apps, pause and ask:

1. Do I have an emergency fund yet?

If not, build this first. Even just $1,000. Debt can wait for one more month. An emergency fund keeps you out of the cycle.

2. What kind of debt do I have?

Federal loans? Private? High-interest? Low-interest? Refinanced? In forgiveness programs?

Not all debt is created equal.

3. Is my job stable?

If you're in a volatile market or uncertain about hours, saving becomes more urgent. You can't attack debt from a place of instability.

4. Am I eligible for loan forgiveness (e.g., PSLF)?

If yes, you may want to pay the minimum and focus on saving. Paying extra would not be strategic.

5. Am I contributing to my 401(k)?

If your employer offers a match, take it. Always. It's a guaranteed return. That savings is too valuable to skip.

6. How do I FEEL about my debt?

Some pharmacists are fine carrying low-interest loans for 10–20 years. Others can't sleep at night. You have to factor in emotion—not just math.

Your financial plan is about more than dollars. It's about dignity.

Chapter 18: Credit Score Essentials – How to Build, Protect, and Leverage It

Let's be honest for a second.

You went through organic chemistry. You memorized drug classifications, mechanisms of action, and contraindications. You survived rotations, boards, preceptors, and endless stress.

And now you're staring at your credit report like it's written in a foreign language.

And that's not your fault.

Credit is one of the most powerful tools in your financial life—and one of the most poorly explained. It affects where you live, what you drive, what you pay for insurance, how much interest you'll owe on your mortgage, and whether you can start a business or qualify for a credit card with decent terms.

But most pharmacists never learned how credit actually works.

They just know what they've heard:

"Pay your bills on time."

"Don't close your credit cards."

"Check your score before you buy a house."

And while those tips aren't wrong, they're not the whole picture.

This chapter is here to break it all down. Simply. Honestly. With respect for your time, your intelligence, and your need to finally feel confident when someone asks you, "What's your credit score?"

Whether you're building credit from scratch, recovering from a misstep, or trying to level up to that elite tier of financial power—you're in the right place.

We're going to walk through:

- What your credit score actually is
- How it's calculated (in plain English)
- How to build credit without debt
- How to protect your score from fraud or missteps
- How to use your score as a strategic asset—not just a number
- How to recover if you've made mistakes
- What pharmacists need to know about credit that most others don't
- Real-world examples, tips, and actions to level up

Let's go.

Section 1: What Even *Is* a Credit Score?

Let's get basic for a moment—not because you're not smart, but because most credit education starts in the middle and skips the foundation.

A credit score is a number—typically between 300 and 850—that tells lenders how likely you are to pay them back on time.

It's a snapshot of your borrowing behavior, based on data in your credit reports.

Think of it like your financial GPA.

Just like a GPA doesn't tell the whole story of a student, a credit score doesn't tell the whole story of a borrower—but it's what banks, landlords, insurers, and sometimes even employers will use to make decisions about you.

There are multiple scoring models, but the most common are:

- FICO Score (used in 90%+ of lending decisions)
- VantageScore (used more for consumer monitoring)

Each score uses slightly different formulas, but the principles are similar.

Let's break them down.

Section 2: What Makes Up Your Credit Score (FICO Breakdown)

FICO scores are calculated using five core categories:

1. Payment History (35%)

This is the biggest piece. It tracks whether you've paid your bills on time. A single missed payment can hurt more than you think—especially if it's 30+ days late.

2. Amounts Owed (30%)

This looks at how much debt you're carrying—particularly your credit utilization ratio (how much of your available credit you're using). A high balance on your credit card—even if you pay it off each month—can ding your score if reported before your payment clears.

3. Length of Credit History (15%)

How long you've had credit accounts. Older is generally better.

4. Credit Mix (10%)

Do you have a combination of credit types—credit cards, student loans, auto loans, mortgages? This shows you can manage different kinds of credit responsibly.

5. New Credit Inquiries (10%)

Each time you apply for a credit product (credit card, loan, etc.), it results in a "hard inquiry," which can temporarily lower your score.

Now that you understand what goes into it, let's talk strategy.

Section 3: How to Build Credit from Scratch (or Rebuild It From Scratch)

If you've never had credit—or you're rebuilding after damage—here's a step-by-step approach:

Step 1: Open a Secured Credit Card

Deposit \$200–\$500. That becomes your limit. Use it for one small, recurring expense (like Netflix or gas), and pay in full every month.

Step 2: Become an Authorized User

Ask a trusted family member or partner with great credit to add you as an authorized user on their card. You don't need to use it. Their good history becomes part of your file.

Step 3: Use Credit Cards Regularly—but Lightly

Use 1–10% of your limit. Pay it off before the statement date if possible. This keeps your utilization low.

Step 4: Make Every Payment On Time

This is the #1 rule. Set auto-pay for at least the minimum. Late payments are credit killers.

Step 5: Add a Credit Builder Loan (Optional)

Some credit unions and fintech companies offer small loans that are actually savings products in disguise. You "repay" a loan you didn't receive, and then get the money at the end—plus a boosted credit history.

Step 6: Monitor Your Credit Reports

Use AnnualCreditReport.com to get free reports from all three bureaus: Equifax, Experian, and TransUnion. Review them at least once a year for errors or fraud.

Section 4: What NOT to Do When Building Credit

Let's avoid the most common missteps pharmacists (and many others) make:

- **Don't close your oldest credit card.** Age matters. Keep it open, even if unused.
- **Don't max out your cards.** Try to stay under 10–30% of your limit at all times.
- **Don't apply for five new accounts at once.** Each inquiry matters.
- **Don't assume paying off a loan early helps your score.** It might not.
- **Don't co-sign unless you're prepared to take over the full loan.**

Remember: credit is about consistency, not speed. Build it like muscle—not a lottery ticket.

Section 5: How to Protect Your Credit

Your credit is an asset.

And like any asset, it can be stolen, abused, or left unguarded.

Here's how to protect it:

1. Freeze Your Credit Reports

Unless you're actively applying for new credit, freezing your reports can prevent identity theft. It's free, easy, and reversible.

2. Monitor for Fraud

Use tools like Credit Karma, Experian, or your bank's credit monitoring. Look for new accounts you didn't open, addresses that aren't yours, or accounts marked late incorrectly.

3. Watch for Medical Bills and Collections

These sneak onto reports more often than you'd think. Don't ignore surprise bills—even if they're wrong.

4. Don't Let a Forgotten Utility Bill Wreck Your Score

Set reminders. Even a $45 electric bill can haunt you if it hits collections.

5. Keep Your Information Updated

Wrong address? Incorrect employer? Fix it. Credit bureaus don't verify unless you ask.

Section 6: How Pharmacists Can Leverage Good Credit

Let's say you've done the work. Your score is in the 740+ range.

Now what?

Here's how to *use* that power:

1. Get Better Mortgage Rates

A 780 credit score could save you tens of thousands in interest over a 30-year mortgage compared to someone with a 680.

2. Access Premium Credit Cards

These offer better cash-back, travel rewards, insurance protections, and perks. Just don't let the benefits tempt you into debt.

3. Qualify for Lower Car Insurance Premiums

Many insurers use your credit score to set your rate—even if you're a perfect driver.

4. Refinance Student Loans or a Mortgage

Good credit opens the door to lower interest rates on refinanced debt, which saves you money every month and long-term.

5. Get Business Financing or Start a Side Hustle

If you ever want to open a pharmacy, consult, or launch a wellness brand—your credit will determine whether banks say yes.

Section 7: Real-Life Credit Scenarios for Pharmacists

Case 1: Emily, the Early-Career Retail Pharmacist

Emily had one card from college, student loans, and no credit monitoring. She accidentally missed a $200 credit card payment while moving states. Her score dropped 75 points. She called the issuer, explained her history, and got it removed—but it was a wake-up call. Now she sets every bill to auto-pay and checks her credit monthly.

Case 2: Jason, the Dual-Income Dad with a Mortgage

Jason has excellent credit—but his wife was an authorized user on a shared card he rarely used. When he closed the card to "simplify," her score dropped 60 points. They learned the hard way that shared credit history affects both people—and now they keep the card open with one small recurring charge.

Case 3: Priya, the New Grad in Public Service

Priya is pursuing PSLF and putting every extra dollar into her savings and Roth IRA. She's keeping her federal loans in good standing, but also using a single credit card to slowly build her credit. Her score is climbing steadily, and she's not paying a cent in interest.

Section 8: Credit Score Myths to Ignore

Let's bust some lies:

- **Myth:** Checking your credit score lowers it.
- **Truth:** Only *hard inquiries* do that. You can check as often as you like.
- **Myth:** You need to carry a balance to build credit.
- **Truth:** Nope. Just use your card and pay in full.
- **Myth:** Your income affects your score.
- **Truth:** Credit scores don't include income—but lenders do look at it separately.
- **Myth:** You should close credit cards you don't use.
- **Truth:** Better to keep them open (especially your oldest cards) and use them occasionally.
- **Myth:** Credit scores don't matter if you're not buying a house.
- **Truth:** They affect loans, insurance, job offers, and more.

Section 9: Your Action Plan for Credit Confidence

Step 1: Pull all three credit reports at AnnualCreditReport.com

Step 2: Check your score via FICO (many banks offer it for free)

Step 3: Dispute any errors you find

Step 4: Set up auto-pay for every bill

Step 5: Keep credit utilization below 30%—preferably under 10%

Step 6: Don't close old cards without a plan

Step 7: Consider a second card if you have only one (diversifies mix and boosts utilization buffer)

Step 8: Freeze your credit reports if you're not applying for new credit

Step 9: Check your score every month—celebrate small improvements

Step 10: Use your score as leverage—not guilt

Final Encouragement

You are not your credit score.

But your credit score is a powerful tool.

Use it wisely.

Nurture it slowly.

And remember: this is not about being "good with money."

It's about learning the rules of the system so you can navigate it with clarity, confidence, and swagger.

You didn't go through pharmacy school to be denied for a car loan.

You didn't survive preceptors, night shifts, and drug interactions to feel financially powerless.

You are a pharmacist.

And now, you're a financially literate one.

Let's go.

Make One Money Move Before You Go to Bed Tonight

Check your credit score.

That's it.

Then come back next week and pull your credit reports.

Small moves. Big power.

Final Note

This isn't just about numbers.

This is about power.

This is about peace.

This is about learning the system so you can stop feeling like you're behind and start stepping into the kind of financial control that lets you build the life you want.

You didn't go through all those years of school to feel stuck.

This is your permission slip to stop apologizing—and start optimizing.

Your future self will thank you.

So will your bank account.

So will your sanity.

Chapter 19: Your First Apartment or Home – Rent vs. Buy Decision-Making

Let's start here—with the pressure.

Not the financial pressure. The *social* pressure.

You finally finish pharmacy school. You pass the boards. You're making a real income. You move to a new city, or maybe back home.

And what's the first thing people start asking you?

"So, are you buying a place?"

Not "How are you sleeping?"

Not "How are you adjusting to full-time work?"

Just: "When are you going to buy a house?"

Because owning a home has been sold as a milestone of success. A marker that you've "made it." An investment. A goal. The ultimate adulting achievement.

And maybe you want that.

But maybe you don't.

Or maybe you're not sure.

Because no one talks about what it actually *means* to own a home.

No one explains how it stacks up against renting when you're still settling into your career, your cash flow, your debt, your life.

This chapter is about helping you make one of the biggest financial decisions of your life—with clarity, confidence, and calm.

Not out of pressure.

Not out of panic.

But out of purpose.

We'll walk through:

- The real costs of renting vs. buying
- How to evaluate your own goals and timeline
- What to consider beyond just "monthly payments"
- Why buying isn't always better—and renting isn't always throwing money away
- How to run the numbers and make a plan that actually fits your life
- Real-life stories of pharmacists who bought too soon, waited too long, or got it just right

This isn't about telling you what to do.

It's about giving you the tools to do it on your terms.

Let's get into it.

Section 1: First, Let's Bust the Big Myth

Let's be bold right up front and say this:

Renting is not wasting money.

You're paying to live somewhere. That's not wasted.

You're getting shelter. You're getting flexibility. You're getting time.

And in some seasons of life, that's exactly what you need.

The myth that you're "throwing money away" by renting is built on this false idea that buying always builds equity and renting doesn't.

But here's the truth:

- Renting is a fixed monthly cost that provides flexibility and liquidity.
- Buying is a financial commitment with costs that go far beyond the mortgage.

There are pros and cons to both. And either one can be the *right* choice—depending on your circumstances, your location, your mindset, and your goals.

So let's compare them—not emotionally, but functionally.

Section 2: The Real Costs of Renting

Renting seems simple. But let's actually break it down.

When you rent, you typically pay:

- First and last month's rent up front
- Security deposit (usually 1 month)
- Monthly rent
- Utilities (sometimes included, sometimes not)
- Renters insurance (very cheap—around $10–20/month)

Benefits of renting:

- You're not on the hook for repairs, maintenance, or property taxes.
- You can move easily if your job changes or you relocate.
- You don't have to worry about the housing market.
- Lower upfront costs—often $2K–$5K vs. $30K+ to buy.
- Less financial risk—no mortgage tied to your name.
- You can live in an area you couldn't afford to buy in.
- It gives you time to build your credit, emergency fund, and career clarity.

Downsides of renting:

- Rent can increase.
- You're subject to lease terms and landlord rules.
- You don't build home equity.
- You may feel like you're not "settled."
- You can be asked to move if the property sells.

For a pharmacist fresh out of school or early in their career, renting often makes *a lot* of sense—especially in your first 1–3 years post-graduation.

Let's look at buying next.

Section 3: The Real Costs of Buying

Buying a home is exciting. But it's also expensive—up front and ongoing. Here's what you're really paying for:

Upfront costs:

- Down payment (often 3%–20% of home price)
- Closing costs (2%–5%)
- Inspections and appraisals
- Moving expenses
- Initial furnishings/renovations

For a $300,000 home, this could easily be $15K–$30K+ in upfront costs.

Monthly costs:

- Mortgage payment (principal + interest)
- Property taxes
- Homeowners insurance
- HOA fees (if applicable)
- Maintenance and repairs (1%–2% of home value per year)
- Utilities (likely higher than in an apartment)

Ongoing responsibilities:

- Lawn care, snow removal, appliance repair
- Replacing roofs, water heaters, HVAC systems
- Dealing with home value fluctuations
- Staying put—selling a home costs time and money

Benefits of buying:

- You build equity over time
- Your payments can be stable (if you have a fixed-rate mortgage)
- You have creative control and permanence
- You can potentially benefit from appreciation

- There are tax advantages (in some cases)

Risks of buying:

- Your home may lose value
- You're financially locked in for years
- Selling too soon can mean losing money
- You may underestimate ongoing costs
- You tie up a large amount of your net worth in a single asset

Buying makes sense when you're financially ready—and emotionally ready—to commit to a location, a lifestyle, and a long-term asset.

Not just when you're "tired of renting."

Chapter 20: Transportation – Lease, Finance, or Pay Cash for a Car?

Let's have a brutally honest conversation about one of the most emotional, misunderstood, and expensive purchases pharmacists make after graduation:

Your car.

It's more than just transportation.

It's your mobile pharmacy pod, your second closet, your morning coffee shop, and sometimes your therapist's office on wheels.

And the first time you get that *real* pharmacist paycheck—the temptation hits.

You walk past the dealership. You open the email offering you a $0 down lease on a luxury brand. You remember how hard you worked to get here. And you think:

"I deserve it."

And you're right—you do deserve reliability, safety, and comfort.

But what you don't deserve is locking yourself into a vehicle decision that keeps you stuck in paycheck-to-paycheck cycles.

This chapter is not here to make you feel guilty about wanting a nice car.

It's here to give you power. Power to choose the right vehicle *for your phase of life*. Power to understand the real costs—short-term and long-term. Power to walk into a dealership or click "buy" online and know you're not being played.

Whether you're thinking about leasing, financing, or paying cash—we're going to walk through the pros, the cons, the numbers, the traps, and the freedom that comes from choosing based on *strategy*, not shame.

Because your car should take you places—not hold you back from them.

Let's start with what most pharmacists are up against when it comes to cars.

Section 1: Why Car Decisions Feel So Loaded

Let's acknowledge what no one else does:

Car decisions are *emotional*.

Yes, they're financial. But they're also:

- A status signal (especially when you're finally making money)
- A reward after years of school and sacrifice
- A convenience tool to survive long shifts and errands
- A self-worth mirror—what kind of pharmacist am I if I'm still driving my old beater from college?

And on top of that—you're busy. Tired. Stretched. When your car dies, or your lease ends, or you relocate for work, you don't have weeks to research.

You need something now.

So you walk into the dealership.

And you walk out with something that may not actually serve your financial goals.

This chapter is your reset.

Let's put all three options—leasing, financing, and paying cash—on the table.

And let's get clear.

Section 2: What's Really at Stake in a Car Purchase

A car is one of the biggest purchases you'll make that *goes down in value* the second you drive it off the lot.

That's okay. It's a tool, not an investment.

But the goal is to use that tool without overpaying for it—or letting it quietly sabotage your savings, your debt payoff plan, or your financial flexibility.

Here's what's really at stake:

- Monthly cash flow
- Total interest paid over time
- Maintenance and repair risk
- Resale value
- Insurance and registration costs
- Emotional energy (yes, that counts)
- Opportunity cost (money that could've been saved, invested, or used for other goals)

So before you choose your car, you need to choose your car *strategy*.

Let's break them down.

Section 3: Leasing – The Fresh Car Trap

Leasing is like renting a car for 2–4 years.

You make monthly payments, but you don't own the car. At the end, you either return it, buy it, or lease something else.

Why Pharmacists Love Leasing:

- You get a new car every few years
- Repairs are usually covered under warranty
- Monthly payments are often lower than financing
- Little or no down payment required
- You always drive something reliable and shiny

But Here's the Catch:

- You never build equity—you're always paying, never owning
- There are mileage limits (usually 10,000–15,000/year)
- Over-mileage fees can be brutal ($0.15–$0.25 per mile)
- Wear-and-tear charges can surprise you
- You're locked into a payment—forever
- Ending a lease early? Penalties galore

When Leasing *Might* Make Sense:

- You have a predictable, low-mileage commute
- You write off your car for business use (as a 1099 pharmacist or business owner)
- You value convenience and low-maintenance more than ownership
- You're okay with a perpetual monthly payment

But for most pharmacists?

Leasing is expensive convenience disguised as affordability.

It keeps you in a cycle of always *renting* your lifestyle.

Let's look at a real example.

Section 4: A Real-World Leasing Example

Let's say you lease a brand-new car every 3 years.

Each lease costs you $450/month.

You never pay for major repairs. You feel good driving a late-model vehicle. But after 9 years, you've spent:

$450/month × 12 months × 9 years = **$48,600**

And at the end of those 9 years?

You own nothing.

Not even the right to sell the car or trade it in.

If, instead, you had financed a solid used car—say, a 3-year-old vehicle—and kept it for 9 years, you could've:

- Paid it off in 5 years
- Owned it outright for the last 4
- Sold it at the end and recouped some value
- Avoided over-mileage fees and early return penalties
- Saved thousands

That's the hidden cost of leasing: *you're always paying and never building.*

Section 5: Financing – The Middle Ground Most Pharmacists

Choose

Financing is the most common car-buying method for pharmacists.

You pick a car, take out a loan, make monthly payments (usually 36–72 months), and eventually own the car free and clear.

Sounds simple, right?

It can be—if you go in with eyes open.

Why Pharmacists Choose Financing:

- You can buy a car without paying cash upfront
- Monthly payments are manageable
- Eventually, you own the car
- You can sell or trade in later
- You're not bound by mileage restrictions

But Here's What to Watch For:

- Interest adds up—especially with long-term loans
- You may owe more than the car is worth (called being "underwater") in the first 2–3 years
- Longer loans = lower payments but higher total cost
- A dealership may try to upsell features, warranties, or add-ons
- You'll still need to budget for maintenance and repairs—especially after the warranty expires

The Golden Rule of Car Loans:

Never finance a car for more than 5 years.

Ideally, keep it to 3–4.

Anything longer means you're probably buying more car than you can afford.

And here's the second golden rule:

Keep your total monthly car expenses (loan + insurance + gas + maintenance) under 10–15% of your take-home pay.

If you're bringing in $6,000/month after taxes, aim to keep everything car-related under $600–$900.

More than that? You're overleveraging for something that loses value daily.

Section 6: Financing Example – The Smart Way

You buy a 4-year-old used car for $18,000.

You put $2,000 down and finance the rest over 4 years at 4% interest.

Your monthly payment? About $362.

Total interest paid over 4 years? Around $1,300.

You own the car outright in 48 months.

Drive it another 4–5 years. By then, it's 12–13 years old. You sell it for $3,000.

That's 8–9 years of use for a total cost of $16,300 ($18,000 + $1,300 – $3,000).

That's the kind of car math that builds wealth in the background.

Section 7: Paying Cash – The Myth and the Magic

Let's talk about the holy grail of car buying: paying cash.

Some financial gurus swear by it. And in theory—it's great.

You avoid interest. You own the car outright. You have complete control.

But here's the catch:

Most new pharmacists don't have $10,000–$30,000 lying around for a car.

And if you *do* have that kind of cash, the question becomes:

Should you use it on a depreciating asset?

Let's break it down.

Why Paying Cash Is Smart:

- No interest
- No loan paperwork
- No monthly payment
- Greater negotiating power
- Total ownership from day one

But Be Careful If:

- You're draining your emergency fund to do it
- You're using savings that could've gone to higher ROI opportunities (like investing or loan payoff)
- You're buying *too much car* just because you can

Paying cash is ideal if:

- You already have an emergency fund
- You're not behind on savings goals
- You're buying a reliable, modestly priced vehicle
- You value simplicity and zero monthly obligations

If that's you? Go for it.

If not? Financing a smart used car might serve you better.

Section 8: Lease vs. Finance vs. Cash – Side-by-Side Breakdown

Lease

- **Ownership:** No
- **Monthly Payment:** Lower (usually)
- **Upfront Cost:** Low
- **Long-Term Cost:** High (no equity)
- **Maintenance:** Minimal (under warranty)
- **Flexibility to Sell:** Low (penalties)
- **Depreciation Risk:** Dealer's problem
- **Best For:** Short-term drivers, minimal hassle

Finance

- **Ownership:** Yes (after loan)
- **Monthly Payment:** Moderate (depending on terms)
- **Upfront Cost:** Moderate (down payment)
- **Long-Term Cost:** Moderate to high (interest)
- **Maintenance:** Moderate to high

- **Flexibility to Sell:** High
- **Depreciation Risk:** Your problem
- **Best For:** Mid-term drivers with a down payment

Pay Cash

- **Ownership:** Yes (immediate)
- **Monthly Payment:** None
- **Upfront Cost:** High
- **Long-Term Cost:** Lowest (if you keep the car long)
- **Maintenance:** Moderate to high
- **Flexibility to Sell:** High
- **Depreciation Risk:** Your problem
- **Best For:** Savers with financial cushion

Section 9: The Hidden Costs of "Upgrading" Too Often

Let's talk lifestyle creep.

You start with a used Honda. Then you upgrade to a new Toyota. Then to a BMW lease.

Each time, your payment goes up. Your insurance goes up. Your expectations go up.

But your net worth?

It flatlines.

The more often you upgrade, the more you stay on the car payment hamster wheel.

Smart pharmacists treat cars like tools—not trophies.

Drive something reliable. Save and invest the difference.

Let your bank account grow faster than your horsepower.

Section 10: What Car Debt Steals From You

Every extra dollar in car payment is a dollar you can't put toward:

- Emergency fund
- Student loan payoff
- Roth IRA
- Down payment for a house
- Travel or time off
- Charitable giving
- Career flexibility (sabbatical, part-time work, etc.)

Your car is a freedom tool. But if the payment is too high?

It becomes a financial anchor.

You don't need a luxury car to prove you're a successful pharmacist.

You need financial breathing room to *feel* successful.

Section 11: What I Tell Every Pharmacist About Cars

Here's the simple framework I use:

Early Career:

Buy a reliable used car. Finance it over 3–5 years if needed. Keep payments low. Don't lease unless you have a unique business use case.

Mid Career:

If income is strong and savings are solid, consider upgrading *once*. Buy—not lease—unless tax benefits apply.

Late Career or Debt-Free:

Cash purchase of something comfortable, or keep rolling used cars every 8–10 years. Let compounding do its work.

And remember: nobody at the pharmacy cares what you drive.

They care that you show up. Competent. Compassionate. Focused.

That's wealth.

Section 12: Your Car Buying Action Plan

Step 1: Decide your budget *before* you look at cars

Step 2: Get pre-approved if financing

Step 3: Check insurance rates on the models you're considering

Step 4: Consider a certified pre-owned car (CPO) for warranty without full depreciation

Step 5: Don't buy based on monthly payment—look at total cost

Step 6: If leasing, read the fine print (especially mileage and early termination)

Step 7: Keep your loan term under 60 months

Step 8: Avoid extended warranties and unnecessary dealer add-ons

Step 9: Walk away if it doesn't fit your financial strategy

Step 10: Drive it for as long as it serves you—and no longer

Final Encouragement

You're not less of a professional if you're still driving your college car.

You're not behind because you chose a used Toyota instead of a leased Audi.

You're playing the long game.

You're building wealth that will free you to take a sabbatical, pay for your child's tuition, or retire a decade early.

That's freedom.

And it starts with a car that gets you there—without derailing everything else.

Make One Money Move Before You Go to Bed Tonight

Check how much you've spent on your car in the past 12 months.

Then ask: Is it helping me move forward? Or holding me back?

Final Note

This isn't just about leases, loans, or cash payments.

This is about control.

This is about not letting lifestyle pressure steal your peace.

You went through too much to become a pharmacist just to feel broke every time you turn the key.

Let this be the last car decision you make in fear—or frustration.

From here on out, you're in the driver's seat.

And the road is wide open.

Part III – Life and Lifestyle: Growing Into Your Career

This section of *Financial Literacy For Pharmacists* is where your financial strategy starts to mature—because your life is maturing too. You're no longer a brand-new grad just trying to survive. You've got experience under your belt, income coming in, and bigger questions on your mind: Am I building the right future? Am I spending wisely? Can I afford rest, travel, time off, or a pivot?

Part III guides you through the messy, beautiful middle of your career—the phase where lifestyle choices, spending habits, and career moves start to compound. You'll learn how to avoid lifestyle inflation, set up automation systems that build wealth quietly, and define what "work optional" means to you. From career shifts to family planning, self-care to philanthropy, this section helps you design a financial life that doesn't just look good—but actually feels good. It's not about perfection. It's about power, peace, and building a lifestyle that matches your values, not just your income.

Chapter 21: Should You Pursue a Residency or Additional Certifications?

Let's be real.

You didn't spend four years grinding through pharmacy school, drowning in exams, therapeutics, and OSCEs, just to coast.

You're here because you care.

About excellence.

About growth.

About building a career that matters.

But somewhere along the way—after graduation, or maybe in the middle of your fourth-year rotations—you started hearing the question:

"Are you going to do a residency?"

And later, it became:

"Are you going to get your BCPS?"

"Are you thinking about a teaching certificate?"

"What about pharmacogenomics? MTM? Compounding? Informatics?"

It never ends.

And the question behind all of it—the real question—is this:

"Will this investment in my training actually pay off?"

That's what this chapter is here to explore.

Because here's the truth:

There's no one right answer.

For some pharmacists, residency is the gateway to their dream role.

For others, it's an expensive delay that leads to burnout.

For some, certifications open doors.

For others, they sit unused on a resume and never generate a return.

We're going to help you figure out where *you* stand.

We'll walk through:

- The real financial cost of residencies and certifications
- The income differences (and whether they justify the time)
- Pros and cons of residency vs. direct-to-work paths
- Who needs certifications—and who doesn't
- How to evaluate ROI (return on investment) like a boss
- Real-world examples from pharmacists in different career tracks
- The "quiet costs" nobody talks about—like stress, delay, and lifestyle impact
- How to make a decision that supports your *goals,* not your guilt

Let's start with what's really on the table.

Section 1: What Is a Residency—Really?

Residency is a post-graduate, year-long (or two-year) training program designed to expand your clinical skills, research ability, and professional network.

It's often required or preferred for hospital, clinical, ambulatory care, or academic roles—especially in competitive settings.

PGY1 is your generalist year.

PGY2 is a specialized track—cardiology, oncology, psych, peds, etc.

Residency means:

- Lower income (average PGY1 stipend = ~$45K)
- Long hours (often 50–60+ hour weeks)
- High expectations
- Steep learning curve
- Heavy focus on projects, presentations, and research
- Less financial freedom for 1–2 years

But it can also mean:

- A pathway to high-level clinical roles
- Earlier promotions in health system jobs
- Exposure to new areas of pharmacy
- Networking that lasts your entire career
- A competitive edge for certain credentials (like BCPS)

So should you do one?

Let's get honest about the numbers.

Section 2: The Financial Cost of Residency

Let's say you get a full-time job out of pharmacy school making $115,000/year.

Your friend does a PGY1 residency for $47,000.

That's a **$68,000 opportunity cost** in the first year alone.

If they do a PGY2? Add another year at ~$52,000.

That's **$136,000+ in lost wages** over two years—plus potential retirement savings, loan payments, and missed investment opportunities.

On the flip side...

If they land a hospital clinical role at $135,000 post-residency that you *can't* get without one?

Over time, the gap may close—or reverse.

Let's do the math.

Section 3: Residency ROI Scenario – Worth It or Not?

Option 1: No Residency

Start at $115K → 3% raises yearly

Year 1 salary: $115,000

Year 5 salary: ~$129,000

Total 5-year income: ~$635,000

Option 2: PGY1 + PGY2

Year 1: $47,000

Year 2: $52,000

Year 3: $135,000

Year 5: ~$143,000

Total 5-year income: ~$563,000

That's a $72,000 difference over 5 years—*in favor of skipping residency.*

BUT—by Year 7–10, the higher clinical salary could surpass yours.

The tipping point is usually around **year 8–10**.

If you *know* you want clinical or academic work long-term, the short-term loss may be worth the long-term positioning.

But if you're not sure?

That's an expensive maybe.

Section 4: The Emotional and Lifestyle Trade-Offs

Money isn't the only factor.

Residency also costs:

- Nights and weekends
- Sleep
- Time with your family or partner
- Opportunities to travel, rest, or explore
- The ability to start aggressively paying off loans

Some residents report burnout before they even start their first full-time job.

You're working hard—for *less* pay, *more* hours, and often, unclear job outcomes.

So ask yourself:

Am I choosing this for the right reasons?

Or because I'm scared to "fall behind"?

Do I *want* this job track long-term?

Or am I hoping this residency will help me figure that out?

If it's the latter—you might be better off working, learning, and reassessing.

Section 5: Certifications – Real Assets or Resume Filler?

Let's shift to the alphabet soup.

BCPS. BCACP. BCGP. BCIDP. CDE. CSP. RPhS. AAHIVP. CPP. MTM.

Certifications can:

- Strengthen your clinical skill set
- Open doors in hospitals and academic centers
- Boost your credibility with patients or peers
- Help you meet job requirements

But they're not always necessary.

And they're *definitely* not always worth the cost.

Consider:

- Exam fees ($600–$1,000+)
- Prep materials ($200–$800)
- Time investment (100–300+ study hours)
- Renewal fees and CE requirements
- The job market (Will this actually lead to more income?)

If your current or future role *requires* a certification—or gives a pay bump—it might be worth it.

But don't collect credentials like Pokémon cards.

Collect them strategically.

Section 6: The Questions That Really Matter

Before you pursue a residency or certification, ask:

1. What specific roles am I targeting?
2. Do those roles *require* a residency or cert?
3. Can I achieve that lifestyle or salary *without* one?
4. How long will it take to break even?
5. How will this affect my debt payoff timeline?
6. Will this increase my job satisfaction—or just my workload?
7. Do I feel pressured, or genuinely excited?

Section 7: Real-Life Pharmacist Paths (No Shame Either Way)

Tasha – Retail to Ambulatory Care (Residency Required)

Did PGY1 + PGY2 → landed an ambulatory care position → now earns $140K, loves her work-life balance, and precepts students. Residency was her bridge.

Marcus – Clinical Without Residency

Went straight to a hospital job → found a great mentor → studied hard, learned on the job → later earned BCPS → no regrets about skipping residency.

Sarah – Cert Collector

Earned 4 certifications in 6 years—but only uses one in her current retail role. "I thought more letters would mean more options. What I really needed was a clearer goal."

Jordan – Switched Mid-Career

Started in retail, got burned out, took a 25% pay cut for a PGY1 years later. Struggled financially during that year—but now works 9–5 with weekends off. Worth it? Yes—for him.

Section 8: Final Framework – Decide Like a CFO

Think like the Chief Financial Officer of *your life.*

Ask:

- What's the return on investment (ROI)?
- What are the real costs—time, money, energy, mental health?
- What are the opportunity costs (what else could I do with those resources)?
- Does this align with my long-term career and life goals?

Residency is not a flex.

Certifications are not trophies.

They are tools.

Use them wisely.

Final Encouragement

You're not less of a pharmacist if you don't do a residency.

You're not more of a pharmacist if you have six certifications.

You're a pharmacist either way.

What matters is that you build a career that makes *sense*—for your life, your goals, and your definition of success.

Don't let fear or peer pressure drive your decisions.

Let clarity do the driving.

Call to Action

Make one decision about your career development this week.

One.

- Research a certification.
- Talk to someone who did a residency.
- Map out a 5-year vision.
- Say no to something that's not aligned.
- Say yes to something that lights you up.

Then do another next week.

Final Note

This isn't just about career advancement.

This is about *ownership*.

Of your time.

Your energy.

Your expertise.

Your future.

You didn't go through all those years of school just to follow someone else's path.

Financial Literacy For Pharmacists is your permission slip to build a career that's not just profitable—but peaceful, powerful, and *yours*.

Your future self will thank you.

So will your bank account.

So will your sanity.

Chapter 22: Career Paths in Pharmacy – Retail, Clinical, Industry, Academia, and Beyond

Section 1: Retail Pharmacy – The Starting Point for Many, but Not the Final Destination for All

Let's begin with the most common entry point for pharmacists in the U.S.—retail.

You already know this world.

The drive-thru. The flu shots. The rush between the register, the phone, and the consultation window.

Retail is where many pharmacists cut their teeth—and where many feel stuck.

Retail is often framed as the "default" job if you don't pursue a residency.

But here's the reality: there's nothing "less than" about choosing retail.

What matters is whether it's the right *fit*—financially, emotionally, and long-term.

The Pros:

- High starting salaries (often \$110K–\$140K+)
- Job availability across the country
- Clear advancement structure (staff → PIC → DM)
- No need for post-grad training
- Great for building communication and crisis management skills
- Union representation in some regions

- Flexibility in location if you want to relocate

The Cons:

- High stress, fast-paced environment
- Heavy workload—often with staffing shortages
- Weekend and holiday hours
- Limited clinical growth
- Can feel transactional and repetitive over time
- Lower job satisfaction reported in surveys
- Career plateau risk if no additional training or pivot

Financial Outlook:

Retail pharmacists often make strong early income, but raises can plateau. Bonuses and stock options are inconsistent. The real trap? Getting stuck without a pivot plan if burnout hits.

Questions to Ask Yourself:

- Is this pace sustainable for me long-term?
- Do I have an exit strategy if I decide to leave?
- Am I using this job to fund a longer-term goal—or just surviving each shift?
- What am I doing with the income I earn here?

If You Stay in Retail:

- Max out your retirement contributions
- Pay down debt aggressively
- Build a "Work Optional" fund in case you need to step away
- Develop transferable skills (leadership, operations, communication)
- Explore side income options or certifications to keep doors open

If You're Looking to Pivot:

Use your income stability to *invest in change*—courses, shadowing, certifications, or even time off to reassess.

Retail can be a launchpad—or a trap.

It depends on whether *you* are steering the ship.

Section 2: Clinical Pharmacy – More Rewarding? Yes. More Complicated? Also Yes.

This is the dream job for many students.

The white coat. The rounding team. The chance to truly "practice at the top of your license."

But it comes with trade-offs.

The Pros:

- Deeper clinical involvement
- More collaboration with healthcare teams
- Often no nights, weekends, or holidays (depending on setting)
- Better work-life balance in some roles
- Opportunity to precept, teach, and research
- Greater professional satisfaction for many

The Cons:

- Requires PGY1 (and often PGY2)
- Lower starting salary during residency years
- Job market is competitive
- Less geographic flexibility
- May require relocation
- Not always a huge pay jump compared to retail

Financial Outlook:

After residency, clinical roles range from $115K–$145K, depending on region and setting. Long-term growth is slower, but retirement plans, benefits, and job satisfaction can make up for that.

Questions to Ask Yourself:

- Am I passionate about patient care and clinical decision-making?
- Am I willing to sacrifice short-term income for long-term fulfillment?
- Will I enjoy research, documentation, and protocols?
- Is my personality a fit for hospital culture?

Tips If You're Considering It:

- Talk to at least 3 clinical pharmacists in different settings
- Ask about their day-to-day—not just what they love, but what they *tolerate*
- Research the residency match process *early*
- If you're already practicing, look into non-traditional PGY1 or fellowship programs

Section 3: Ambulatory Care – The Middle Ground That Feels Like a Sweet Spot

Think of ambulatory care as the outpatient cousin of clinical pharmacy. It's patient-facing. It's chronic care. It's highly collaborative.

And it's growing.

The Pros:

- Longitudinal patient relationships
- No weekends or holidays
- Better work-life balance
- Autonomy and protocol-based prescribing (in some states)
- High impact on chronic disease management
- Fulfilling work with vulnerable populations

The Cons:

- Requires residency and/or board certification
- Often tied to grants or short-term funding
- Less pay than inpatient hospital roles in some regions

- May require dual responsibilities (admin, teaching, clinic)
- Some jobs can be hard to come by

Financial Outlook:

Average salaries are $110K–$130K. But benefits, job stability, and job satisfaction can be strong. Not a "get rich" path—but often a "stay sane and purposeful" path.

Section 4: Academia – Teach, Research, Inspire

Teaching is a calling.

You won't get rich in academia. But if you love mentoring, writing, presenting, and shaping the next generation—this could be your zone.

The Pros:

- Stable schedule (often M–F)
- Summers can be lighter depending on institution
- Deep involvement in professional development
- Access to academic resources, conferences, research
- Potential for sabbaticals, international work, or adjunct projects
- Often strong retirement matching or pension

The Cons:

- Salaries are lower—often $85K–$120K to start
- Lots of meetings, service requirements, and admin tasks
- Pressure to publish or pursue grants
- Teaching + research + service = full plate
- Some faculty feel disconnected from real-world pharmacy practice

Financial Outlook:

Don't do it for the money. Do it for the legacy, the lifestyle, and the opportunity to multiply your impact through students.

Chapter 23: Budgeting for Lifestyle Inflation – How to Avoid the Trap

Section 1: What Lifestyle Inflation Actually Looks Like in Real Life

Let's start by naming it.

Lifestyle inflation is when your spending increases as your income increases—sometimes on purpose, sometimes silently.

It's not evil. It's not foolish. It's *natural.*

You get your first job out of pharmacy school.

You're earning $110K. Then $120K. Then $130K.

But you're still just barely saving anything.

Why?

Because every raise becomes an invitation to upgrade.

And those upgrades sneak in quietly:

- You stop cooking because you're always tired—so you order Uber Eats 3x/week.
- You get promoted, so you reward yourself with a nicer car—because "you deserve it."
- You finally have weekends off, so you start saying yes to events, trips, and Amazon Prime splurges.
- Your apartment gets a little bigger.
- Your clothes get a little more stylish.
- Your habits get a little more expensive.

Each change feels justified. Small. Harmless.

But over time, your budget fills up.

Until suddenly, you realize:

"I make $130,000. And I still feel broke."

Section 2: Lifestyle Inflation vs. Lifestyle Alignment

Let's be clear: not all upgrades are bad.

You *should* be able to enjoy your money.

The goal isn't to live like a student forever.

But the key distinction is this:

Lifestyle inflation is automatic.

Lifestyle alignment is intentional.

Lifestyle inflation is reacting to income increases with spending.

Lifestyle alignment is designing your spending around your values.

Inflation says, "I make more, so I spend more."

Alignment says, "I spend on what matters—and I let the rest go."

The problem isn't the latte. It's the *autopilot*.

If your spending grows without a plan, you lose control.

And when you lose control, you lose confidence.

Let's take that back.

Section 3: Why Pharmacists Are Especially Vulnerable to the Trap

There are a few unique reasons lifestyle inflation hits pharmacists hard:

1. Delayed Gratification Burnout

You've been in school for years. You've sacrificed sleep, fun, time, and freedom.

Once the money finally comes in, there's a powerful urge to "make up for lost time."

2. High Starting Salaries, No Financial Training

You go from making $0 to six figures overnight—with no formal education about how to manage it.

3. Financial Survivor's Guilt

Especially if you came from a lower-income background, there's pressure to help family, look successful, or "repay" your past in visible ways.

4. Social Comparison

You're surrounded by other high-earning professionals. The optics of success—nice cars, white kitchens, vacations—start to feel like requirements.

5. Student Loans Feel Like Monopoly Money

When you owe $180K, what's another $800/month car payment? You already feel behind, so you give up on catching up.

But here's the truth:

You can enjoy your income *and* build wealth.

You can live well now *and* plan for later.

It just takes structure. And a mindset shift.

Section 4: The Emotional Side of Lifestyle Creep

We have to talk about shame.

Because that's what makes lifestyle inflation so dangerous—it hides under pride, but it feeds off shame.

You start thinking:

"I make good money. I *shouldn't* feel stressed."

"If I admit I can't afford this, people will think I'm bad with money."

"If I scale back, does that mean I failed?"

No. It means you're self-aware.

Lifestyle creep thrives in silence.

It wants you to keep pretending everything is fine, while quietly draining your energy and your bank account.

But when you name it?

You take the power back.

Section 5: A Story You Might Recognize

Meet Elena.

She's 30. She's a retail pharmacist making $127,000.

She drives a $600/month SUV, lives in a luxury apartment, and takes 2–3 trips a year.

She contributes 3% to her 401(k) because that's what the company matches.

She pays her loans on auto-pay.

On the outside, things look great.

But Elena is stressed.

She has no emergency fund.

Her credit card balance is creeping up.

She hasn't looked at her loan balances in 6 months.

And the idea of changing anything makes her feel like a failure.

She's not a failure.

She's caught in lifestyle inflation.

What she needs isn't a lecture. It's a system.

Let's build one.

Section 6: How to Budget *with* Lifestyle Growth (Not Against It)

Here's the framework I use with pharmacists who want to live well *and* grow wealth.

It's called the **30-30-30-10 Rule**:

- 30% → Fixed Needs (housing, transportation, insurance, utilities)
- 30% → Financial Priorities (retirement, loans, savings, investing)
- 30% → Flexible Wants (restaurants, travel, shopping, hobbies)
- 10% → Generosity and Growth (gifts, donations, courses, therapy, coaching)

This model lets you upgrade *intentionally*.

You want a nicer car? Cool—do it within the 30% fixed cap.

You want more trips? Great—use the 30% fun budget.

You want to invest more? Expand the second 30% by shrinking the others.

It's not restrictive. It's *directive*.

You don't have to ask, "Can I afford this?"

You ask, "Which category does this fall into—and is there space?"

Simple. Clear. Powerful.

Chapter 24: Buying a Home as a Pharmacist – How Much House Can You Afford?

Section 1: The Real Cost of Buying a Home (Hint: It's Not Just the Mortgage)

When most pharmacists think about home affordability, they zero in on one number:

"How much is the mortgage payment?"

But your mortgage is just the beginning.

Here's what else you'll need to account for:

- Property taxes (can be thousands per year depending on your location)
- Homeowners insurance (mandatory for most lenders)
- Private mortgage insurance (PMI), if your down payment is under 20%
- HOA fees (common in condos and planned communities)
- Utilities (typically higher than in apartments)
- Maintenance and repairs (expect 1–2% of home value per year)
- Furniture, appliances, landscaping, upgrades (often underestimated)

A $2,500/month mortgage could easily become $3,200/month in total housing costs.

That's why "approval amount" is misleading. Banks don't care about your budget—they care about their risk.

You have to define *your* limit.

Section 2: Approval vs. Affordability – Know the Difference

Let's be blunt:

The bank will almost always approve you for more than you should actually spend.

They don't know about your student loans, your plans to start a family, your desire to travel, or your dream to retire at 55.

They use your gross income and your debt-to-income (DTI) ratio. That's it.

Many pharmacists are approved for homes with mortgage payments that are 35%–40% of their gross income.

That's too high.

If your housing costs more than 28–30% of your *net* income (after taxes), you're stepping into "house poor" territory.

Here's a safer rule of thumb:

- Keep your all-in housing cost at or below 25% of your take-home pay.
- That leaves room for savings, investing, loan repayment, and lifestyle.

Remember: being house rich and cash poor is a terrible feeling.

Section 3: How to Calculate a Realistic Housing Budget

Let's break it down with a sample formula.

Let's say you're a pharmacist making $120,000 per year.

After taxes and deductions, your monthly take-home pay is about $7,000.

Using the 25% rule:

- 25% of $7,000 = $1,750
- That's your **maximum recommended monthly housing budget**—and that includes mortgage, taxes, insurance, HOA fees, and maintenance.

That might mean shopping for homes under $350,000 in some markets.

In others, it might mean waiting or renting longer while you build a stronger down payment.

Section 4: Down Payments – What You Need to Know

You've probably heard that 20% is the gold standard.

And it is—for avoiding PMI (private mortgage insurance) and reducing your total loan cost.

But pharmacists often face a tough choice:

Save for a down payment while paying student loans

vs.

Buy sooner with a lower down payment and take on PMI

There's no one right answer.

But here are your options:

- **20% down**: Ideal. No PMI. Lower interest rate. Lower monthly payment.
- **10% down**: Common. PMI applies. Still fairly strong equity position.
- **5% down**: Some conventional loans allow this. PMI will be higher.
- **0–3.5% down**: Available through VA loans (if applicable) or FHA loans. These can work—but the monthly costs are high.

If you're putting down less than 10%, make sure your emergency fund is solid.

Don't drain your savings to become a homeowner.

Section 5: How Student Loans Affect Your Home Buying Power

This is where pharmacists hit a wall.

You're earning good money—but you're carrying $150K–$250K in federal student loans.

How does that impact your mortgage?

Lenders look at your DTI (debt-to-income) ratio. That includes:

- Your minimum student loan payment
- Your proposed mortgage
- Any car loans, credit card debt, personal loans

If your DTI exceeds 43%, many lenders will deny the loan—or charge a higher interest rate.

Strategies to reduce your DTI:

- Use income-driven repayment for federal loans
- Pay off credit cards or car loans before applying
- Increase your income or save for a larger down payment

Quick note: federal loans in deferment *may still count* toward your DTI. Check with your lender.

Section 6: Renting vs. Buying – Which One Is Smarter Right Now?

Buying a home is not always better.

Renting offers:

- Flexibility to move
- Lower upfront costs
- No maintenance stress
- Opportunity to invest more aggressively
- Protection in high-cost housing markets

Buying offers:

- Potential equity growth
- Tax deductions
- Predictable monthly payments (fixed-rate loans)
- A sense of stability

Here's the truth:

If you're staying in a location for less than 3–5 years? Renting often wins.

If your job feels uncertain? Renting may be safer.

If your financial foundation is shaky? Buying can turn stress into disaster.

There's no shame in renting.

Renting while investing, saving, and getting your financial house in order? That's powerful.

Section 7: First-Time Homebuyer Programs – Should You Use One?

As a pharmacist, you might not think you qualify for first-time buyer help. But you'd be surprised.

Let's unpack what's out there—and what's worth considering.

What counts as a first-time homebuyer?

According to the U.S. Department of Housing and Urban Development (HUD), a first-time homebuyer is someone who hasn't owned a principal residence in the last three years.

That means if you've been renting or living with family—or sold your last house more than three years ago—you might still qualify.

Types of programs to look for:

- **FHA loans** – Low down payment (as little as 3.5%). Great for lower-credit buyers, but includes mortgage insurance premiums for the life of the loan.
- **Conventional 97** – Requires just 3% down. Best for good credit.
- **Physician or "Medical Professional" loans** – Some lenders offer special loans to pharmacists with low or zero down payment and no PMI—even with high student loans.
- **State and local grants or deferred loans** – Many cities or states offer cash assistance for down payments or closing costs.
- **Good Neighbor Next Door** – For pharmacists who also hold other community roles (rare, but worth checking).

Questions to ask before saying yes to any program:

- What's the interest rate compared to conventional options?
- Are there income limits?
- What fees, insurance, or stipulations apply?
- Will this increase my monthly housing cost over time?

Not all help is helpful.

But if the program truly reduces your *out-of-pocket cost without inflating your long-term cost,* it can be a smart first step.

Section 8: Dual-Income Households – Avoid the Two-Person Trap

Let's talk about something common—but rarely discussed:

Dual pharmacist couples.

On paper, it looks like a dream.

Two high incomes. Maybe no kids yet. Possibly $200K–$300K in annual income combined.

But here's where things go wrong:

- You buy a house based on *both* incomes.
- You borrow to the max.
- You upgrade your lifestyle hard and fast.
- Then—life happens.

One of you wants to go part-time.

One of you gets laid off.

You want to have a child and need flexibility.

You want to move closer to family or switch job settings.

But the house won't let you.

It's locked to a two-income budget.

Here's a safer way to approach it:

Base your house affordability on one income.

Or at least make sure *one person's income* could cover the mortgage and essentials if needed.

That's what creates freedom.

Two incomes should build margin, not pressure.

Section 9: The Hidden Costs of Homeownership

Most first-time buyers only look at the mortgage payment.

Let's list the other expenses—so they don't catch you off guard.

1. Closing Costs:

Typically 2%–5% of the home's price. That's $8,000–$20,000 on a $400,000 home.

2. Move-In Expenses:

Truck rental, new locks, appliances, deposits, internet installation, etc.

3. Furniture:

Even if you're keeping your old stuff, a new space often calls for more. Budget at least $3,000–$10,000 depending on size.

4. Ongoing Maintenance:

Roof, HVAC, appliances, plumbing, yardwork, pest control. Rule of thumb: budget 1%–2% of the home's value annually.

5. Property Taxes and Insurance Increases:

These often go up over time. Even with a fixed-rate mortgage, your monthly payment can climb.

6. Repairs and Surprises:

You'll have a year with 3 HVAC calls and a burst pipe. Ask any homeowner.

7. Opportunity Cost:

Every dollar tied up in a home is a dollar *not* invested elsewhere. That doesn't make homeownership bad—but it makes liquidity important.

Section 10: How to Make Your Home Part of Your Wealth Plan (Not a Detour From It)

Buying a house is an emotional decision.

But it has to serve your *financial* life—not hijack it.

Here's how to keep the balance:

1. Budget backwards.

Start with your ideal financial life—investing, saving, traveling, margin—and *then* see how much house you can afford without giving those things up.

2. Set a ceiling.

Before you talk to a realtor, define your max purchase price and monthly housing budget. Stick to it—even if you "fall in love" with a place outside your range.

3. Build equity intentionally.

If you buy, make extra principal payments when you can. Don't stretch too thin, but even $200/month adds up over time.

4. Keep an emergency fund for the house.

Not just for life—but for *the house itself.* That's how you avoid putting home repairs on a credit card.

5. Track your net worth quarterly.

It'll remind you that your house is *one piece* of the wealth puzzle—not the whole game.

Section 11: Emotional Discipline – Stay Grounded in the Process

Home buying is not just financial—it's deeply *emotional.*

It represents arrival. Stability. Success.

It's easy to get caught up in comparisons, open house emotions, and pressure from agents or family.

Take a breath.

Here are some mindset reminders:

- Don't buy for Instagram. Buy for your peace.
- Don't buy to prove something. Buy when you're ready.
- Don't feel rushed. The market will always fluctuate—but wisdom is always in style.

Your dream home should fit *your* dream life.

Not force your life to revolve around it.

Final Encouragement

Homeownership can be powerful.

It can create stability. It can build wealth. It can give you roots.

But only when done with clarity, intention, and enough breathing room to still live your life.

Don't let a mortgage become your master.

Let your home serve your freedom—not strangle it.

You've already done the hard work of becoming a pharmacist.

Let your money reflect that excellence—not just in what you earn, but in how you decide.

Call to Act

Do this tonight:

- Run the numbers. What's 25% of your monthly take-home pay?
- Plug in local property tax and insurance estimates.
- Look at your savings. Could you afford a down payment and still keep a 3-month emergency fund?

That's your clarity. That's your line.

Stick to it like your peace depends on it—because it does.

Then, next week?

Interview a lender. Explore rent-vs-buy tools.

Or start a "future down payment" fund—even if you're not ready yet.

Every step counts.

Final Note

This isn't about owning a home.

It's about owning your decisions.

Financial literacy is freedom.

And no home—no matter how beautiful—should cost you that.

You deserve a home that fits your life.

Not one that takes it over.

Your future self will thank you.

So will your bank account.

So will your Saturday mornings.

Chapter 25: Relationship Money Talk – Combining Finances with a Partner

Section 1: Why This Conversation Feels So Hard

You're not bad with money.

You're not bad at relationships.

But combine the two?

And suddenly things get weird.

Why?

Because money represents more than dollars.

It represents identity.

Security.

Freedom.

Success.

Control.

Shame.

And for some—trauma.

Your partner didn't just grow up with different spending habits.

They grew up with a different money *story*.

Maybe they had parents who fought about money—or never talked about it.

Maybe they watched someone lose everything in a divorce.

Maybe they were taught that money was meant to be spent, not saved.

Or saved, not enjoyed.

You bring your story. They bring theirs.

And unless you talk about it—you'll live by accident instead of by design.

Let's flip that.

Section 2: How to Start the Money Conversation Without Causing a Fight

Money talks don't have to be awkward.

But they do need structure.

Try this:

1. Set the tone.

"Hey—I've been thinking a lot about how we can build something strong together financially. I'd love for us to have a calm, clear talk—not because anything's wrong, but because I care about us."

2. Pick the right moment.

Not after a fight.

Not during a budget crisis.

Not at 11:00 PM when you're both exhausted.

Try a "money date"—scheduled, chill, maybe even over coffee or takeout.

3. Focus on shared goals.

"What do we want life to look like in 1 year? 5 years? 10 years?"

Use dreams as your anchor—not debt.

4. Stay curious.

Instead of: "Why do you spend so much on DoorDash?"

Try: "Tell me more about what those food deliveries do for you. Convenience? Comfort? A break in the day?"

This is about *understanding*, not control.

Section 3: The Three Models of Combining Finances

You've got options.

There's no one "right" way to manage money as a couple—but there *is* a right way for your relationship.

Here are the big three models:

1. Fully Combined

All money goes into joint accounts. Shared budgets. Total transparency.

Best for:

- Couples who want full partnership and simplicity
- Similar money values
- Long-term or married couples

Risk:

- Can feel invasive or controlling if one person is much more frugal or dominant

2. Fully Separate

Each person manages their own income, debts, and expenses. Shared bills are split down the middle or based on income.

Best for:

- Newer couples
- Second marriages
- Couples with very different money styles

Risk:

- Can feel like roommates
- May cause resentment if one person earns significantly more

3. Hybrid Model

A combination. You each keep your own accounts for personal spending, but also contribute to a joint account for shared expenses and goals.

Best for:

- Couples who want both autonomy and unity
- Partners with different debt or financial responsibilities
- Dual-income households managing a home or family

How it looks:

- Joint account for rent/mortgage, groceries, vacations, kids
- Separate accounts for personal spending (no judgment zones)
- Optional third account for shared saving goals

This model is increasingly popular among pharmacists because it blends partnership with personal freedom.

Section 4: How to Handle Income Differences Without Resentment

You might both be pharmacists.

Or maybe one of you is in retail making $115K and the other is in industry making $175K.

Or maybe one partner isn't in pharmacy at all.

Income imbalances don't have to break the relationship—but they *do* have to be addressed directly.

Here's what works:

1. Contribute proportionally, not equally.

Let's say your take-home pay is $7,000/month, and your partner's is $4,000/month.

A 50/50 split on all bills would feel unfair—and likely unsustainable.

Instead, consider a **percentage split**.

You each contribute the same % of your income—say, 60%—to a shared account, and keep the rest for personal use.

That way, both of you feel invested—but no one feels penalized for earning less.

2. Respect what each partner brings.

Money is one form of value.

But emotional labor, domestic work, caretaking, and long-term planning all matter too.

Don't measure contribution *only* by income.

3. Name the emotion underneath.

Jealousy? Shame? Pride? Guilt?

Talk about it—not just the spreadsheet.

Section 5: Student Loans, Past Debts, and Financial Baggage

When you combine lives, you don't just combine assets.

You combine *baggage.*

Maybe one of you has $220,000 in student loans.

Maybe one of you has credit card debt.

Maybe one of you comes in with an inheritance, a divorce settlement, or a financial wound.

The question is: how do you move forward without judgment or confusion?

1. Get it all on the table.

Make a spreadsheet.

List every account, debt, balance, and interest rate.

You don't need to merge right away—but you do need transparency.

2. Decide what's joint and what's personal.

Maybe you pay off your student loans separately.

Maybe you attack them together.

Maybe you split them by who earns more.

There's no perfect way.

But silence builds shame.

Clarity builds teamwork.

3. Protect each other.

Even if you're not legally married, it's smart to have agreements in place—especially if one partner is contributing heavily to joint assets or debt payments.

Prenups and postnups aren't cold. They're grown-up.

Chapter 26: Managing Income-Based Repayment While Planning a Life

Section 1: Understanding the Four Major Income-Driven Repayment Plans

Let's get this straight from the top.

If you're a pharmacist with federal student loans, and you're not going for full aggressive repayment, your life probably revolves around one of the four major IDR plans:

- IBR (Income-Based Repayment)
- PAYE (Pay As You Earn)
- REPAYE (Revised Pay As You Earn)
- SAVE (Saving on a Valuable Education – the newest and most flexible)

Here's how they differ—and why you might choose one over the other.

IBR

- 10%–15% of discretionary income
- 20–25 years to forgiveness
- Capped at the 10-year Standard Plan amount
- Good for high-debt, moderate-income borrowers
- Still available, but largely outdated unless you're grandfathered in

PAYE

- 10% of discretionary income
- 20 years to forgiveness
- Monthly payment capped at what the 10-year plan would've been
- Only available if you borrowed after 2007 and had a disbursement after 2011

REPAYE (now replaced by SAVE)

- 10% of discretionary income
- No payment cap
- Offers interest subsidies that reduce unpaid interest accumulation
- Great for single borrowers or those early in careers

SAVE (the evolution of REPAYE)

- Replaces REPAYE as of 2024
- 5%–10% of discretionary income depending on loan type
- Raises the income exemption to 225% of the poverty line
- Massive interest subsidy (unpaid interest doesn't capitalize)
- Likely the best plan for most pharmacists unless pursuing PSLF

Section 2: The New SAVE Plan – Why It's a Game-Changer

The SAVE plan changes the landscape for pharmacists in several ways:

1. Lower Monthly Payments

Because it raises the income protection threshold and reduces the payment percentage for some loans, many borrowers see significantly lower monthly payments—even on six-figure incomes.

2. No More Ballooning Interest

In the past, if your payment didn't cover the interest, that interest would stack up. Under SAVE, any unpaid interest is forgiven monthly. That means your balance doesn't grow—even if you're not paying enough to cover interest.

3. Spousal Income Treatment

Previously, REPAYE included both incomes for married borrowers—even if you filed separately. SAVE now allows you to exclude your spouse's income if you file taxes separately.

4. Loan Forgiveness After 20–25 Years

Under SAVE, undergraduate loans are forgiven after 20 years, and graduate loans (like most pharmacy programs) after 25 years.

So is SAVE right for you?

It might be if:

- You're early in your career and want cash flow flexibility
- You're not pursuing PSLF
- You have high debt relative to income
- You're building a life—home, kids, retirement—and need space to grow

Section 3: PSLF vs. Long-Term IDR Forgiveness – Which Path Are You On?

Let's stop pretending this is a simple choice.

Public Service Loan Forgiveness (PSLF) offers forgiveness after 120 qualifying payments (10 years) while working full-time at a government or nonprofit employer.

But many pharmacists either:

- Don't work for qualifying employers
- Change jobs mid-career
- Have breaks in employment or inconsistent eligibility
- Want the flexibility to pivot, start businesses, or relocate

So what's the play?

If you're PSLF-eligible:

- Maximize it.
- File taxes separately if it lowers your payment.
- Track employment certifications annually.

- Keep pristine records.
- Consider staying put long enough to lock it in.

If you're not PSLF-eligible:

- Look at SAVE as your path.
- Plan around the 20–25 year forgiveness mark.
- Be ready for the "tax bomb" (more on that next).
- Don't assume this is "worse"—it's just different.

Section 4: The Tax Bomb – What to Expect and How to Prepare

Under current law, loan balances forgiven under long-term IDR plans (like SAVE) are considered **taxable income**.

That means if you're forgiven $150,000 in year 25, the IRS might say: "Cool, now pay taxes on that like it's income."

Depending on the tax bracket and your financial situation at that time, this could mean owing $30,000–$60,000+ in one year.

Ways to plan for it:

1. **Open a "forgiveness sinking fund"**
2. Start setting aside $100–$200/month into a separate savings or investment account.
3. Let it grow alongside your forgiveness timeline.
4. **Reassess every five years**
5. If your income grows dramatically, your plan might shift.
6. You may decide to switch to aggressive repayment or refinance.
7. Keep it flexible.
8. **Watch for legislative changes**
9. This tax bomb could be repealed or altered—especially for low-income earners or healthcare workers. Stay informed.

Section 5: Managing Your AGI – Legally Lowering Your Payment

Your monthly IDR payment is based on your **Adjusted Gross Income**

(AGI).

And here's the trick:

You have control over your AGI.

Ways to lower AGI (and thus your student loan payment):

- Max out **pre-tax retirement contributions** (401k, 403b, 457b)
- Contribute to an **HSA** (Health Savings Account)
- Deduct eligible **student loan interest**
- Claim other above-the-line deductions (self-employed health insurance, educator expenses, etc.)

Example:

Let's say your gross salary is $120,000.

You contribute $22,500 to your 401(k) and $3,850 to your HSA.

Your AGI drops to $93,650—saving you thousands over time in student loan payments *and* taxes.

Retirement planning + loan strategy = boss move.

Chapter 27: Financial Red Flags in the Pharmacist Community

Section 1: Red Flag #1 – High Income, Low Net Worth

Let's start here.

You're making $120K.

You're contributing to your 401(k).

You drive a reliable car.

You're doing everything "right"—and yet your net worth is… negative.

Why?

Because six-figure income doesn't guarantee wealth.

What matters is what you keep—and where it goes.

Too many pharmacists are asset-light, liability-heavy, and emotionally exhausted.

Here's the red flag:

You're making good money, but you can't tell me your net worth within $10K.

That's the first sign you're building a lifestyle, not a legacy.

Start tracking it.

- Assets: cash, investments, retirement accounts, property
- Liabilities: loans, credit cards, mortgages, any money you owe

Net worth = assets – liabilities

If the number is negative or not growing, that's your cue: time to course-correct.

Section 2: Red Flag #2 – You Don't Know Where Your Money Is Going

Here's the hard truth:

If you don't have a budget—or at least a system—you're leaking cash.

Every time you say "I think I'm doing okay…"

Or "I pay my bills, so I must be fine…"

That's a red flag.

Especially if you:

- Can't say how much you spent on food last month
- Don't know your fixed vs. variable monthly costs
- Have no system for automating savings or investments
- Rely on credit cards "just until next payday"

Most pharmacists need clarity, not complexity.

Try this:

- Fixed costs: 50% or less
- Financial goals (savings, debt, investing): 30%
- Flexible spending: 20%

Track for 30 days. See the patterns. Adjust accordingly.

Section 3: Red Flag #3 – Treating the Loan Payment as a Life Sentence

If you say, "I'll be paying these loans forever," that's a mindset issue *and* a planning issue.

Too many pharmacists choose the minimum payment with zero plan beyond it.

Or they throw extra cash at loans with no regard for interest rate, tax implications, or forgiveness eligibility.

Here's what matters:

- Do you have a defined repayment strategy?
- Are you pursuing PSLF, SAVE forgiveness, or payoff in 10 years or less?
- Are you organizing your budget around your loan plan—or just reacting?

The red flag is **avoidance**.

You don't have to pay it off today. But you do have to know the strategy.

No plan = no power.

Section 4: Red Flag #4 – You Don't Know What's in Your Benefits Package

You wouldn't dispense a med without reading the label.

So why are you ignoring the document that controls your income protection and retirement future?

If you don't know:

- What your 401(k) match is
- Whether your disability insurance is own-occupation
- What life insurance you have (or don't)
- Whether your employer offers a 457(b)
- How much vacation or sick time you're accruing

That's a red flag.

Your benefits are compensation. If you're not maximizing them, you're losing money.

Action step: Block off 1 hour. Log into your HR portal. Read everything. Ask HR to explain what you don't understand.

Own your benefits like you'd own your license.

Section 5: Red Flag #5 – You're Living Like You'll Never Retire

Another sign something's off?

You're 32, making six figures—and saving nothing for retirement.

Or you're 45, with $300K in a 401(k)—and no clue if it's enough.

Or you're 60, wondering if you'll ever be able to walk away.

Pharmacists get tunnel vision: survive school, get the job, keep the job.

But if your retirement strategy is "work until I drop," that's not a plan. That's avoidance.

Signs of trouble:

- No retirement projections
- No Roth strategy (IRA or 401(k))
- You've never increased your 401(k) contribution beyond the match
- You haven't spoken to a planner or run your own numbers

Start now. Even $200/month into a Roth IRA in your 20s–30s changes the game.

Don't wait until burnout forces you to rethink everything.

Section 6: Red Flag #6 – Lifestyle Inflation Has You Trapped

We talked about this in the lifestyle inflation chapter—but it bears repeating here:

When your expenses grow with your income, your freedom shrinks.

If you:

- Bought a home that eats more than 30% of your net income
- Lease a luxury car while carrying credit card debt
- Take trips you can't actually afford, "because I need a break"
- Feel like you have to say yes to every invitation, gift, or purchase "because you're a pharmacist"

That's a red flag.

You deserve comfort. You deserve fun.

But not at the cost of freedom.

Section 7: Red Flag #7 – You're Taking Financial Advice from Facebook Comment Sections

If your financial plan is built off advice from pharmacist forums, Facebook groups, or DMs from "wealth coaches" with no licenses, pause.

Not all peer advice is bad.

But a lot of it is:

- "Refinance now! Rates are low!" (Without context)
- "My advisor said put it all in whole life insurance!"
- "Crypto will fix your student loan problem!"
- "I just do PRN jobs and Venmo all my money—works for me."

Before you take advice:

- Check the source
- Ask what their credentials are
- Ask who benefits if you follow that advice

Because bad advice doesn't show up as a scam.

It shows up as an opportunity that "worked for my friend."

Protect yourself. Be skeptical. Be slow. Ask questions.

Chapter 28: How to Say "No" Financially – Boundaries with Family and Friends

Section 1: Why This Is So Hard for Pharmacists

Let's start with the real reason this chapter hits a nerve:

You worked your tail off to get here.

You survived organic chemistry, late-night rotations, seven years of school, maybe $180K in debt—and now you finally have a real paycheck. You're licensed. You're respected. And in your family or friend circle, you might be the first.

The first one with a "stable" job.

The first one who can afford to pick up the check.

The first one who "makes good money."

And people notice.

They ask for help.

They assume you're okay.

They reach for your generosity, your guilt, or both.

You want to be supportive. That's part of who you are.

But now you feel torn—between the life you're building and the people who helped you get here.

That's not a character flaw. That's a crossroad.

And most pharmacists never get taught how to stand at that crossroad with love, clarity, and a backbone.

That's what we're going to build.

Section 2: What Saying "Yes" Can Actually Cost You

It seems harmless, right?

A couple hundred here.

A quick loan to cover their car note.

You'll get paid back—eventually.

But here's what it *actually* costs you:

- **Your savings rate.** What you give away is money not invested in your Roth IRA, your emergency fund, or your mortgage principal.
- **Your peace of mind.** The stress of wondering, "Will they ask again?" or "What if I say no next time?" eats up your mental bandwidth.
- **Your relationships.** Ironically, money given in guilt tends to *strain* relationships, not strengthen them.
- **Your confidence.** Over-giving makes you feel powerless, especially when your goals keep getting pushed back.
- **Your boundaries.** Every unspoken "no" that becomes a "yes" reinforces a pattern that's hard to reverse.

Here's the test:

If you're giving money but secretly feel anxious, resentful, or trapped—it's not generosity.

It's self-sacrifice. And it's unsustainable.

Section 3: The Most Common Scenarios—and How to Navigate Them

Let's walk through what pharmacists face regularly, and exactly how you can respond.

Scenario 1: "Can you help me out this month? I'm short on rent."

Before you respond:

- Ask yourself: Can I give this *without* needing it back?
- Ask: Will this solve their issue—or is this a recurring pattern?
- Ask: Will this impact my own bills or goals?

What you can say:

"I care about you, and I want to support you. Right now, I'm not in a position to help financially, but I can help you look at resources or brainstorm solutions if you'd like."

Alternate version if it's someone you *want* to help (with limits):

"I'm able to help with $150 this month—but beyond that, I have to stay focused on my financial responsibilities. Let's also talk about how you can avoid being in this spot next month."

Scenario 2: "You're a pharmacist—can't you just pay for the hotel/vacation/gift?"

This is lifestyle inflation wrapped in peer pressure.

Try saying:

"I'd love to go, but that trip doesn't fit into my budget right now."

Or, if they keep pushing:

"I'm working toward some big financial goals this year, and I've made the decision not to stretch beyond them—even for fun things. It's a boundary I've set for myself."

Scenario 3: "You make more than me—can't you just spot me this time?"

This one's tricky—especially among friends. But the issue isn't income. It's boundaries.

Say this:

"I know it might seem like I can afford more because of my job, but I have a plan for every dollar right now—loans, savings, and future goals. I'm trying really hard to stick to that."

Section 4: Scripts for Saying "No" With Love and Clarity

Let's simplify.

Here are some ready-to-use, pharmacist-friendly scripts you can adapt anytime someone pushes your boundaries:

Polite + Clear:

"I'm so sorry—I'm not able to help financially right now."

Polite + Redirect:

"I'm not in a place to contribute, but I'd be happy to help you think through other options."

Polite + Personal:

"I've made a commitment to stick to my financial goals this year, which means I've had to say no to things I'd normally say yes to—including this."

Polite + Firm:

"I care about you. But I can't give or lend money right now. Please understand that it's not about you—it's about staying disciplined with my finances."

Polite + Empowering:

"I've had to set some strong boundaries to stay on track financially, especially with my loans and long-term goals. It's hard, but I've realized it's necessary. I hope you can respect that."

Section 5: Generosity vs. Enabling – Where's the Line?

Generosity uplifts.

Enabling weakens.

The difference?

Generosity:

- Respects your boundaries
- Supports temporary needs
- Honors mutual respect
- Is given freely, without expectation

Enabling:

- Erodes your goals
- Feeds dependency
- Creates resentment
- Feels obligatory or guilt-driven

You are *not* a bad daughter, son, sibling, or friend for saying no.

Sometimes the most loving thing you can do is to stop funding dysfunction.

Section 6: What to Do When They Ask to Borrow Money (Again)

Let's face it—this won't be a one-time request.

You say yes once, and suddenly you become The Bank of You. Even if you meant it as a one-time favor.

The second or third request is the moment to pause.

Ask yourself:

- Has the first loan been repaid—or even acknowledged?
- Is this helping them become more independent—or keeping them dependent?
- Am I feeling stress, frustration, or anxiety about this?

Here's what you can say:

If you're done loaning money:

"I know I helped out before, but I've realized I can't be in a position to lend money anymore. It's not sustainable for me. I care about you, but I have to make a different decision this time."

If you're willing to help with boundaries:

"I can help with $200 this month, but this has to be the last time. I'm tightening up my budget for long-term goals."

If it's emotional:

"I've been feeling stressed about how often we've had money conversations. I don't want our relationship to be about loans. Can we figure out a new way for me to support you that doesn't involve money?"

Section 7: Cultural Expectations, Family Ties, and Guilt

Let's talk about the heavy stuff.

In many communities—especially immigrant, minority, and close-knit cultures—there's a deeply rooted sense of financial responsibility to "take care of everyone."

The unspoken rule is:

"If you make it, you lift others with you."

And that's beautiful—until it becomes a burden.

It becomes:

- Paying your cousin's rent every month
- Buying your mom a car you can't afford
- Skipping your own savings to support someone else's dream
- Feeling guilty every time you say "not right now"

Here's the truth:

You can love your family.

You can be proud of where you came from.

And you can still say:

"I'm not the financial solution to every problem."

Your success should not come with a lifetime tax.

What you *can* do is build **a generosity plan** (we'll get to that in a moment) that allows you to help in a sustainable way.

But here's your mantra:

"I can support you—but I won't sacrifice my financial peace to do it."

Say it again. Say it until it feels like freedom.

Section 8: The Sustainable Generosity Plan

Now let's flip the script.

Let's say you *want* to be generous. You want to give back, support family, or even invest in your community—but you also want to stay on track.

That's where the **Sustainable Generosity Plan** comes in.

Here's how to build it:

1. Decide your annual giving amount.

Just like you budget for groceries or rent—budget for generosity.

It could be $1,000 a year.

It could be 5% of your after-tax income.

It could be a one-time gift fund of $10,000 you refill every 3 years.

The key is: set a **cap** that fits your financial plan.

2. Make it a line item—not a reaction.

Generosity given in guilt isn't generosity—it's obligation.

By planning for it, you take back the power. You give with intention, not pressure.

3. Define your rules.

- Will you give to individuals or only nonprofits?
- Will you help with one-time emergencies or monthly support?
- Will you require a conversation or budget before giving?

You don't owe anyone a blank check. Even family.

4. Create a system.

Example: You create a "Family Support Fund" with $2,500/year.

- If someone asks for help, you can say, "Let's talk—here's what I can offer from the fund this year."
- When it's gone, it's gone. You're not saying no—you're saying, "I've already said yes to my limit."

This framework is how you stay generous *and* financially sovereign.

Section 9: What If You've Already Given Too Much?

If you're reading this thinking, "I've already made the mistake—I've already given too much," you're not alone.

Here's how to course-correct with grace:

Step 1: Acknowledge it—without shame.

You were trying to help. That came from love. Don't beat yourself up.

Step 2: Reset the relationship.

This conversation might sound like:

"I realized I've been giving more than I can really afford, and it's starting to impact my goals. I need to take a step back from financial help for now—not because I don't care, but because I need to stabilize things on my end."

Step 3: Offer alternatives.

"I can't help financially anymore, but I can help you build a plan or connect with resources."

This shift helps the other person feel seen and supported—even without money.

Step 4: Protect your future.

Start saving and investing again. Build your emergency fund. Adjust your boundaries moving forward.

You are allowed to change your mind. You are allowed to grow.

Section 10: When "No" Is the Greatest Act of Love

Let's finish with this:

You didn't work this hard to live paycheck to paycheck *because* of other people's expectations.

You didn't study for your NAPLEX, survive 3 AM shifts, or grind through rotations to stay broke forever.

You have dreams too.

You deserve the right to:

- Retire comfortably
- Raise kids with options
- Take a vacation without guilt
- Say "yes" to the future you want
- Live without resentment

And sometimes, the best way to love someone else is by modeling what self-respect looks like.

Because your "no" is not rejection.

It's a declaration: **"I value myself. And I trust you to find your way, too."**

You've got this.

Final Encouragement

Boundaries aren't walls. They're doors.

Doors that let love in, while keeping chaos out.

Doors that open to generosity—but close to guilt.

Start small.

Make one boundary clear this week.

Say no once with kindness and confidence.

Create one system that protects your peace.

Then do another next week.

Because financial freedom isn't just about the numbers.

It's about the life you create when you finally realize—

You're allowed to build a future that works for you.

And when you do?

Everyone around you rises, too.

Chapter 29: Lifestyle Planning – Travel, Shopping, Self-Care, and Balance

Section 1: You Deserve Joy—Let's Start There

Here's what I want you to hear loud and clear: You didn't become a pharmacist to live in restriction.

You didn't sacrifice your twenties, survive rotations, and graduate with six figures of debt just to spend your life telling yourself "no."

You became a pharmacist because you care. Because you're smart. Because you value stability, service, and legacy.

And you deserve to experience joy on the journey—not just once you've "made it."

But here's what often happens:

- You spend years in survival mode.
- You finally start making money—and immediately feel pressure to use it only for debt, savings, or obligations.
- You ignore your needs, delay your desires, and end up either burned out or binge-spending.

This isn't balance. It's a cycle.

This chapter is about breaking that cycle by creating a **lifestyle plan** that includes joy on purpose.

Not in rebellion. Not in guilt. But as part of your financial health.

Section 2: Create Your Personal Lifestyle Budget – The 3 Joy Buckets

Let's build your **Lifestyle Budget Framework** using three core categories:

1. **Travel & Experiences**
2. **Shopping & Aesthetics**
3. **Self-Care & Wellness**

The goal here is to set **intentional spending parameters** in each of these areas—based on your current financial priorities, your personality, and your season of life.

Ask yourself:

- What level of spending in each category feels satisfying?
- What triggers guilt, shame, or impulse behavior in each category?
- How often do you want to engage with each joy bucket?

Here's a sample plan:

- Travel & Experiences: $300/month (saved monthly, used for 2-3 trips/year)
- Shopping & Aesthetics: $150/month (used for wardrobe refreshes, skincare, home upgrades)
- Self-Care & Wellness: $100/month (used for therapy, massages, gym, books, etc.)

Total: $550/month of joy, **baked into the budget**. No guilt. No chaos.

Start there, and adjust up or down as your goals shift.

Section 3: Travel Like a Pharmacist (Not Like an Influencer)

Here's the trap: You scroll through IG, see someone lounging in Bali, and think, "Why can't I take a trip like that?"

And maybe you can. But maybe that influencer doesn't have student loans, or they put the whole trip on a 25% APR credit card.

Travel is about **freedom**, not **flex**.

Let's talk strategy:

1. Plan Your Travel Fund Like a Pro

Set an annual travel goal—say $3,000/year.

That's $250/month saved automatically into a travel fund.

Use a high-yield savings account or a travel-specific sinking fund.

2. Get Good at Off-Peak Planning

Pharmacists often have unique schedules. Use your non-traditional availability to travel off-season and save 30–50%.

3. Credit Card Points: Friend or Foe?

Use travel rewards **only** if you pay the balance in full monthly. Otherwise, that "free" flight is costing you interest.

4. Ask: Is This Escape or Experience?

Are you booking this trip because you need rest, connection, exploration—or are you trying to run away from burnout?

Be honest. Then book accordingly.

Bottom Line: Travel is allowed. Budgeted joy is responsible joy.

Section 4: Shopping – It's Okay to Want Nice Things

Let's talk about money and aesthetics.

You want the designer bag. The fresh sneakers. The Dyson hair dryer.

And part of you says, "This is dumb—I should be throwing this money at debt."

Pause.

Shopping isn't bad.

But **mindless spending** is.

Retail therapy that hides burnout is.

Buying to impress others is.

Here's the reframe: Shopping can be art, expression, and empowerment—if it's done **on purpose.**

Tips:

- Create a **Style & Aesthetic Fund**—your guilt-free wardrobe/hobby/u pgrade budget
- Use the **72-Hour Rule**: Wait 3 days before non-essential purchases.

Want it still? Cool.
- Choose 1–2 "splurge items" per year that you save for intentionally
- Unfollow accounts that make you feel less-than or pressure you to overspend
- Budget for **fun**—don't just restrict. Assign joy a number.

You're not reckless for caring about how you look or feel in your space.

But don't let the algorithm tell you what you need.

Section 5: Self-Care Is Not a Luxury

You work long hours.

You stand all day.

You hold people's health and safety in your hands.

Self-care is not optional.

But here's the thing: self-care isn't just massages and facials.

It's therapy. It's rest. It's quitting toxic jobs. It's hiring a house cleaner. It's saying no.

Build your **Self-Care Budget** intentionally.

Some examples:

- Therapy sessions: $120/month
- Massage or bodywork: $80/month
- Yoga or gym: $60/month
- Digital detox day: Free but essential
- "Pharmacist Sabbath" (a full day off weekly): Invaluable

Ask yourself:

- What replenishes me the most?
- What am I using to numb instead of heal?
- What's missing from my self-care that *actually* supports my wellbeing?

Then build that into your budget like it's your mortgage—non-negotiable.

Chapter 30: Keeping Up With the Jones's in a Profession with Prestige

Section 1: When the Title Comes with Unspoken Expectations

Becoming a pharmacist comes with a cultural weight—not just the white coat, but the image of stability, intelligence, and affluence.

You hear it all the time:

"She's a pharmacist? Oh, she must be doing well."

"They've got money—he works in healthcare."

The moment people hear your title, they assume you've *arrived.*

And if you've spent years struggling through school, taking out loans, hustling through residencies or retail shifts, it's tempting to *want* to look the part. You might not feel rich—but you want to appear "on track."

That's where the prestige trap starts.

Because here's the truth: **You don't owe the world a performance of wealth.**

You owe yourself financial peace, dignity, and options.

Section 2: Signs You Might Be Caught in the Prestige Trap

Not sure if this is you?

Here are the red flags:

- You feel pressure to upgrade your car every few years, even though your current one runs fine.
- You bought a home based on what you thought a pharmacist should own—not what your budget could comfortably handle.

- You say yes to expensive dinners, vacations, or weddings because you "don't want to look cheap."
- You feel behind or less successful because your colleague drives a luxury SUV or posts about their second home.
- You're constantly spending to maintain an image—but you have no idea what your net worth is.

Here's the thing: The people you're trying to "keep up with"?

They might be drowning in debt. They might be leasing their lifestyle. They might be insecure too.

But none of that shows up on Instagram. Or in the parking lot. Or at the alumni reunion.

You only see the highlight reel. You don't see the balance sheet.

Section 3: Why It Happens—The Psychology Behind It

This isn't just about ego. It's about identity.

When you spend a decade in training, your identity gets wrapped up in what you *do.* And when that identity finally earns income, you want to express it.

You think: "I worked so hard. I deserve this."

And you do.

But if your desire to "look successful" is bigger than your desire to *be financially free,* the trap wins.

Social comparison is hardwired into the human brain. It's a survival mechanism—"Do I belong? Am I doing enough? Am I safe?"

But in the age of curated digital lives and inflated job titles, that mechanism gets hijacked.

And what was once "community" becomes competition.

Section 4: Real-Life Case Study - Same Title, Very Different Outcomes

Let's meet two fictional (but very real-feeling) pharmacists:

Dr. Smith:

Retail pharmacist, age 36

Makes $128,000/year

Leases a luxury SUV ($650/month)

Lives in a $625K home with high HOA fees

Takes multiple financed vacations per year

Has $187,000 in student loans still outstanding

No retirement contributions for past 2 years

Total net worth: **–$95,000**

Dr. Patel:

Clinical pharmacist, age 34

Makes $110,000/year

Drives a paid-off used Honda

Lives in a $375K condo

Takes one annual trip paid in cash

Aggressively paying down loans ($75K left)

Maxes out Roth IRA, contributes to 401(k)

Total net worth: **$78,000**

On paper? Dr. Smith looks more "successful."

But if both lost their jobs tomorrow—only one of them could breathe.

It's not about income. It's about *what you do with it.*

Section 5: Reclaiming Your Financial Narrative

Here's what it takes to break out of prestige pressure:

1. Decide whose approval actually matters.

Your life isn't a performance. The only audience you need to please is Future You. The one who wants options. Who wants rest. Who wants dignity. Choose them every time.

2. Know your numbers.

Prestige is loud. Net worth is quiet. But it's the number that tells the truth. Track it quarterly. Watch it grow.

3. Automate your goals.

Before you upgrade your car or join the expensive gym, make sure you've already automated:

- Roth IRA contributions
- Emergency fund deposits

- Debt repayment
- "Joy" spending (so you don't binge-spend)

4. Create "Jones-Free" zones.

Unfollow the accounts that trigger comparison. Set spending boundaries with colleagues. Find friends who *value values.*

5. Anchor to your *real* definition of wealth.

Write it out: "Wealth, to me, means…"

Then build from there.

Part IV: Building Wealth – Investment Strategies for Pharmacists

You've made it through school. You've built a career. You've paid your dues, and your debt. Now it's time to build wealth—not just a higher income, but true, lasting financial strength that buys you freedom, flexibility, and options.

Part IV of *Financial Literacy for Pharmacists* is where your money starts working for *you.*

In this section, we take pharmacists beyond budgeting and into smart, pharmacist-specific investment strategies. You'll learn how to build a portfolio while juggling student loans, family planning, and demanding schedules. We'll cover foundational concepts like stocks, bonds, and compound interest—but we won't stop there. You'll also explore Roth IRAs, backdoor strategies for high earners, employer retirement plans, HSAs, real estate, and whether you really need a financial advisor or not.

Most importantly, you'll learn how to align your investment decisions with your *actual* life—whether you're a retail pharmacist with side gigs, a hospital pharmacist considering early retirement, or a mid-career professional finally ready to catch up.

We'll walk you through:

- What to invest in, when, and how much
- How to avoid common investment traps and sales pitches
- How to grow wealth without sacrificing today's quality of life

- How to use automation to stay on track—even during burnout seasons
- How to think long-term in a profession that can be high-pressure and unpredictable

This isn't Wall Street talk. It's pharmacist-proof investing: clear, empowering, and built around your reality.

Because your income alone won't make you wealthy. But how you *use* it? That's the game-changer.

This section is your blueprint. Let's start building.

Chapter 31: Investing Basics – Index Funds, IRAs, and Diversification

Let's be real.

Nobody handed you a guide to investing when you graduated pharmacy school. You were given a diploma, a white coat, a license to practice—and a silent expectation that you'd somehow know what to do with your money now that you were finally making some.

And yet, here you are.

Maybe you've got a decent paycheck, but no idea what a Roth IRA really is.

Maybe you've been "meaning to start investing" for the last five years, but keep putting it off because it feels overwhelming.

Or maybe you've got money sitting in your savings account earning 0.01% interest while inflation eats it alive—and you know there has to be a better way.

This chapter is that better way.

It's not a lecture. It's not a hype pitch. It's a calm, clear, empowering breakdown of how investing actually works—what to do, what to avoid, and how to build long-term wealth without becoming a finance bro or day trader.

Because here's the truth: investing isn't just for the rich.

It's how people become rich.

And pharmacists, with your consistent income and high earning potential, are perfectly positioned to invest with impact—if you learn how to play the game.

We're going to walk through:

- What investing is—and what it isn't
- Why most pharmacists overestimate the risk of investing but underestimate the risk of doing nothing
- How compound interest can change your life
- Why index funds are one of the most pharmacist-friendly tools on the planet
- How to use Roth IRAs, Traditional IRAs, and your employer's 401(k)
- How to diversify like a pro (without needing a finance degree)
- How to avoid analysis paralysis, fear, and toxic advice
- Real-life scenarios for investing at different career stages
- A pharmacist's investing checklist you can start using today

No charts. No hype. No shame. Just clean, powerful investing wisdom designed for the realities of your life.

You didn't go to school for this—but now you're about to learn it like a boss.

Let's start building your wealth.

Section 1: What Investing Is (And What It Isn't)

Let's start by untangling a myth.

Investing is not gambling.

It's not just "playing the market."

It's not something only rich people do once they've "made it."

Investing is what turns income into wealth.

It's the process of using your money to earn more money—by owning things that grow in value or pay you cash flow (like dividends or interest). It's not about timing the market, guessing trends, or picking the next Amazon.

It's about consistent, long-term ownership in the economy.

When you invest in a broad stock index fund, for example, you're buying small pieces of hundreds or thousands of real companies. When they grow, you grow.

Compare that to simply saving money in a bank account. You're preserving cash, yes—but that cash is losing value every year because of inflation. That's a hidden cost. That's the real risk.

Here's the bottom line: if you're not investing, you're falling behind.

Section 2: Compound Interest – Your Quiet Superpower

Let's talk about magic.

Albert Einstein allegedly called compound interest "the eighth wonder of the world." Whether he said it or not, the truth holds. Compound interest is the most pharmacist-friendly financial concept out there—because it rewards people who are consistent and patient.

Here's how it works:

You invest $5,000.

It earns 8% in a year. That's $400.

Next year, you earn interest not just on the $5,000—but on $5,400.

Repeat this process for 30 years—and your investment snowballs.

$5,000 invested once at 8% becomes over $50,000 after 30 years—with no additional contributions. Now imagine what happens when you invest $5,000 every year. You become a millionaire, quietly, while you're working your day job.

Compound interest rewards time, discipline, and consistency. That's it. You don't need to be a genius. You don't need to beat the market. You just need to get in, stay in, and let time do its thing.

Section 3: Index Funds – Simple, Smart, and Powerful

Let's get practical. What do you actually invest in?

If there's one tool that belongs in almost every pharmacist's investing toolkit, it's the index fund.

An index fund is a collection of stocks that tracks a particular segment of the market. Instead of trying to pick individual winners, you invest in the whole market—or a large slice of it.

For example:

- The S&P 500 index includes 500 of the largest U.S. companies.
- A total market index fund includes thousands of companies of all sizes.
- An international index fund gives you exposure to global markets.

When you buy an index fund, you're diversifying instantly. You're not putting all your eggs in one basket. And because these funds are passively managed, they have very low fees—which means you keep more of your returns.

Why index funds are ideal for pharmacists:

- You're busy. You don't want to spend hours researching stocks.
- You value consistency and reliability.
- You understand systems—and index funds are one of the most efficient investing systems out there.

You can own index funds through your 401(k), your IRA, or a brokerage account. They're flexible. They're low maintenance. And they work.

More to come…

Section 4: Roth vs. Traditional IRAs – Picking the Right Tool

As a pharmacist, you've probably heard of IRAs—individual retirement accounts. But the difference between a Roth IRA and a Traditional IRA? That's where things get fuzzy for a lot of people.

Let's break it down simply.

Traditional IRA:
- You contribute with pre-tax dollars (may lower your taxable income now).
- Your money grows tax-deferred.
- You pay taxes when you withdraw in retirement.

Roth IRA:
- You contribute with after-tax dollars (no tax break now).
- Your money grows tax-free.
- You pay no taxes when you withdraw in retirement.

Which one is better?

Here's a rule of thumb:

If you're early in your career and expect your income (and tax rate) to rise over time, the **Roth IRA** is usually the better choice. You pay tax on a smaller amount now, and enjoy tax-free growth for life.

If you're already in a high tax bracket and want to reduce your current tax bill, the **Traditional IRA** might make more sense—especially if you expect a lower income in retirement.

Contribution limits for both are currently $6,500/year (or $7,500 if you're over 50). These numbers can change, so check annually. You must have earned income to contribute, and there are income limits for the Roth IRA.

Pro tip: Some high-earning pharmacists use a "backdoor Roth IRA" strategy to get around those income limits. We'll cover that in a later chapter.

Section 5: Diversification – Your Risk Management Plan

If you only remember one thing about investing, let it be this: **Don't put all your eggs in one basket.**

Diversification means spreading your money across different types of investments so that one bad event doesn't tank your entire portfolio.

Ways to diversify:

- Across asset classes: stocks, bonds, real estate, cash
- Within stocks: large-cap, small-cap, international, sector-based
- Across time: investing consistently over many years (this is called dollar-cost averaging)

A well-diversified portfolio protects you from catastrophic losses while allowing your wealth to grow steadily over time.

Example pharmacist portfolio:

- 60% U.S. stock index fund
  - 20% international stock index fund
  - 15% bond fund or fixed income
  - 5% cash or high-yield savings for short-term goals

This setup is low-maintenance, low-cost, and time-tested.

Diversification won't make you rich overnight. But it will keep you in the game long enough to win.

More to come: case studies, emotional investing traps, and action checklists...

Section 6: Real-Life Scenarios – Investing at Every Stage

Let's make this real. Here are some investing roadmaps for pharmacists at different stages of their careers.

New Grad (Age 26–30):
  - Income: $100K
  - Student loans: $180K
  - Goal: Start investing without ignoring debt

Plan:
  - Contribute enough to 401(k) to get the full employer match (free money!)
  - Open a Roth IRA and automate $200/month
  - Build a $1,000 starter emergency fund

- Focus on aggressive debt repayment with leftover cash

Mid-Career (Age 35–45):

- Income: $130–150K
- Family responsibilities growing
- Goal: Build real wealth, balance retirement with kids' needs

Plan:

- Max out 401(k) ($23,000/year if 50+)
- Continue Roth IRA or Backdoor Roth
- Open a brokerage account for additional savings
- Consider 529 for kids' college
- Rebalance investments annually

Late-Career (Age 50+):

- Income: $150–180K
- Mortgage nearly paid, kids in college
- Goal: Retirement planning and tax optimization

Plan:

- Max catch-up contributions (401(k), IRA)
- Review asset allocation to reduce risk
- Consider working with a fee-only financial advisor
- Start learning about required minimum distributions (RMDs)
- Consider legacy planning

Section 7: Emotional Investing Traps (and How to Avoid Them)

Let's talk about fear and greed—the two emotions that derail even smart pharmacists.

Fear Trap: "What if I lose all my money?"

Reality: A diversified portfolio isn't a casino—it's ownership in the economy. It goes down sometimes, but over time it grows.

Greed Trap: "I heard about a stock that doubled last year—I should get in."

Reality: Chasing hot stocks or market timing is how people lose money. Stay the course.

Comparison Trap: "My coworker just bought a Tesla and brags about crypto gains."

Reality: You don't know their debt. You don't know their plan. Stick to yours.

Rule: **Ignore the noise. Trust the math.**

Section 8: Pharmacist's Investment Checklist – Start Here

Let's keep it practical. Here's your step-by-step starter list:

1. Contribute to your employer's 401(k) or 403(b)—at least up to the match
2. Open a Roth IRA and automate monthly contributions
3. Choose index funds (S&P 500, Total Market, International)
4. Reinvest dividends automatically
5. Review your accounts quarterly
6. Don't check your balance daily
7. Diversify, diversify, diversify
8. Stay invested through the ups and downs
9. Learn as you go—but don't wait until you feel 100% confident
10. Never invest in something you don't understand

Final Word:

You are capable of building wealth. You don't need a six-figure inheritance, a trust fund, or a finance degree.

You need a system. You need discipline. And you need to believe that financial freedom is for you.

This chapter gave you the tools.

Now, take action. Automate your first $100. Open your IRA. Ask your HR about your plan. Pick your index fund. Learn by doing.

The best time to invest was ten years ago.
The second-best time? Today.

Section 2: Compound Interest – The Pharmacist's Best Friend

Compound interest is what makes investing magical.

When you earn interest on your investments, and then that interest earns interest, and then *that* interest earns more—your money grows not in a straight line, but in an upward curve. Slowly at first. Then quickly.

Let's say you invest $200 a month from age 27 to 65, and it earns 7% annually.

You don't just end up with $91,200 (your total contributions).
You end up with over $500,000.

Why? Because of compound interest.

Time is your greatest asset. Start early. Stay consistent. Let the math work.

Section 3: Index Funds – Simple, Powerful, and Built for Busy Pharmacists

An index fund is a basket of investments designed to mirror the performance of a specific market index—like the S&P 500.

Instead of trying to pick winners, an index fund buys them all.

Why this matters:

- It's diversified (you're spreading your risk across hundreds of companies)
  - It's low-cost (because it's passively managed)
  - It performs better than most actively managed funds over the long term

Index funds are the perfect solution for pharmacists who want to grow their wealth without obsessing over the market. You're not trying to beat the market. You're trying to own the market—and go to sleep at night.

Top choices:
- Vanguard Total Stock Market Index (VTSAX or VTI)
- Fidelity ZERO Total Market Index (FZROX)
- Schwab U.S. Broad Market ETF (SCHB)

Want international exposure too? Add:
- Vanguard Total International Stock Index (VTIAX)
- Fidelity International Index Fund (FSPSX)

Own. The. Market. Then let it work for you.

Would you like to move on to emotional investing traps, advanced strategies, or pharmacist-specific wealth building tips next?

Section 4: Emotional Investing Traps – Outsmarting Fear, Greed, and Comparison

You're a logical person. You trust evidence. You went through years of scientific training.

And yet—money makes people emotional.

That's why even smart pharmacists can fall into these common traps:

The Fear Trap:
You hear a recession is coming. The market drops 10%. You panic-sell your index funds and move everything into cash. A year later, the market rebounds and you miss the recovery.

The Greed Trap:
You see a meme stock exploding on Reddit. A friend made 5x their money on crypto. You throw $5,000 into something you don't understand. A month later, it's worth $900.

The Comparison Trap:
Your classmate just posted about buying a vacation home. You're still renting. You feel behind, so you overspend to catch up.

The solution?

Create a system.
Stick to your plan.
Invest regularly, no matter the headlines.

And remember: wealth is quiet.
It's the pharmacist who maxes their Roth IRA every year—not the one flashing a new BMW on Instagram.

Section 5: Pharmacist Wealth-Building Strategies – From Steady Paycheck to Financial Freedom

You may not be a Silicon Valley tech mogul, but you have something they don't: **income predictability.**

Here's how to turn that into power:

1. Automate Your Investing
Set up automatic contributions to your 401(k), IRA, and brokerage accounts. Build wealth while you sleep.

2. Invest Raises, Not Just Paychecks
Every time you get a raise, increase your savings rate before upgrading your lifestyle.

3. Diversify Your Income
Consider side gigs, real estate, consulting, or teaching. More income = more investing fuel.

4. Build a "Work Optional" Fund
This isn't about early retirement—it's about *freedom*. Having enough saved to walk away from burnout and toward something better.

5. Revisit and Rebalance Annually
Adjust your portfolio as you age and grow. Get help if needed. The key is to stay involved.

Section 6: Call to Action

Tonight, do one thing:
- Open your Roth IRA.
- Increase your 401(k) contribution by 1%.
- Watch a 10-minute video on index funds.
- Review your last three months of spending.

Just one move. Then another next week.

Your investing journey is yours to design.
You've got the tools. You've got the knowledge.
Now build the future that fits your life—not someone else's Instagram.

Section 7: Your Pharmacist Investing Roadmap – Milestones to Mark

Let's map it out. Here's what your investing journey might look like over the next few decades.

Year 1–3: Getting Started
- Open your Roth IRA and contribute monthly
- Contribute to your 401(k) to get the full match
- Choose 1–3 index funds to invest in
- Build your emergency fund
- Read one investing book or course per year

Year 4–7: Growing Consistency
- Increase 401(k) and IRA contributions each year
- Open a taxable brokerage account if you've maxed the others
- Rebalance your investments annually
- Ignore market noise and keep contributing through all cycles

Year 8–15: Wealth Accumulation
- Explore advanced tax planning
- Consider real estate investing or passive income streams
- Meet with a financial planner for strategy check-ins
- Track your net worth every quarter

Year 16+: Financial Independence Zone
- Optimize your portfolio for stability and withdrawal strategies

- Explore charitable giving, trusts, or legacy planning
- Decide when work becomes optional
- Help others—mentor, teach, or pay it forward

Section 8: Final Encouragement

You've got the knowledge. Now you need the rhythm. The commitment. The *why.*

Investing isn't about being perfect.
It's about being consistent.

It's not about predicting the market.
It's about owning it.

It's not about having a finance degree.
It's about giving your future self options, peace, and power.

So tonight:
Log into your account.
Make a small move.
Pick one index fund.
Set up that automatic contribution.
Open the Roth IRA.
Ask your HR about the 401(k).
Whatever your next step is—take it.

Your pharmacist paycheck is a tool.
Your investments are your power.

Don't just work for your money.
Make your money work for you.

Chapter 32: Advanced Investing – Roth IRAs, Backdoor Roths, and Tax Strategy

You've worked hard to get where you are. You've got the degree, the job, the paycheck.

Now it's time to go beyond the basics.

Because real wealth-building doesn't just happen when you make good money. It happens when you *keep* it, *grow* it, and protect it from taxes.

This chapter is your next-level guide to one of the most powerful, misunderstood tools in your investing toolbox: the Roth IRA.

It's also about strategic tax planning—not tax evasion, but legal optimization.

If you've ever said:

- "I make too much to contribute to a Roth..."
- "I have no idea what the pro-rata rule is..."
- "My CPA said not to mess with backdoor Roths..."
- "Taxes feel like a black box I'll deal with later..."

Then this chapter is for you.

We'll walk step-by-step through:

- Why Roth IRAs are the financial cheat code for retirement
- What makes Roth money different (and better) than traditional retirement accounts
- How to legally sidestep the Roth income limit
- Common mistakes with backdoor Roths (and how to avoid them)
- The hidden tax advantages of Roth conversions
- When to use Traditional vs. Roth—and why "it depends"
- How to run your own Roth vs. pre-tax projection as a pharmacist
- Roth laddering for early retirees
- Roth strategies for dual-income pharmacist households

This is where things get strategic, intentional, and tailored to the long game.

Let's build wealth that lasts—and keep more of it.

Section 1: Why Roth IRAs Are a Game-Changer for Pharmacists

Let's begin with the basics—then level them up.

A Roth IRA is a retirement account where you contribute money that's already been taxed. Then it grows. And grows. And when you retire? You withdraw it all—contributions and earnings—**tax-free**.

Why does this matter for a pharmacist?

Because your income is likely to be high now, and you may retire in the same (or higher) tax bracket later. That means paying tax now, at known rates, might be *cheaper* than paying unknown taxes later.

Here's what makes Roth IRAs especially powerful:

- **Tax-free growth**: You'll never owe capital gains taxes or income tax on the investment earnings inside the account
- **No RMDs (Required Minimum Distributions)**: Unlike traditional IRAs, the government won't force you to start withdrawing at age 73
- **Legacy planning**: Your heirs can inherit your Roth IRA tax-free, giving them a head start
- **Flexibility**: You can always withdraw your contributions (not earnings) tax- and penalty-free

The catch? There's an income limit to contribute directly.

In 2024, you can't contribute to a Roth IRA if your modified adjusted gross income (MAGI) is over:

- $146,000 (single)
- $230,000 (married filing jointly)

Which brings us to...

Section 2: The Backdoor Roth – How to Contribute When You Make Too Much

Pharmacists often hit the income limit early in their careers.

That's where the **backdoor Roth IRA** comes in—a completely legal IRS-endorsed strategy that lets high earners contribute to a Roth IRA through a two-step process.

Step-by-step:

1. Contribute to a Traditional IRA (non-deductible)
2. Wait a few days for the funds to settle (optional)
3. Convert the funds to your Roth IRA

You now have Roth money growing tax-free—even if you're "over the limit."

Important:
- This only works smoothly if you have **no other pre-tax IRAs** (Traditional, SEP, or SIMPLE)
- If you do, the **pro-rata rule** applies—causing a portion of your conversion to be taxable
- You'll need to file IRS Form 8606 each year to report the non-deductible contribution and conversion

Avoiding the Pro-Rata Problem:
- Roll your existing pre-tax IRA funds into your 401(k) if your plan allows
- This clears the slate, so your backdoor Roth stays clean

Done right, the backdoor Roth IRA becomes an annual wealth-building ritual.

Next up: Roth conversion strategies, Traditional vs. Roth decision-making, and long-term tax planning tailored for the pharmacist's career arc...

Section 3: Roth Conversions – When and Why to Make the Move

A Roth conversion means moving money from a pre-tax account (like a Traditional IRA or 401(k)) into a Roth IRA—and paying taxes on it now so you can enjoy tax-free growth later.

Why would anyone *voluntarily* pay taxes today?

Because you believe the tax you pay now will be lower than what you'd owe later.

Here's when a Roth conversion might make sense:
- You're in a temporarily low income year (e.g., residency, job gap, early

retirement)
- You want to reduce future Required Minimum Distributions (RMDs)
- You expect higher tax rates later (due to income, legislation, or both)
- You're building a "tax-diversified" portfolio

How to Do It:
- Calculate how much you can convert without pushing yourself into a higher tax bracket
- Convert that amount from a Traditional IRA or old 401(k) into a Roth IRA
- Pay the taxes from a separate savings account (don't use the IRA funds to pay the tax bill)

Tax pro tip:
Use Roth conversions to "fill up" lower tax brackets each year in retirement, especially before taking Social Security or RMDs.

Section 4: Traditional vs. Roth – Which One Should You Use?

The eternal question: Should I contribute to a Roth or a Traditional account?

Here's how to decide:

Use **Roth contributions** when:
- You're early in your career and in a lower tax bracket
- You value tax-free growth more than the deduction today
- You want to build flexibility and avoid RMDs later

Use **Traditional (pre-tax) contributions** when:
- You're in your peak earning years
- You want to reduce your current taxable income
- You have other Roth sources already and want balance

The goal isn't to "guess" perfectly—it's to build *tax diversification*.

That means having a mix of:
- Taxable accounts (brokerage)
- Tax-deferred accounts (Traditional 401(k)/IRA)
- Tax-free accounts (Roth IRA, HSA)

Tax diversification gives you control and flexibility later. That's what makes retirement planning powerful.

Section 5: Roth Laddering – Tax-Free Income in Early Retirement

Let's say you want to retire early—before age 59½—and you've been diligently saving in pre-tax retirement accounts. How do you access that money without penalty?

Enter: the Roth ladder.

Here's the basic strategy:

1. Convert a portion of your Traditional IRA to a Roth IRA each year
2. Wait 5 years (the IRS waiting period)
3. Withdraw the *converted* amount (not earnings) tax- and penalty-free

Repeat this annually, and you create a steady stream of penalty-free withdrawals.

Why this works:
- Roth contributions (and conversions) can be withdrawn after 5 years
- The conversion starts the clock for each "rung" of your ladder
- It gives early retirees control over their tax exposure and income stream

Pro tip: Start your Roth ladder 5 years *before* you want to access the funds.

Section 6: Dual-Income Pharmacist Households – Strategy, Sync, and Savings

If you and your partner are both pharmacists, you've likely crossed the Roth IRA income threshold quickly.

Here's how to optimize:

1. Backdoor Roth x2
- Each of you can do your own backdoor Roth contribution every year
- Double the tax-free growth, double the long-term payoff

2. Staggered Conversions
- Convert one partner's pre-tax assets in low-income years
- Use the other's salary to pay taxes, preserving the investment compounding

3. File Strategically
- Married filing jointly often reduces your effective tax rate
- Use that advantage to plan Roth conversions, fill up lower brackets, or reduce student loan payments (if on IDR)

4. Align Your Risk
- Review both retirement portfolios annually
- Ensure your combined asset allocation isn't overweight in one area

Tax planning as a dual-income household is about *coordination*. Don't optimize in silos—optimize as a team.

Section 7: Building Your Pharmacist Tax Map – A Strategy by Career Stage

New Grad/Residency (Low Income):
- Prioritize Roth contributions
- Consider small Roth conversions if you have existing pre-tax dollars
- Use an HSA as a second Roth (invest the balance, pay for care out of pocket)

Mid-Career (High Income, Peak Earnings):
- Max your 401(k)
- Use the backdoor Roth annually
- Revisit your 401(k) for after-tax contribution options (mega backdoor Roth)

Pre-Retirement (Lower Expenses, Flexible Income):
- Start strategic Roth conversions from pre-tax accounts
- Consider retiring early and "filling the bracket" before RMDs and Social Security kick in
- Revisit asset location (place tax-inefficient funds in Roth or taxable accounts)

Retirement (Decumulation Phase):
- Withdraw from taxable accounts first
- Convert pre-tax dollars to Roth within low tax brackets
- Delay Social Security if possible to control taxable income

This is the roadmap pharmacists rarely get handed. You've got it now.

Case Study: Ashley and Marcus – Dual-Income Roth Strategy for Pharmacists

Ashley and Marcus are both hospital pharmacists in their late 30s. Together, they earn $240,000 annually and have $400,000 combined in Traditional 401(k)s. They've heard about Roth strategies but feel overwhelmed.

Here's how they build their Roth game plan:

1. **Backdoor Roths** – Each opens a non-deductible Traditional IRA, contributes $6,500, and immediately converts it to their Roth IRA. They track this with IRS Form 8606 annually.

2. **Mega Backdoor Roth** – Marcus's 401(k) plan allows after-tax contributions and in-service rollovers. He contributes an additional $20,000 beyond the standard $23,000 limit, then rolls it into his Roth 401(k) quarterly.

3. **Tax Coordination** – In 2024, Ashley takes a short unpaid sabbatical. They convert $30,000 from her Traditional IRA into a Roth while in a lower tax bracket, paying taxes from savings.

4. **Roth Ladder Planning** – They aim to retire at 55. Starting at age 50, they begin converting $25,000/year from Marcus's Traditional IRA to Roth IRA to create 5-year "rungs" for penalty-free withdrawals in early retirement.

5. **HSA Investing** – Their family HSA holds $18,000. Instead of using it for expenses, they pay cash for medical bills and invest the HSA funds in a low-cost index fund.

In 20 years, they'll have built up a powerful Roth base, minimized RMD exposure, and kept their future tax liability flexible.

Worksheet: Roth IRA Strategy Checklist for Pharmacists

☐ Are you eligible to contribute directly to a Roth IRA?
 - 2024 MAGI limit: $146,000 (single), $230,000 (married filing jointly)

☐ If not eligible, have you:
- Opened a Traditional IRA?
- Made a non-deductible contribution?
- Waited 1-3 days for settlement?
- Converted it to your Roth IRA?
- Filed IRS Form 8606?

☐ Do you have other pre-tax IRAs that trigger the pro-rata rule?
- ☐ Yes → Consider rolling them into a 401(k)
- ☐ No → Proceed with clean backdoor Roth

☐ Do you and your partner both contribute (if applicable)?
- Maximize Roth growth with 2 backdoor contributions annually

☐ Do you have a low-income year upcoming?
- Plan a Roth conversion to take advantage of a lower bracket

☐ Have you considered Roth laddering for early retirement?
- Start 5 years before you need funds

☐ Do you have an HSA?
- Max it out
- Invest it
- Pay expenses out-of-pocket (receipts = future reimbursement)

☐ Reviewed with a financial planner or tax professional?

☐ Saved a copy of this checklist for next year?

Chapter 33: Retirement Planning for Pharmacists – 401(k), Roth, SEP, and Solo 401(k)

Retirement isn't a finish line—it's a financial runway. And for pharmacists, it can feel more like a foggy terminal than a well-lit airstrip.

You work long hours. You deal with insurance headaches, patient expectations, corporate metrics, and shifting career paths. But in the middle of all that, you've got to ask one crucial question: Am I building the kind of future I want to retire into?

This chapter is here to help you answer that.

Whether you're 27 or 57, whether you work retail, hospital, academia, or own a consulting firm—you need a retirement game plan that works for you.

We'll cover:

- How your employer 401(k) works—and how to read between the lines
- Whether you should prioritize pre-tax or Roth contributions
- SEP IRAs and Solo 401(k)s for side hustlers and self-employed pharmacists

- Tax-deferred vs. tax-free vs. taxable investing
- How to avoid the "phantom savings" trap (where you save, but not enough to retire free)
- Rules of thumb: contribution targets by decade, what a pharmacist needs to retire comfortably, and where you might be falling behind or surging ahead

By the end of this chapter, you'll know:
- Where your retirement accounts stand
- What your next financial move should be
- How to get from burned-out to "work-optional"

So let's step into it. Let's build the financial runway you deserve to take off on—long before your 60s.

First stop: decoding your 401(k) and employer match.

Section 1: Understanding Your Employer 401(k)

The 401(k) is often your biggest retirement tool—and yet most pharmacists barely scratch the surface of what it can do.

Here's what you need to know:

1. Contribution Limits
- In 2024, you can contribute up to $23,000 if under 50.
- If you're 50 or older, you get an extra $7,500 catch-up contribution.

2. Employer Match
Many employers offer a match like "100% up to 4% of your salary." If you make $120,000 and contribute 4%, that's $4,800. Your employer matches $4,800. That's a 100% return on your money—free.

Never leave that match on the table.

3. Vesting Schedule

Some employers require you to stay for a certain number of years before you "own" the match. That's called vesting. For example, 20% per year for five years. If you leave early, you may forfeit part of the match.

4. Investment Choices

Your 401(k) might offer 10–30 funds. Don't just pick the one with the best 3-year return. Look for:

- Low-cost index funds (e.g., S&P 500 index)
- Target-date retirement funds (good for set-it-and-forget-it investing)
- Diversified options (US, international, bonds)

Avoid high-fee funds unless you have a clear reason.

5. Roth vs. Traditional 401(k)

Most plans now offer both. So which do you choose?

Section 2: Roth vs. Traditional Contributions – The Tax Tradeoff

This is the great fork in the road: Do you want to pay taxes now or later?

Roth 401(k):

- You contribute after-tax money
- It grows tax-free
- You pay $0 in taxes on withdrawals in retirement

Best for:

- Younger pharmacists in lower tax brackets
- Those who believe taxes will rise
- Anyone who values tax-free income later

Traditional 401(k):

- You contribute pre-tax money
- It grows tax-deferred
- You pay ordinary income tax on withdrawals

Best for:

- Mid-career, high-earning pharmacists who want to reduce taxable income
- Those who expect to be in a lower bracket in retirement

You can also split your contributions—for example, 50% Roth and 50% Traditional. This builds *tax flexibility* for the future.

Still not sure? Ask yourself:

- Would I rather pay a known tax today—or an unknown tax tomorrow?
- Am I maximizing other buckets like an HSA or Roth IRA?

Section 3: SEP IRAs and Solo 401(k)s – For Pharmacists with a Side Hustle

If you run a consulting business, MTM practice, independent immunization clinic, or any freelance work on the side—you're not just a pharmacist. You're a business owner.

And that means you have access to retirement accounts that most people don't.

Let's look at your two main tools:

1. SEP IRA (Simplified Employee Pension)

The SEP IRA is simple and powerful.

- You can contribute up to 25% of your net self-employment income, up to $66,000 (2023 limit)
    - Contributions are tax-deductible
    - It's easy to set up through most brokerages
    - You can open one for a side hustle even if you have a 401(k) at your main job

Downside?
    - You can't make Roth contributions
    - It doesn't have a catch-up provision
    - If you have employees, you must contribute the same percentage for them

2. Solo 401(k)

Also known as an individual 401(k), this is for sole proprietors with no employees (except maybe a spouse).

Why it's powerful:
    - You contribute as both employer and employee
    - You can hit the same $66,000 limit—but more easily
    - You can choose Roth or Traditional contributions for the employee portion
    - Some plans allow after-tax contributions and in-plan Roth conversions (aka the mega backdoor Roth)

Solo 401(k)s are more complex to set up than SEP IRAs, but they give you more flexibility. For pharmacists with significant 1099 income, they're often the better option.

Section 4: Coordinating All Your Accounts – Building a Unified Retirement Plan

Here's the problem: Most pharmacists don't have just one account. They have:

- A 401(k) from their current job
- A 401(k) from an old job
- A Roth IRA (maybe)
- A Traditional IRA
- A taxable brokerage account (maybe unused)
- An HSA (hopefully invested)
- A SEP or Solo 401(k) from their side business

And they're not sure how to manage it all.

Here's your game plan:

1. Consolidate When Possible
   Roll old 401(k)s into your current one *if* it has low-cost investment options. Fewer accounts = less paperwork, easier to manage.

2. Maximize Account Efficiency
   - Taxable: For long-term index funds, tax-managed funds, municipal bonds
   - Roth: For high-growth assets like small-cap, emerging markets
   - Traditional: For income-producing assets like REITs or bonds

3. Create an Investment Policy Statement
   Write down your target asset allocation (e.g., 80/20 stocks/bonds), contribution priorities, and rebalance plan. Stick to it.

4. Automate Contributions
   Set up automatic transfers to:
   - Your 401(k)
   - Your Roth IRA
   - Your HSA

- Your brokerage (even if it's just $100/month)

5. Rebalance Annually
Review your total allocation across *all* accounts, not just one. Adjust to keep your investment mix on target.

6. Revisit Quarterly, Not Constantly
Too many pharmacists tinker with their accounts too often. Make small, strategic moves—not reactionary ones.

Section 5: The Decumulation Phase – Withdrawing Without Worry

Most financial advice is focused on getting money *into* your retirement accounts. But what about taking it *out*?

That's called decumulation—and it's just as important.

Pharmacists often ask:
- How do I avoid running out of money?
- When should I take Social Security?
- Which account should I tap first?
- What if I need long-term care or face a market downturn?

Let's break it down.

1. Sequence of Withdrawals – What to Tap First

General rule of thumb:

1. Taxable brokerage account
2. Traditional 401(k)/IRA (after RMD age or as needed)
3. Roth IRA (last)

Why? You want to:
- Allow tax-free accounts (Roth) to grow longer
- Manage your taxable income by spreading withdrawals over time
- Reduce Required Minimum Distributions (RMDs) by drawing down Traditional assets early

2. The 4% Rule – A Starting Point, Not a Gospel

The 4% Rule says you can safely withdraw 4% of your portfolio annually, adjusted for inflation, and your money should last 30 years.

But in real life?
- Markets fluctuate
- Healthcare needs change
- You might want to spend more in early retirement (travel) and less later

Build a plan based on:
- Your fixed vs. variable expenses
- Your guaranteed income sources (Social Security, pension, annuities)
- Your flexibility in spending

3. Roth Conversion Laddering in Early Retirement

If you retire before 59½, Roth conversion laddering is your friend. You convert a small portion of Traditional IRA to Roth each year and wait five years to access it tax-free.

This lets you:
- Reduce RMDs
- Spread tax liability over years
- Build a pipeline of tax-free cash flow

4. Guardrails, Not Guilt

Instead of fixating on "never run out of money," use a guardrail approach:

- Spend more when markets are up
- Cut back slightly if they're down
- Reassess every 6–12 months

This allows you to live life while staying on track.

5. Long-Term Care, Insurance, and Legacy Planning

Late-retirement planning includes:

- Long-term care insurance (or self-funding a cushion)
- Updated estate documents
- Charitable strategies like Qualified Charitable Distributions (QCDs)
- Talking with family or beneficiaries about your financial intentions

Your money isn't just about surviving—it's about stewarding what you've built.

End-of-chapter move: Run your own decumulation simulation. Pick a retirement age, build a 30-year spreadsheet, and plan your withdrawal order.

Section 6: Retirement Planning Across the Decades

Every stage of your career demands a different playbook. Let's break down what retirement planning should look like in your 20s, 30s, 40s, 50s, and 60s.

Your 20s – Start the Engine

This is your financial warm-up. You may not be earning much yet—but time is your greatest asset.

Goals:

- Open a Roth IRA and automate contributions
- Learn how investing works (not just saving)
- Avoid lifestyle creep as income rises
- Don't cash out your 401(k) if you leave a job

Game Plan:

- Save at least 15% of your income between 401(k) and Roth
- Focus on building habits, not perfection
- Choose growth-oriented index funds

Your 30s – Build Momentum

You've got your license, your first few jobs under your belt, and a more stable income.

Goals:

- Maximize employer match and increase savings rate to 20%
- Open an HSA and invest it
- Consider backdoor Roth IRA if income is too high
- Pay off high-interest debt

Game Plan:

- Track your net worth annually
- Start planning for future family/house/kids
- Avoid letting rising income lead to lifestyle explosion

Your 40s – Strategic Accumulation

You're in your prime earning years—and your financial decisions matter more than ever.

Goals:

- Catch-up if you're behind on retirement
- Coordinate taxable, tax-deferred, and tax-free accounts
- Protect your income with adequate insurance

- Build college savings (if applicable) and estate plans

Game Plan:

- Consider working with a fiduciary advisor
- Run retirement projections at least once a year
- Rebalance accounts annually

Your 50s – Sharpen the Focus

Retirement isn't an abstract idea anymore. It's a reality you're getting close to.

Goals:

- Max out all catch-up contributions
- Fine-tune withdrawal strategy
- Pay off consumer debt and assess mortgage timeline
- Decide when (or if) you want to downshift careers

Game Plan:

- Use calculators or a financial planner to model income in retirement
- Evaluate Social Security claiming strategies
- Consider Roth conversions while income is still high

Your 60s – Glide Path and Exit Strategy

Now you're transitioning from accumulation to decumulation.

Goals:

- Set your actual retirement date
- Plan for Medicare and healthcare expenses
- Solidify legacy/estate plans
- Determine drawdown order for accounts

Game Plan:

- Have a withdrawal plan for the first 5–10 years

- Reduce market exposure gradually (but don't go all cash)
- Talk with family and professionals about future decisions

Final encouragement: No matter your age, no matter your past mistakes, it's never too late—or too early—to plan for a dignified, confident retirement.

Chapter 34: Understanding Employer Stock Options and Profit Sharing

Let's talk about one of the most misunderstood forms of compensation in the pharmacist community: equity and profit-sharing.

Whether you work for a large retail chain with a public stock ticker, a hospital system offering 403(b) matching plus bonus incentives, or a start-up compounding pharmacy giving you a slice of the pie—you need to understand what stock options and profit-sharing actually mean.

This chapter is not about guessing stock prices or chasing hot tips. It's about getting crystal clear on what's being offered, what it's really worth, and how it fits into your bigger financial plan.

We're going to cover:

- The difference between stock options, RSUs, ESPPs, and profit-sharing
- Vesting schedules and what happens if you leave your job
- Tax implications (because yes, the IRS is watching)
- Pros and cons of holding employer stock
- Actionable steps to manage, diversify, and use equity wisely

Let's break it down like we're sitting at the kitchen table, not across from a fast-talking broker.

Section 1: What Are Stock Options, RSUs, ESPPs, and Profit Sharing?

1. Stock Options (ISOs and NSOs)

A stock option gives you the right to buy your company's stock at a fixed price, known as the strike price. The idea is that, over time, the value of the stock will rise—and you can profit from the difference.

- ISOs (Incentive Stock Options): Better tax treatment but limited to $100K per year and require holding periods to avoid taxes.
- NSOs (Non-Qualified Stock Options): More common and flexible, but taxed as ordinary income when exercised.

2. RSUs (Restricted Stock Units)

RSUs are shares granted to you by your employer, usually subject to a vesting schedule. Once vested, they're yours—no purchasing required. You'll owe taxes on their value when they vest, even if you don't sell them.

3. ESPPs (Employee Stock Purchase Plans)

These allow you to buy your company's stock at a discount (often 15%), usually through after-tax payroll deductions. Some plans include a "lookback" provision that lets you buy stock based on a lower historical price.

4. Profit Sharing

Unlike equity-based plans, profit sharing is typically a cash contribution to your retirement account (often your 401(k)), based on your employer's profitability. It's not guaranteed every year and varies by company performance.

Section 2: Vesting – The Golden Handcuffs

Vesting determines when you actually "own" your options or RSUs. A typical schedule might look like this:

- 4-year vesting with a 1-year cliff: You get 25% after your first year, then 1/36th each month after that.

What happens if you leave before you're fully vested? You forfeit unvested shares. This can matter a lot if you're considering leaving a job or negotiating a raise.

Section 3: Tax Implications of Stock Compensation

This is where many pharmacists (and even some advisors) get confused. Stock compensation sounds exciting—until you get hit with a tax bill you weren't expecting. Let's fix that.

1. Stock Options (ISOs vs. NSOs)

ISOs:

- No tax when granted or exercised (as long as you don't sell immediately)
- BUT: the "bargain element" (difference between exercise price and fair market value) may be subject to AMT (Alternative Minimum Tax)
- If held at least 2 years after the grant and 1 year after exercise: long-term capital gains

NSOs:

- Taxed as *ordinary income* when exercised (difference between strike price and fair market value)
- Additional capital gains taxes when you eventually sell the stock

Real Talk: Many pharmacists exercise options and forget about the ordinary income taxes due. That tax bill can sneak up on you.

2. RSUs (Restricted Stock Units)

- No taxes when granted
  - Taxed as *ordinary income* when they vest—based on the market value at that time
  - Some employers automatically withhold taxes by selling a portion of shares for you

Tip: Make sure the taxes withheld are sufficient. If not, you may owe additional taxes at filing time.

3. ESPPs (Employee Stock Purchase Plans)

There are two types of dispositions:
  - **Qualifying disposition**: Held at least 1 year after purchase and 2 years after the beginning of the offering period. You'll pay ordinary income tax on the discount and capital gains on the appreciation.
  - **Disqualifying disposition**: If you sell earlier, the discount is taxed as ordinary income, and gains may be short-term or long-term depending on holding period.

4. Profit Sharing

- Treated like any other 401(k) contribution
  - No tax due until you withdraw in retirement
  - If Roth 401(k) option is used, growth may be tax-free

Bottom Line:
Get familiar with IRS Form 3921 (for ISOs), Form W-2 (reporting RSUs), and Form 1099-B (for sales). Or, better yet—work with a tax pro who understands stock compensation.

Section 4: Diversification Strategy and Exit Planning

Let's say you've got RSUs vesting every quarter, your ESPP is filling up, and your 401(k) is looking good. That's awesome. But now it's time to ask a bigger question: How exposed are you to your employer?

Here's the deal: having too much of your wealth tied up in one company—especially the one that also writes your paycheck—is a risk. You need a strategy.

Why Diversification Matters

If your company's stock drops 40% and you're both employed there *and* invested there, you're getting hit twice:

- Your portfolio just shrank
- You might be at risk of layoffs or budget cuts

It's like betting your career and your future wealth on the same horse. Even if it's a strong horse—that's not smart investing.

What's a Safe Exposure Limit?

A common rule of thumb:

- Don't let any single stock (even your employer's) be more than 5–10% of your total investment portfolio.

So if you've got $300K in total investments, try to limit employer stock to $15K–$30K.

How to Diversify Out

1. RSUs: As they vest, sell them immediately and reinvest in low-cost

index funds or diversified ETFs.

2. Stock Options: Consider exercising and selling *in stages* to avoid big tax hits.
3. ESPP: Sell shares after the required holding period and redeploy into your core portfolio.

Exit Planning: When to Sell

This is personal—but here are some prompts to guide you:
- Do you already have enough exposure through your job?
- Would you be devastated if your company's stock dropped 50%?
- Do you need the cash for other goals (house down payment, debt, etc.)?

Don't let loyalty keep you from making a smart financial decision. You can love your company and still reduce your risk exposure.

Section 5: Real-Life Pharmacist Case Studies on Equity Wins and Woes

Let's make this real. These stories are based on composite scenarios from pharmacists I've worked with over the years. The names and details have been changed, but the financial lessons are real.

Case Study 1: Jessica – The RSU Tax Surprise

Jessica was a clinical pharmacist at a mid-sized tech-enabled pharmacy startup. Her compensation package included RSUs, which seemed like a nice perk—until tax season rolled around.

What happened:
- Her RSUs vested quarterly.
- She never sold any shares.
- Her employer withheld taxes, but not enough.

- She owed $8,000 more than expected in April.

Lesson:

Understand the tax timing. Just because you didn't sell stock doesn't mean you don't owe taxes. RSUs are taxed at vesting.

What she did next:

Jessica started selling a portion of her RSUs immediately upon vesting. She also bumped her withholdings on her W-4 to offset future tax bills.

Case Study 2: Malik – The ESPP Windfall

Malik worked for a large pharmacy chain with a generous ESPP. He contributed the max allowed each pay period and took full advantage of the 15% discount and six-month lookback feature.

Over three years:

- He bought $30K worth of stock for $25.5K
- The stock appreciated another 20%
- He walked away with over $40K when he sold strategically

Lesson:

An ESPP can be a low-risk way to build wealth if you follow the rules. Buy at a discount, sell at a gain, and redeploy the cash into diversified investments.

Case Study 3: Aria – The Loyalty Trap

Aria had worked at the same healthcare system for 15 years. Her retirement account included a ton of company stock from profit-sharing and bonuses.

Then her employer faced a scandal that made headlines. The stock dropped 60%.

What happened:

- Aria had 40% of her 403(b) in company stock
- She lost $80K in value overnight
- Her overall retirement plan got set back by at least five years

Lesson:

Even "safe" employers can have stock crashes. Loyalty is admirable, but your financial independence has to come first. Diversify.

Case Study 4: Brandon – The ISO Gamble

Brandon got incentive stock options at a small specialty pharmacy that later went public. He exercised early to start the clock on long-term capital gains. The gamble paid off.

- Strike price: $10
- FMV at exercise: $12 (minimal AMT impact)
- FMV at sale: $45

He sold most of his shares at long-term capital gains rates and used the funds to pay off his mortgage and start a side business.

Lesson:

ISOs can be powerful—but only if you understand the tax rules and time the exercise right. Don't wing it. Work with a CPA.

Final Thoughts on Case Studies

Every story here carries a core message: Stock compensation can build wealth—but only if you respect the rules, understand the risks, and act with intention.

Don't let fear keep you from participating.

Don't let greed keep you from diversifying.
Don't let confusion stop you from asking questions.

Let's bring it all together.

Pharmacists are often offered employer stock perks that seem complicated at first glance—but they don't have to be confusing. Once you understand the vocabulary, tax implications, and strategic value of each type, you move from reactive to proactive. And that's where wealth-building starts.

Here's a recap of the key takeaways:

- RSUs are taxed at vesting, not at sale.
- Stock options (ISOs and NSOs) have specific tax timing. Learn it before exercising.
- ESPPs can be low-risk wealth builders—but only if you sell at the right time.
- Too much company stock = too much risk. Diversify early and often.
- Profit-sharing is retirement gold—don't ignore it.
- Taxes can sneak up fast—especially if you forget the IRS always wants their cut.

Now let's turn insight into action.

Action Steps for Pharmacists with Stock Compensation

1. Locate your equity paperwork.
Find your grant letters, ESPP summaries, and RSU schedules. Know what you've been offered—and when things vest.

2. Set calendar reminders for vesting and sale dates.
Don't let RSUs sit idle without a plan. Schedule check-ins quarterly to review your holdings and tax impact.

3. Talk to your HR and Benefits Team.
   Ask about your ESPP rules, your 401(k) profit-sharing frequency, and how taxes are withheld on RSUs.

4. Work with a CPA who understands equity compensation.
   Not every accountant is familiar with ISOs, AMT, and ESPP rules. Vet your professionals carefully.

5. Set an "Equity Diversification Plan."
   Decide your percentage limit on employer stock (e.g., 10% of total portfolio), and create rules for selling and reinvesting.

6. Use new equity proceeds to build your freedom fund.
   Pay off debt. Start a side hustle. Pad your emergency fund. Max out your IRA. Whatever your next wealth move is—use stock income to fund it.

Stock options and profit sharing aren't just line items on your HR packet. They're keys. They unlock doors to flexibility, wealth, and freedom—if you learn how to use them.

Don't let complexity paralyze you.

Ask questions. Read the paperwork. Make a plan. Take action.

A Call to Act:

Make one money move tonight before you go to bed. Just one.

Maybe that means logging into your ESPP portal. Maybe it means calling HR. Maybe it means blocking 30 minutes on your calendar next Sunday to build your equity plan.

Then do one more thing next week.

Build momentum. Stack confidence. Own your financial future.

You didn't become a pharmacist to stay confused about money. You became a pharmacist to help people, build security, and live well. And that starts with clarity, confidence, and action.

Chapter 35: Real Estate Investing – Should a Pharmacist Go There?

Let's start with a simple truth: Real estate investing is one of the most talked-about ways to build wealth—and also one of the most misunderstood. For pharmacists, it can look incredibly attractive. You've got a stable income, decent credit, and possibly even some cash saved. The real estate gurus on podcasts and social media make it sound like all you need to do is buy a duplex and suddenly you're swimming in passive income.

But the truth? It's not that simple.

This chapter isn't going to sell you a fantasy. It's going to walk you through the real pros, real cons, and real math of real estate investing—specifically for pharmacists.

Because here's the thing: Real estate isn't just an investment. It's a job. A responsibility. A risk. And if it's not aligned with your lifestyle, your career demands, your cash flow, and your goals—it can become a very expensive distraction.

But if done well and done wisely? It can become one of the most powerful vehicles for freedom, wealth, and legacy.

This chapter will walk you through:

- The different types of real estate investments pharmacists consider
- How to evaluate whether real estate is a good fit for your life
- Pros and cons compared to investing in the stock market
- Common red flags, bad advice, and rookie mistakes
- Real-life examples from pharmacists who bought properties—both good and bad
- Tangible action steps to take if you want to explore this further

Before we dive in, one more reminder: you don't have to do real estate to be wealthy.

Let that land.

This chapter isn't here to talk you into it. It's here to help you ask better questions, weigh trade-offs, and decide for yourself.

Let's start with what "real estate investing" even means.

Section 2: Types of Real Estate Investments Pharmacists Consider

When people say they want to "get into real estate," what do they really mean? Often, they're imagining a rental property that magically deposits $1,000 into their checking account every month. But real estate investing isn't one-size-fits-all. There are multiple paths, each with its own requirements, risks, and rewards.

Let's explore some of the most common types of real estate investments pharmacists consider—and what you need to know about each one.

1. Single-Family Rentals (SFRs)

This is the most traditional starting point. You buy a house. You rent it out. Ideally, the rent covers the mortgage, property taxes, insurance, maintenance, and still gives you a little extra.

Why pharmacists like it:

- Easy to understand
- Often aligns with the "starter home" neighborhood they already know
- Seen as a gateway to building equity and passive income

What you must consider:

- Vacancy risk
- Maintenance surprises
- Managing tenants (even if you hire a property manager, you're still the owner)

2. House Hacking

House hacking is when you live in one part of a multi-unit property (or rent out rooms in your own home) while collecting rent from others. Think duplex, triplex, or even renting your basement on Airbnb.

Why pharmacists like it:

- Helps offset personal housing costs
- Easier to qualify for a mortgage since you're an owner-occupant
- Can build wealth while reducing expenses

What you must consider:

- You're living next to your tenants
- Privacy trade-offs
- May not fit every lifestyle or stage of life

3. Short-Term Rentals (Airbnb, VRBO)

Some pharmacists are drawn to vacation rentals, especially in tourist-heavy markets. With the rise of Airbnb, this has become a hot topic—but also a hot mess in some cities with new regulations.

Why pharmacists like it:
- Potential for higher income than long-term rentals
- Fun to design and furnish
- Flexible use (you can stay there too)

What you must consider:
- Heavy management demands
- Regulatory risks
- High turnover = higher wear and tear

4. Real Estate Syndications

Syndications let you invest passively in larger real estate deals (e.g., apartment buildings, storage units) with other investors. You provide capital; someone else handles the work.

Why pharmacists like it:
- Hands-off investing
- Potential for strong returns and tax benefits
- Diversification away from W-2 income

What you must consider:
- Accredited investor requirements (in some cases)
- Due diligence needed on sponsors and deals
- Less liquidity and control

5. Real Estate Investment Trusts (REITs)

REITs let you invest in real estate through the stock market. You can buy them like shares of a company and get exposure to commercial real estate (like office buildings, apartments, warehouses).

Why pharmacists like it:

- Easy entry
- No landlord headaches
- Liquid like a stock

What you must consider:

- Lower upside compared to direct ownership
- Market correlation
- Less tax-sheltered income

Each of these vehicles has pros and cons. What matters is how each fits your time, goals, cash flow, and appetite for complexity.

In the next section, we'll unpack how to evaluate whether real estate investing fits your lifestyle—and what questions to ask before you say yes to a down payment.

Section 3: How to Evaluate If Real Estate Fits Your Life

Let's be honest—just because you can do something doesn't mean you should. And that's especially true with real estate.

Pharmacists are in a unique position: you're high-earning, but often overworked and burned out. Your time is not just valuable—it's maxed out. That's why the "passive income" promise of real estate can be seductive. But the truth is, real estate only becomes passive after a whole lot of upfront hustle.

So before you jump in, ask yourself these questions:

1. Do I have the time and energy to manage a property (or to manage the people managing it)?

Real estate is rarely truly passive—especially at the start. If you're already stretched thin with long shifts, family, or other obligations, consider whether you're solving a money problem or creating a time problem.

2. Am I clear on my financial goals?

Are you trying to build wealth, increase income, or reduce taxes? Real estate can do all three—but not all at once. If your primary goal is simplicity, index funds may be a better fit. If you're chasing tax shelters, syndications might help. Clarity matters.

3. Can I handle uncertainty?

Even the best landlords deal with late payments, broken HVACs, and insurance headaches. If financial surprises stress you out, real estate may not align with your temperament. Stocks go down too—but you don't get a midnight call about a burst pipe.

4. Is my personal financial house in order?

Before buying a rental, make sure your own emergency fund, student loan strategy, and retirement savings are solid. Don't buy a duplex to "invest" if you haven't reviewed your 401(k) match or can't weather a vacancy.

5. How much liquidity do I need in the next 3-5 years?

Real estate is not liquid. If you think you might want to change jobs, move cities, have kids, or take a sabbatical—you want access to cash. Locking money into a house you can't easily sell could backfire.

6. What's my exit strategy?

How will this property help you move closer to your bigger financial vision? Will it cash flow in retirement? Fund your kid's college? Allow you to cut back to part-time work? If you can't articulate the why, don't chase the what.

Now, this isn't to scare you off. It's to ground you. Real estate can be amazing—but only when it aligns with your values, time, risk tolerance, and goals.

Coming up next, we'll walk through the pros and cons of real estate versus the stock market to help you choose your lane with confidence.

Section 4: Real Estate vs. Stock Market – Which Is Better for Pharmacists?

If you're deciding between real estate and the stock market, you're not alone. Pharmacists often feel torn between these two worlds. One seems tangible, grounded, and maybe even "passive." The other is abstract, volatile, and sometimes intimidating. But the truth is, both are just tools. And every tool depends on the user.

Let's compare real estate and the stock market in ways that matter to you.

1. Accessibility

- Real Estate: You typically need a larger upfront investment—down payment, closing costs, repairs, reserves. It takes planning and time.
- Stocks: You can start investing with as little as $50. You don't need to qualify for a mortgage. You don't need good tenants. You just need time in the market.

Winner: Stocks for accessibility.

2. Time Commitment

- Real Estate: This is an active asset class unless you're purely in syndications or REITs. Even with a manager, you are responsible.
- Stocks: Once you automate your investing strategy, it runs in the background. Rebalancing once or twice a year is often enough.

Winner: Stocks for busy pharmacists.

3. Leverage and Control

- Real Estate: You can use a mortgage to buy a property with 20% down and still capture 100% of the appreciation. You can renovate it, raise rents, add value.
- Stocks: You don't control what happens inside the companies. You're a shareholder, not a decision-maker.

Winner: Real estate for control and leverage.

4. Tax Treatment

- Real Estate: Offers depreciation, 1031 exchanges, and deductions that can offset other income. Huge win for tax strategy.
- Stocks: Tax-advantaged accounts like Roth IRAs help—but ordinary brokerage accounts are subject to capital gains and dividend taxes.

Winner: Real estate for tax-savvy investors.

5. Liquidity

- Real Estate: Hard to sell quickly. Deals take time. Emergencies can turn into fire sales.
- Stocks: Can be sold in minutes. Great in a crisis or if your financial

plans change.

Winner: Stocks for liquidity.

6. Cash Flow and Income

- Real Estate: Can produce consistent cash flow—if managed well.
- Stocks: Dividends exist, but most stock growth is through appreciation.

Winner: Real estate for monthly income.

7. Volatility

- Real Estate: Less volatile in the short term, but values can stagnate for years.
- Stocks: More volatile day to day but generally grow over time with the economy.

Winner: Depends on your nerves.

The Verdict?

You don't have to choose just one. Many pharmacists use stocks for automated, long-term retirement wealth—and dabble in real estate to create cash flow and tax benefits.

In the next section, we'll explore how to get started with your first real estate investment—from prep work to purchase to property management.

Section 5: How to Get Started with Your First Property

So you've run the numbers, assessed your lifestyle, and you're feeling ready to make your move into real estate. Now what?

This section walks you through the major steps to purchasing your first investment property—without burning yourself out or blowing up your budget.

Step 1: Get Clear on Your Why

Are you buying this property for cash flow? Appreciation? Tax benefits? A future home for your kids? Your "why" determines everything—from the location you choose to the financing structure. If you don't have a strong "why," stop here. The work isn't worth it without purpose.

Step 2: Set Your Budget (and Buffer)

Determine how much you can invest—including the down payment, closing costs, emergency repairs, and holding reserves. Most lenders want 20–25% down for investment properties. Add 3–6 months of expenses for unexpected issues. This isn't optional—it's essential.

Step 3: Choose Your Market Wisely

You don't have to buy where you live—but you should buy where you understand. If you're investing out of state, build a team first: a trusted real estate agent, property manager, and contractor. Look for areas with:

- Job growth
- Low vacancy rates
- Landlord-friendly laws
- Affordable price-to-rent ratios

Step 4: Run the Numbers Like a Pharmacist

You're trained to analyze details—put that skill to work. For each property, calculate:

- Gross rent
  - Mortgage payment
  - Taxes and insurance
  - Maintenance and vacancy reserves
  - Property management fees (even if self-managing—your time is not free)
  - Net cash flow

If the deal doesn't pencil out on paper, it won't magically perform better in real life.

Step 5: Assemble Your Real Estate Team

Don't DIY this. You'll need:

- A lender who understands investment properties
  - A real estate agent with investor experience
  - A property manager (or a clear plan to manage it yourself)
  - A home inspector
  - A CPA or tax advisor familiar with real estate

Step 6: Start Small, Learn Fast

Your first property is your classroom. Don't swing for the fences. A single-family home or small duplex in a stable neighborhood can teach you everything you need to know—without risking your entire savings.

Step 7: Expect the Unexpected

Things will break. Tenants will leave. Regulations will change. That's real estate. Don't let it derail your plan—build the setbacks into your budget and timeline.

Step 8: Track and Optimize

Every month, review your income and expenses. What's working? What's bleeding money? What needs to be delegated or automated? Just like running a pharmacy, running a property requires systems and accountability.

Step 9: Decide What's Next

One property might be enough. Or it might be the beginning of a portfolio. Either way, pause after your first deal to evaluate. Did this investment get you closer to your freedom goals—or just busier?

In the next section, we'll look at common mistakes pharmacist investors make and how to avoid them—so you can protect your peace while growing your wealth.

Section 6: Mistakes Pharmacists Make in Real Estate – And How to Avoid Them

You've seen it happen. A colleague gets excited about real estate, buys a property quickly—and then regrets it. The dream of passive income turns into a full-time headache. Real estate can work, but it doesn't forgive ignorance or arrogance.

Let's break down some common mistakes pharmacists make when diving into real estate—and how you can sidestep them with confidence.

Mistake 1: Chasing Cash Flow Without a Plan

You see a property with $500/month in "cash flow" and think it's a steal. But then you forget to budget for maintenance, vacancies, and property management. Suddenly, your $500 turns into -$200/month.

Avoid it: Always run conservative numbers. Use a pro forma. Add buffers. Assume the worst—and if the deal still works, you've got something.

Mistake 2: Thinking You're "Too Smart to Fail"

Pharmacists are highly educated, so it's tempting to assume you'll naturally succeed in real estate. But this field doesn't care about degrees. It rewards experience, relationships, and humility.

Avoid it: Learn from real estate mentors. Read books, join forums, attend local meetups. Approach your first deal as a student, not a savior.

Mistake 3: Skipping Due Diligence

It's easy to fall in love with a house, especially after seeing a good price or pretty kitchen. But hidden issues—bad roofs, foundation problems, HOA rules—can destroy your ROI.

Avoid it: Always get inspections. Review all financials. Walk the neighborhood. Call the city. Vet every part of the deal before signing.

Mistake 4: Overleveraging

Just because a bank will give you the money doesn't mean you should take it. If you're maxed out on every property, you're one emergency away from disaster.

Avoid it: Maintain strong reserves. Use financing wisely. Don't stretch just to buy more doors.

Mistake 5: Not Treating It Like a Business

Real estate isn't just buying a house. It's managing tenants, handling repairs, planning taxes, and growing equity. It requires systems and decisions.

Avoid it: Set up a bookkeeping system from day one. Open a separate bank account. Have clear contracts and tenant screening processes.

Mistake 6: Investing for the Wrong Reasons

Buying just to look successful, beat a friend's portfolio, or escape your job never ends well. These motivations create rushed decisions and poor investments.

Avoid it: Make sure your investing goals are rooted in your financial plan—not your ego.

Mistake 7: Doing It All Yourself

You might be the pharmacist who also becomes the landlord, handyman, accountant, and negotiator. That might save money, but it can cost you time, peace, and performance.

Avoid it: Build a team. Delegate what you can. Spend your time where it has the most value.

Mistake 8: Ignoring Taxes

Rental income, depreciation, capital gains, cost segregation—real estate has tax advantages, but also complexity. Many pharmacists miss deductions or create tax headaches.

Avoid it: Work with a CPA who understands real estate. Don't wait until tax season to plan.

Mistake 9: Not Thinking Long-Term

You get frustrated after one bad tenant or a year without appreciation and sell. But real estate is a long game. Most investors win by holding for 10+ years, not flipping in 10 months.

Avoid it: Commit to your plan. Review your goals annually. Be patient.

Mistake 10: Losing Yourself in the Process

You started investing for freedom. But now you're exhausted, overwhelmed, and wondering if it was worth it.

Avoid it: Protect your time. Say no to bad deals. Remember: You're not building an empire. You're building a life.

In the next section, we'll look at how to integrate real estate investing with the rest of your financial plan—so it works for you, not the other way around.

Section 7: Integrating Real Estate into Your Overall Wealth Plan

Too often, real estate gets treated like an isolated side hustle—separate from the rest of your financial life. But to make it truly work for you, it needs to fit into your bigger wealth-building strategy. Let's explore how to harmonize your real estate decisions with your broader financial goals.

Think of your finances as a full orchestra—your 401(k), Roth IRA, emergency fund, insurance, savings accounts, and yes, real estate, all playing different instruments. Your job isn't to make one section louder. It's to conduct them in balance.

Step 1: Start with Your Goals

Why are you even investing in real estate?

- To retire early?
- To generate extra income?
- To reduce taxes?
- To leave a legacy?

If you're not clear on your "why," it's easy to end up with the wrong "what." The property itself doesn't matter until your goals are clear.

Step 2: Know Your Time Horizon

Real estate is often best for long-term investors. If you're planning to move, change careers, or go back to school in the next 2-5 years, buying property might not be the best move right now.

On the other hand, if you've got job stability, a strong emergency fund, and a plan to stay put, it might be the perfect time.

Step 3: Prioritize Safety First

Before you tie up cash in a down payment, ask:

- Do I have 3–6 months of emergency expenses saved?
- Am I contributing at least enough to my 401(k) to get the full employer match?
- Have I tackled high-interest debt?

If not, real estate can wait. Build a strong base before adding complexity.

Step 4: Align Your Accounts

If you own real estate, that's an asset. But don't let it replace your retirement accounts. You still need to:

- Contribute to a Roth IRA or backdoor Roth if eligible
- Maximize your 401(k) if you're self-employed (via a Solo 401(k) or SEP IRA)
- Rebalance your portfolio annually to manage risk

Real estate can complement your stocks and bonds—but it shouldn't be the only thing in your plan.

Step 5: Consider Tax Strategy

Real estate offers tax advantages: depreciation, 1031 exchanges, cost segregation, etc. But they don't replace retirement tax planning.

Work with a CPA or tax strategist who understands both real estate and pharmacist income.

Ask them:

- How do I report rental income?
- Can I write off part of my home if I run a business?
- Should I hold the property in my name or an LLC?

Step 6: Protect What You're Building

Real estate means liability—so don't forget insurance and asset protection.

- Have umbrella liability insurance (especially if you own multiple properties)
- Make sure each property has landlord insurance
- Consider forming an LLC for legal protection (talk to a professional first)
- Have a will, living trust, and estate plan that includes your real estate

Step 7: Keep It in Perspective

You're not investing in real estate to become a landlord for life (unless that excites you). You're doing it to create freedom, options, and long-term wealth.

So revisit your strategy annually. Make sure your properties still serve your goals. Sell or 1031 exchange if they don't. Don't get emotionally attached to an asset that no longer fits.

Step 8: Balance with Life Goals

Maybe you love real estate, but you also want to:

- Travel for three months each year
- Save for your kids' college
- Reduce clinical hours in five years

Make sure your real estate doesn't block those dreams. It should support them.

Create buckets in your plan:

- Income for today (job)
- Income for the future (retirement accounts)
- Growth (index funds, real estate equity)
- Flexibility (cash savings, side income)

Step 9: Use Real Estate to Fund Other Dreams

One of the most powerful uses of real estate is recycling your equity. You can use:

- Cash-out refinances
  - Home equity lines of credit (HELOCs)
  - 1031 exchanges
  - Appreciation plays

...to roll that money into new investments, business ideas, or lifestyle upgrades (responsibly).

It's not about buying and holding forever. It's about making strategic moves to fund a life that feels rich—not just looks rich.

Step 10: Build a Team

To integrate real estate with the rest of your plan, you'll want:

- A fee-only financial planner
  - A real estate-savvy CPA
  - A real estate attorney (if investing actively)
  - A lender who understands your strategy

This isn't about doing it alone. It's about building a team that helps you stay on track.

Next, we'll walk through a full example of a pharmacist's real estate strategy—from first purchase to retirement vision—and how it all connects.

Section 8: Sample Strategy – A Pharmacist's Real Estate Journey from Purchase to Purpose

Let's bring it all together through the story of a fictional pharmacist named Dr. Maya Carter. Maya is a 33-year-old clinical pharmacist earning $128,000 a year. She has about $140,000 in student loans, a Roth IRA with $25,000, a 401(k) with $85,000, and a dream to someday create more flexibility in her work-life balance.

She's curious about real estate but isn't sure how to start. Over the next 15 years, here's how Maya integrates real estate into her wealth-building plan—without losing focus or burning out.

Year 1: Foundation First

Before Maya even thinks about buying property, she focuses on her foundation:

- Builds a 6-month emergency fund
  - Contributes 6% to her 401(k) to get her full employer match
  - Maxes out her Roth IRA ($6,500)
  - Consolidates student loans and sets up income-driven repayment

She decides to "house hack" to dip her toe into real estate without overextending. She buys a duplex, lives in one unit, and rents out the other.

Down payment: $25,000 (from savings and a gift from her parents)
Monthly mortgage: $1,750
Rental income from other unit: $1,400
Her effective housing cost: $350/month + maintenance

Year 3: Rinse and Repeat

The duplex performs well. Maya learns the basics of landlord-tenant law, maintenance, and budgeting for vacancies. She takes a real estate investing course and joins a local investor meetup.

She buys a small single-family rental in a nearby town:

- Purchase price: $175,000
  - Down payment: $35,000
  - Rent: $1,500/month
  - PITI (Principal, Interest, Taxes, Insurance): $1,050/month
  - Net cash flow: $300/month

Year 6: Scaling with Caution

Maya now owns 3 units and continues contributing to her Roth IRA and 401(k). She increases her 401(k) contributions to 15%, focuses on tax strategy, and creates an LLC for her rental properties.

She meets with a CPA to:

- Track expenses and depreciation
  - Set up a Solo 401(k) for side income from consulting work
  - Plan her tax deductions properly

Year 9: Lifestyle Goals, Not Just Property

Maya wants more freedom. She buys a short-term rental near a national park—a passion project. It cash flows well and gives her a place to stay for vacations.

But she's not obsessed with "more doors." She focuses on:

- Paying off one mortgage aggressively
  - Keeping a low debt-to-income ratio
  - Hiring a property manager so she can step back

Year 12: Shifting Gears

Maya decides to cut back to 32 hours a week at her pharmacy job. Her rental income now covers $2,800/month in expenses. She still contributes to her Solo 401(k) and Roth IRA.

She now owns:

- 1 duplex (house hack)
- 2 long-term rentals
- 1 short-term rental

She's not retired, but she's work-optional. That's the goal.

Year 15: Purpose, Not Just Profit

Maya mentors younger pharmacists. She creates a small online course about real estate and wealth building. She sells her first rental and uses a 1031 exchange to buy a small multifamily closer to home.

Her net worth has grown to over $1 million.

- $340,000 in retirement accounts
- $200,000 in equity from real estate
- $60,000 in a high-yield savings account
- $400,000 in property value appreciation

But more importantly—she has peace of mind, options, and time.

What Maya Did Right:

- Started small and learned with each step
- Never sacrificed retirement for real estate
- Built a team: CPA, agent, attorney, property manager
- Stayed focused on lifestyle, not just hustle
- Always revisited her goals

This is one example—but it's a blueprint you can adapt to your own dreams, values, and timelines.

Next, we'll wrap up the chapter with rules of thumb, red flags to avoid, and how to decide if real estate truly fits your financial life.

Section 9: Rules of Thumb, Red Flags, and Final Guidance

By now, you've seen how real estate can be a tool for pharmacists to create financial flexibility—but it's not one-size-fits-all. Before you take the leap (or the next leap), let's lay out some rules of thumb, red flags to watch for, and a framework for deciding what role real estate should play in your life.

Rules of Thumb for Real Estate Investing

1. **Don't Invest If You're Still in Survival Mode**
   If you're living paycheck to paycheck, real estate can wait. Build your emergency fund, stabilize your income, and gain financial clarity first.

2. **Never Bet the Farm on Appreciation**
   Real estate should cash flow now. Appreciation is a bonus, not a guarantee.

3. **Cash Flow First, Equity Later**
   Buy property that makes money today—not just someday.

4. **House Hack if You Can**
   Especially early in your career, house hacking (living in one unit and renting out others) is a low-risk, high-learning investment.

5. **20–25% Rule**
   After accounting for expenses, aim for 20–25% of rent as positive monthly cash flow. If rent is $1,500, shoot for $300–$375 monthly net.

6. **Don't DIY Everything**

Learn the basics, but build a team. Get a great CPA, a trustworthy contractor, and an attorney who knows landlord-tenant law.

7. **Leverage Responsibly**

Use financing, but don't over-leverage. If one bad month would bankrupt you, you're stretched too thin.

8. **Diversify**

Real estate shouldn't be your only wealth-building tool. Keep contributing to your Roth, 401(k), and taxable accounts.

Red Flags to Avoid

1. **Overhyped Gurus**

If someone's selling you a $10,000 weekend seminar or course that promises millions—run. Real wealth-building is slow and intentional.

2. **"No Money Down" Tricks**

These work for maybe 1% of people, and often lead to legal, tax, or financing issues. If it sounds too good to be true, it probably is.

3. **Underestimating Expenses**

Many new investors forget about vacancies, maintenance, management fees, and capital expenditures (new roof, new HVAC, etc.).

4. **Buying for Ego, Not Income**

Don't buy a beach house to flex on Instagram unless it also fits your plan. Real estate is a business.

5. **Neglecting the Numbers**

Fall in love with the math, not the property. If it doesn't work on paper, walk away.

6. **Ignoring Local Laws**
   Some cities are hostile to landlords. Always research local zoning, short-term rental ordinances, and tenant protections.

7. **Unrealistic Time Commitments**
   If you already work 60-hour weeks as a pharmacist, don't add a second full-time job as a landlord. Start small or go turnkey.

Should You Go There?

Ask yourself:

- Do I have the financial bandwidth for this?
  - Am I willing to learn?
  - Is this a stepping stone to my goals—or a distraction?
  - Do I want more freedom, or more work?
  - Am I romanticizing real estate because of someone else's journey?

You don't need real estate to become wealthy—but it can be a powerful ally if you do it right.

Your job as a pharmacist is demanding. You're already contributing to society in a major way. If you want to expand your wealth and options, real estate might help. If it doesn't fit your vision, that's okay too.

Either way, the principles still apply: clarity, consistency, and confidence.

You don't need 10 doors and 6 spreadsheets to win. You need a plan that matches your purpose.

Start by running the numbers on one property. Talk to one trusted advisor. Attend one local real estate meetup. Get one book from the library. Watch one video. Then, if it still excites you—take one step forward.

Just one.

This is how you build a life with leverage, not just loans.

And don't forget:

You didn't go to pharmacy school to be financially stuck.
You went to change lives—including your own.

So let's build a real estate plan that respects your license, your lifestyle, and your legacy.

Your future self is already proud of you.

Chapter 36: Investing While Paying Off Debt – Rules of Thumb

You worked hard to earn your PharmD. You survived clinicals, board exams, and all-night shifts. Now you're making money—but you've also got debt, maybe a lot of it. And somewhere in between paying rent, buying groceries, and treating yourself to something nice on your day off, there's that nagging question:

"Should I invest now or wait until my loans are gone?"

You're not alone. This chapter is your guide to that very dilemma. We're going to talk about real numbers, real strategies, and real peace of mind.

This is not a binary decision. It's a dance. And we're going to teach you the rhythm.

Let's get one thing clear right away—being in debt doesn't mean you can't build wealth. It just means you need a strategy. This isn't about choosing between your future and your present. It's about building a bridge between the two. That bridge is made of cash flow, confidence, and clear decisions. And that's what we're about to unpack—together.

SECTION 1: WHY THIS DECISION FEELS SO HARD

Let's be honest—pharmacists are under a unique kind of pressure.

You're making more than most new grads. You're also often carrying more debt than most new grads. And because of that, you feel stuck. It's like watching two trains leaving the station in opposite directions—one labeled "Financial Freedom" (investing), and one labeled "Debt-Free" (repayment). You're expected to jump on both at the same time.

Here's the truth: You can. But you need to be intentional.

You've been told that "debt is bad" and "you should never invest until all debt is paid off." That's not entirely true. Some debt is toxic. Some is tolerable. Some is even strategic. The key is knowing which is which—and when to prioritize one over the other.

This chapter will give you the tools to do just that.

SECTION 2: UNDERSTANDING THE MATH—AND THE MINDSET

Let's look at the cold, hard numbers first.

If your student loan has a 6.8% interest rate, and your investments might earn an average of 7–8% over time, it sounds like a wash. Why not just pay off the loan?

But investing doesn't just earn a return. It earns *compound* return. That means your money earns money, and then that money earns more money. Over time, that snowballs into something powerful.

And beyond the math—there's mindset.

Paying down debt feels like relief.
Investing feels like power.

You want both.

This is why the goal isn't to pick one. The goal is to build a system that lets you move toward both, without burnout.

SECTION 3: RULES OF THUMB THAT ACTUALLY WORK

Let's lay out some practical, pharmacist-friendly rules of thumb:

1. **If your loan interest rate is over 7%, prioritize extra payments.**
That's a high rate. If your investments are unlikely to beat that consistently, you're better off wiping that debt out fast.

2. **If your interest rate is under 5%, prioritize investing.**
A diversified investment portfolio will likely beat 5% over time. The sooner you get money into the market, the better.

3. **If your loan is between 5–7%, consider a 50/50 split.**
Balance is your friend. You don't have to choose one path. You just need to keep moving in both directions.

4. **Always grab your employer match before anything else.**
If your company offers a 401(k) match and you're not contributing enough to get it, you're leaving free money on the table.

5. **Build your emergency fund before you go big on either.**
If you don't have 3–6 months of expenses set aside, that's priority number one. Otherwise, one emergency turns into new debt.

6. **Automate your investing and debt payments.**

Set up automatic transfers. This turns discipline into default behavior.

7. **Use bonuses, raises, and windfalls intentionally.**
Don't inflate your lifestyle. Allocate 50% to debt, 30% to investing, and 20% to treat yourself. Or some version that feels right to you.

SECTION 4: SCENARIOS THAT BRING IT TO LIFE

Scenario A: Mia, 27, $190K in student loans, just landed a job in retail pharmacy earning $124K/year.

- Her loan interest is 6.2%.
  - She gets a 4% 401(k) match.
  - She lives in a moderate-cost area.

What we'd tell her: Contribute enough to get the match. Put a small amount into a Roth IRA each month ($200–$300). Make aggressive extra payments on her highest-interest loans, especially if she's not pursuing forgiveness.

Scenario B: Dan, 35, clinical pharmacist, married, household income $210K, two kids, owes $85K in student loans at 4.6%.

What we'd tell him: Maximize retirement contributions (401(k), Roth IRA). Continue minimum loan payments. He's in the wealth-building stage, and his lower-rate loans shouldn't hold him back from growing investments.

Scenario C: Priya, 43, in pharma industry, making $180K, has $40K left in loans at 7.5% but no retirement savings yet.

What we'd tell her: That interest rate is a fire. Throw water on it fast.

But still set aside at least 10% of income into a Roth or Traditional IRA while paying that loan down as fast as possible.

Building Momentum: Stacking Habits for Long-Term Growth

Let's talk about momentum. Financial momentum isn't about one grand slam move—it's about stringing together singles until you're consistently scoring. Paying off debt while investing isn't an all-or-nothing game. You don't have to choose one or the other forever. You just have to start—and stack.

Here's what stacking habits look like for a pharmacist:

- You set up a $100/month automatic transfer into your Roth IRA.
- You commit to throwing every bonus and tax refund at your highest-interest debt.
- You stop adding new debt by creating a spending plan that includes fun money—so you don't have to swipe for happiness.
- You check your net worth every quarter—not to judge yourself, but to understand your trajectory.

Stacking isn't sexy. It's not flashy. But it's how real pharmacists build wealth. And over time, that momentum creates options—early retirement, a sabbatical, a home you love, or the power to walk away from a toxic work environment.

What If You're Starting Late?

Maybe you're 38 with six figures of debt and no retirement savings. Maybe you're 45 and just now getting serious. Here's what I need you to hear:

It's not too late. But it is time to get serious.

You'll need to be more aggressive about savings. You'll need to understand the trade-offs of each dollar. But you don't need to panic. You need a plan.

You may:
- Max out your employer's retirement plan and open a Roth IRA.
- Refinance student loans for a better interest rate if forgiveness isn't a fit.
- Cut unnecessary expenses ruthlessly—but keep the things that bring joy and sustainability.

It's not about guilt. It's about making the next decade count—because when pharmacists focus, their earning power can shift their entire trajectory.

Closing Thoughts

You don't have to be perfect to build wealth. You just have to be intentional. And you don't need a million-dollar windfall—you need a strategy that matches your reality. That's what this chapter was about.

Debt and investing aren't enemies. They're just tools. Your job is to learn how to use them wisely.

So tonight—before your head hits the pillow—do one thing. One financial move. Whether it's logging into your retirement account, making an extra debt payment, or setting up a money date. Just one. Stack it. Then do another next week. That's how you win.

And if you ever feel stuck—reread this chapter. Let it remind you of your power.

You've got this, pharmacist.

Your future self is already cheering.

How to Know When to Shift Your Focus

One of the hardest parts of managing debt and investing at the same time is knowing when to rebalance. When should you shift more energy toward debt? When should investing take the lead? Let's talk strategy.

You might shift more toward investing when:
- You've paid off all high-interest debt (anything over 7–8%).
- You have an emergency fund with at least 3–6 months of expenses.
- Your employer offers a 401(k) match and you're not maxing it out.
- You're approaching your 30s, 40s, or 50s without much in retirement savings and time is now your most valuable asset.

You might focus more heavily on debt when:
- You have credit card balances or personal loans with interest rates over 10–15%.
- Your debt is keeping you up at night or creating significant anxiety.
- You're planning a major life change (new job, starting a business, moving) and want to reduce financial obligations.
- Your net worth is negative and you need to reset your foundation.

This isn't about shame. This is about sequencing. Just like pharmacy has its protocols, so does personal finance. Sometimes the right first step is killing the chaos. Sometimes it's claiming free money through employer retirement matches. You don't have to do it all at once—but you do have to do it on purpose.

How to Avoid the Trap of False Progress

Ever feel like you're doing all the right things, but nothing's changing? Welcome to false progress. It looks like:
- Saving money in one account while carrying a balance on a high-interest credit card.

- Making the minimum payment on loans while spending freely on lifestyle upgrades.
- Starting five financial goals but completing none.

Here's the truth: Progress is simple, but not always easy. It requires trade-offs. Saying "no" to now so you can say "yes" later. So if your financial life feels foggy, simplify it. Pick one move and nail it. Then stack another.

Up next, let's walk through sample scenarios for real pharmacists and how they chose to strike the balance between debt and investing...

Real-Life Scenarios: Pharmacists Striking the Balance

Scenario 1: The Early-Career Retail Pharmacist

Meet Sarah. She's 27, making $118,000 as a retail pharmacist in a mid-size city. She's got $170,000 in student loans at 6.8% interest, no credit card debt, and a small emergency fund of $3,000.

At first, Sarah threw every extra dollar toward her student loans, trying to crush them. But then she realized she was missing out on her employer's 5% 401(k) match. She paused, met with a financial advisor, and adjusted.

Now, Sarah contributes 5% to her 401(k) to get the full match, puts $100/month into a Roth IRA, and pays an extra $500/month toward her student loans. She still lives with roommates and drives a used car—not because she has to, but because she's playing the long game.

Sarah's strategy: Balance long-term investing with aggressive debt payoff while leveraging employer benefits.

Scenario 2: The Dual-Income Pharmacist Couple

Eric and Melissa are both pharmacists in their late 30s. Combined, they bring in $225,000 annually. They still owe about $90,000 in student loans between them and just bought their first home.

Their pain point? Cash flow. Between mortgage payments, daycare, and the desire to save for their kids' education, they felt stuck.

Their solution: automation and clarity. They maxed out both of their Roth IRAs ($6,500 each), contribute 10% to their 401(k)s, and funnel any bonuses toward student loan payments. They also use a sinking fund strategy for vacations and home repairs to avoid relying on credit.

Eric and Melissa's strategy: Prioritize future savings through automation while staying flexible on how aggressively they pay off debt.

Scenario 3: The Midlife Pharmacist in a High-Cost Area

Jason is 45, earning $160,000 at a hospital in San Francisco. His student loans are paid off, but he's late to investing. He has only $65,000 saved for retirement and worries it won't be enough.

He considered throwing every dollar into investments but paused. First, he built a 6-month emergency fund. Then, he started maxing out his 403(b), and opened a brokerage account with automatic monthly transfers of $500.

Jason's strategy: Play catch-up with disciplined investing and avoid lifestyle inflation despite a strong income.

These stories aren't perfect, but they're real. And real wins over perfect every time. Up next, let's walk through the most powerful tools to automate and organize your money so it works while you sleep...

Systems That Save You – Automating Your Way to Wealth

If you're trying to invest while paying off debt, the last thing you need is mental fatigue. That's where automation becomes your secret weapon.

Why automation matters:

1. It removes willpower from the equation.
2. It protects you from lifestyle inflation.
3. It helps you stick to your goals even when life gets busy.

Let's break it down into an automation plan you can tailor to your situation.

1. Direct Deposit Distribution

Instead of having all your paycheck go into one checking account, split it up.

- 85% to your checking (for bills, living expenses)
- 10% to a high-yield savings account (for emergency fund or short-term goals)
- 5% to an investment account (Roth IRA or brokerage)

2. Automatic Transfers

Set your savings and investing on autopilot. Have $200/month go to your Roth IRA and $100 to your brokerage account, no matter what. Treat it like a bill you can't skip.

3. Debt Payoff Autopilot

Set your minimum payments to auto-pay. Then set up a separate auto-payment for your extra principal payment—say, $300/month. This ensures you're always making progress, even if life gets hectic.

4. Expense Tracking That Doesn't Suck

Use tools like:

- YNAB (You Need A Budget) – great for zero-based budgeting
- Empower (formerly Personal Capital) – excellent for net worth tracking
- Mint (if still functioning in your area)

5. Sinking Funds for Sanity

Create sub-savings accounts for:
- Holidays
- Car maintenance
- Vet bills
- Travel

This prevents you from blowing up your budget when irregular expenses hit.

6. Set It and Forget It Reviews
- Monthly: Review your accounts and upcoming expenses.
- Quarterly: Check on progress with debt/investments.
- Annually: Reset goals and rebalance your investments.

This system may feel like overkill now. But once it's humming, you'll barely have to think about money—and that's the goal. Financial peace doesn't come from spreadsheets. It comes from knowing your money is working for you while you work for everything else.

Up next, let's get into the myths about debt and investing that hold pharmacists back—and what to believe instead.

Debt vs. Investing Myths That Mess with Your Mind

Even smart, well-educated professionals like pharmacists can fall into mindset traps when it comes to debt and investing. Let's dismantle some of the most toxic myths out there—and replace them with truths that empower.

Myth #1: "You shouldn't invest until all your debt is paid off."

Reality: That sounds responsible, but it's often short-sighted. If you wait 10 years to start investing while paying off loans, you lose a decade of compound growth. A better strategy? Tackle high-interest debt while still contributing something—anything—to retirement and investments.

Myth #2: "All debt is bad debt."

Reality: Not all debt is created equal. Credit card debt at 25% APR? Bad. Federal student loans at 4–6% with forgiveness potential? Not the same monster. Mortgage debt at 3%? Might be the cheapest money you'll ever borrow. The key is managing debt strategically, not fearfully.

Myth #3: "I'll invest later when I make more money."

Reality: That's the trap of lifestyle inflation. You'll always find a reason to delay. The earlier you start—even with small amounts—the more power your dollars have to work for you. Waiting for the "perfect time" is the perfect way to stay behind.

Myth #4: "If I can't max out my accounts, it's not worth it."

Reality: It's not all or nothing. Contributing $100/month to a Roth IRA adds up over time. Don't let perfectionism paralyze progress. Something beats nothing, always.

Myth #5: "Investing is gambling."

Reality: Randomly picking stocks? Sure, that's gambling. But a well-diversified, long-term index fund strategy? That's disciplined wealth-building. The market rewards consistency and time in the market—not timing the market.

Myth #6: "My loan interest is higher than the stock market return."

Reality: Sometimes yes—but that doesn't account for taxes, liquidity, risk tolerance, and opportunity cost. It also ignores employer 401(k) matches, tax-deferred growth, and psychological wins from dual progress. You don't need a spreadsheet to justify peace of mind.

Bottom Line:

Stop choosing between the two. Instead, design a plan that does both. The pharmacists who build wealth long-term aren't the ones who waited for perfect conditions. They're the ones who took consistent action.

Let's finish this chapter with a set of tailored, pharmacist-specific money moves you can take—starting today.

Pharmacist-Specific Money Moves You Can Make This Week

Let's bring it home with practical, low-stress, high-impact steps pharmacists can take right now to balance debt payoff and investing. Pick one and get moving.

1. Set Up Automatic Transfers:

Even $50–$200/month into a Roth IRA or high-yield savings account can change your life over a decade. Automate it so you don't have to think about it.

2. Calculate Your "Debt-to-Investment" Ratio:

If you're putting $1,000/month toward loans, can you carve out $200 to invest? A healthy ratio keeps momentum on both fronts.

3. Refinance High-Interest Private Loans:

If you're paying more than 7–8% interest, shop around. Don't refinance federal loans unless you're sure you're not using PSLF or IDR plans.

4. Check for 401(k) Match—and Max It:

If your employer offers a match, that's free money. Don't leave it on the table. Contribute at least enough to capture every dollar.

5. Open a Roth IRA:

Ideal for young pharmacists in lower tax brackets. Tax-free growth + tax-free withdrawals in retirement = future you will cheer.

6. Split Your Raises:

When you get a raise, increase your loan payments by half the raise and invest the other half. That way, you enjoy some of it, but most goes toward freedom.

7. Start a "Freedom Fund":

Separate from retirement or debt—this is your stash to buy options, not things. Could be for a sabbatical, career shift, or your own consulting gig.

8. Pay Off Small Debts for a Quick Win:

Use the snowball method to knock out a lingering credit card or small personal loan. That emotional victory builds momentum.

9. Schedule a "Money Date":

You + your budget. Once a month. Pour a drink, play a playlist, and check in. Celebrate your wins and adjust your strategy.

10. Get Professional Guidance:

Don't wing this stuff alone. Consider talking to a fiduciary financial advisor who understands pharmacists, student loans, and long-term strategy.

Final Call to Action:

You don't need to have it all figured out. You just need to start. Make one money move before you go to bed tonight. Just one. And then do another next week.

Let's build a life where your money works for you—not the other way around.

Chapter 37: Financial Advisors – When to Hire One and How to Vet Them

You went to school to master pharmacology, not portfolio management. And yet here you are—with a six-figure income, student loans, a demanding job, and the nagging sense that you should be doing more with your money. The truth is, financial success isn't just about earning a good paycheck. It's about making intentional decisions with that paycheck, and sometimes, you need a seasoned guide to help you do that. That's where a financial advisor comes in.

But hiring one can feel overwhelming. There are different types, different fee structures, and wildly different levels of quality and ethics. Some people swear by their advisor. Others feel burned. So how do you know when you need one? How do you find a good one? And how do you make sure you're not overpaying for something you could be doing yourself?

This chapter will walk you through everything you need to know—with no jargon, no pressure, and no shame.

Understanding the Role of a Financial Advisor

At its core, a financial advisor is a professional who helps you plan and manage your money. That might include:

- Setting financial goals
- Budgeting and cash flow planning
- Investment strategy and portfolio construction
- Tax optimization

- Insurance analysis
- Estate planning
- Retirement planning
- Student loan repayment strategies

Not every advisor does all of these. Some specialize in investments. Others take a comprehensive approach (often called "financial planning").

When Should a Pharmacist Consider Hiring an Advisor?

Here are common scenarios when it might be time to seek out professional help:

- You just landed your first full-time job and have no idea what to do with your 401(k).
- You make good money but feel like it disappears each month.
- You want to start investing, but you're afraid of making mistakes.
- You're married (or getting married) and need help combining finances.
- You're saving for multiple goals: retirement, a house, kids' college.
- You're starting a side business and want to structure it wisely.
- You're approaching retirement and want to build a withdrawal plan.

Types of Financial Advisors: Fee-Only, Commission-Based, Hybrid

Here's the breakdown:

- **Fee-Only:** Paid directly by you. No commissions. Often charge hourly, by project, or as a percentage of assets. Fiduciary by law.
- **Commission-Based:** Paid when they sell products (like insurance or mutual funds). Not always required to act in your best interest.
- **Fee-Based/Hybrid:** Charge both fees and earn commissions. Must disclose conflicts of interest, but you'll need to stay alert.

What Services Can a Financial Advisor Provide?

- **Investment Management:** Rebalancing, diversification, risk tolerance alignment.

- **Tax Planning:** Strategies to reduce taxable income, tax-loss harvesting.
- **Insurance:** Evaluating life, disability, long-term care, umbrella policies.
- **Student Loans:** Choosing between PAYE, REPAYE, PSLF, and private refinancing.
- **Cash Flow:** Helping you create and maintain a spending plan.
- **Estate Planning:** Coordinating with attorneys on wills, trusts, and beneficiary designations.

Pros and Cons of Working with an Advisor

Pros:

- Expertise you may not have time to develop yourself
- Accountability to follow through on financial goals
- Objectivity during emotional decisions (like market downturns or life changes)

Cons:

- Cost: Can range from a few hundred to thousands per year
- Mismatch: Some advisors aren't a good fit or have incentives that aren't aligned with yours
- False security: Having an advisor doesn't mean you can stop being financially literate

How to Vet an Advisor: Credentials, Background, Fiduciary Duty

- Look for **CFP® (Certified Financial Planner)**, **CPA/PFS**, or **CFA** designations.
- Ask if they are a **fiduciary 100% of the time**.
- Check their **ADV Form** (on the SEC's Investment Adviser Public

Disclosure website).

- Ask about their **disciplinary history**.
- Look up reviews, but be cautious—regulations limit what advisors can publish.

Questions to Ask in the First Meeting

1. Are you a fiduciary all the time?
2. How do you get paid?
3. What services are included?
4. Do you specialize in working with pharmacists or medical professionals?
5. How often do you meet with clients?
6. Can I see a sample financial plan?

Red Flags and How to Spot a Bad Fit

- Pressure to buy products or move quickly
- Lack of transparency around fees
- Over-promising investment returns
- Discouraging your questions
- No credentials or relevant experience

Do-It-Yourself vs. Delegation: Knowing What You Want

There's no shame in handling your finances yourself—especially if you have the interest, time, and discipline. But many pharmacists are time-poor and energy-depleted. Delegating to a trusted professional can free up mental space for what matters most. The key is knowing what you want: oversight? a second opinion? full-on planning?

How to Integrate an Advisor into Your Financial Plan

- Start by defining your goals: Are you trying to retire early? Buy a home? Pay off loans?

- Decide what you want help with: Just investments? Or full financial planning?
- Be open: Your advisor needs honest information to give solid advice.
- Stay engaged: Review your plan annually and ask questions often.

Case Studies: Different Pharmacists, Different Needs

- **Sarah, Retail Pharmacist, Age 30:** Needed help setting up a Roth IRA, choosing her 401(k) allocation, and refinancing student loans. Worked with a fee-only CFP for a one-time plan.
- **Mike & Alicia, Hospital Pharmacists, Married with Kids:** Needed help budgeting, saving for college, and understanding their employer stock options. Chose a financial planner on retainer.
- **Greg, Independent Consultant:** Runs a consulting side hustle and wanted help with tax strategy, SEP IRA contributions, and business structuring. Hired a financial planner with tax expertise.

Checklist: Is It Time for You to Get an Advisor?

- Do you feel stuck, confused, or overwhelmed with your money?
- Are you juggling multiple goals with no clear plan?
- Do you have more income than time?
- Have you experienced a major life event recently (new job, marriage, baby, inheritance)?
- Are you nearing retirement or wanting to retire early?

If you answered yes to two or more of these, it might be time to explore a conversation with a trusted advisor.

Words of Encouragement and Final Thoughts

Getting help with your money is not a sign of weakness—it's a sign of wisdom. Just like your patients come to you because they need expert guidance, you can (and should) seek out expert help when it comes to your finances.

You worked hard to become a pharmacist. You deserve a financial plan that works just as hard for you.

Call to Action:

Make one move tonight: look up one fee-only financial advisor in your area. Or write down the three things that stress you out the most about money. That's your starting point.

Final Note:

Financial literacy is not about doing everything alone. It's about knowing when to ask for help, what to ask, and who to trust. Your wealth deserves strategy. And your peace of mind deserves protection.

Your future self will thank you.

So will your bank account.

So will your sanity.

Chapter 38: DIY Investing vs. Working With a Professional

Let's be honest: You probably didn't get a PharmD to spend your nights and weekends watching financial markets, analyzing portfolio allocations, or researching the pros and cons of dividend-paying stocks. But you *do* care about your future, your finances, and making sure all that hard work turns into wealth, security, and peace of mind.

So the question is: Should you invest on your own, or work with a professional?

Welcome to one of the most misunderstood debates in personal finance. This chapter isn't about picking sides. It's about equipping you with the clarity, confidence, and criteria to decide what works best *for you* at different stages of your career. You might DIY your investments in your 20s, hire a professional in your 40s, and go back to DIY in your 60s. That's fine. This isn't dogma—this is decision-making.

And as a pharmacist, you're already a highly trained professional. You understand the value of precision, planning, and delegation. So let's unpack this with that same mindset.

Why This Chapter Matters

Whether you choose to manage your investments yourself or partner with a pro, the cost of getting it wrong is high: lost time, missed returns, unnecessary stress, and even costly mistakes. This chapter gives you the knowledge to:

- Understand the responsibilities and trade-offs of managing your own investments.
- Evaluate the *real* value a financial advisor brings (and when it's worth it).
- Learn how to vet, hire, or even *fire* a financial advisor.
- Build a hybrid approach that keeps you informed and empowered.

You didn't go to school to be average. Let's make sure your investing game isn't either.

The Case for DIY Investing

Let's start with the upside. DIY investing is empowering. It gives you full control, transparency, and customization. You can open an account, research index funds, automate contributions, and track your progress.

Pros of DIY:

- **Cost-Effective:** No advisor fees. You keep more of your returns.
- **Full Control:** You decide what you invest in, when, and why.
- **Learning Opportunity:** You deepen your financial literacy by managing your money.
- **Immediate Action:** No meetings, no waiting for someone to get back to you.

Cons of DIY:

- **Time-Consuming:** Researching investments, managing tax strategy, and staying current on markets takes time.
- **Risk of Emotional Mistakes:** Fear and greed can lead to bad decisions (panic selling, chasing hot trends).
- **Overconfidence:** It's easy to underestimate what you don't know.
- **No Accountability:** You have no one helping you course-correct if you're off track.

DIY investing *can* work extremely well—especially if you stick to index funds, automate your savings, and stay consistent. But don't let pride or fear keep you from asking for help when you need it.

The Case for Working With a Professional

You already outsource things in life that matter: medical care, car repairs, tax filing. Investing can be the same. A good financial advisor is more than a stock picker—they're a guide, a strategist, a coach, and sometimes a therapist with a calculator.

Pros of Working With an Advisor:

- **Expertise Across Many Areas:** Investments, taxes, insurance, estate planning, retirement.
- **Personalized Planning:** A good advisor tailors your financial plan to your goals, values, and timeline.
- **Accountability and Coaching:** Helps you stay the course during market volatility.
- **Saves Time and Energy:** Lets you focus on your career, family, and life.

Cons of Working With an Advisor:

- **Cost:** Most charge a percentage of assets under management (usually 1%). Some charge hourly or flat fees.
- **Quality Varies:** Not all advisors are equal. Some are glorified salespeople.
- **Less Control:** You may have to relinquish some decision-making.

The best advisors earn their fee and then some. But you have to choose carefully.

How to Vet a Financial Advisor

This is non-negotiable. If you're hiring someone to help you build wealth, protect your family, and plan your future, do your homework.

Here are the must-ask questions:

1. **Are you a fiduciary?** This means they're legally obligated to act in your best interest.
2. **How do you get paid?** Fee-only (no commissions) is usually best for transparency.
3. **What services do you offer?** Look for comprehensive planning, not just investment management.
4. **Who is your typical client?** Make sure they understand pharmacists, healthcare professionals, or high-income W2 earners.
5. **What's your investment philosophy?** Look for consistency, not market timing or hype.
6. **Do you use proprietary products?** Be wary. This can be a red flag for conflicts of interest.

Also, trust your gut. Do they listen more than they talk? Do they respect your questions? Are they educating you, or just trying to sell you something?

A Hybrid Approach

Many pharmacists take a hybrid route: DIY in the early years, hire an advisor when life gets more complex, and maybe even go back to managing it themselves in retirement.

You could:

- Manage your IRA and 401(k) while hiring an advisor for tax and estate planning.
- Use a robo-advisor for simplicity and supplement it with a fee-only planner.
- DIY your core investments but meet annually with a pro to sanity-check your plan.

There's no one right way. There's only *your* way.

When DIY Might Be Best:

- You're under 35, have under $100K invested, and want to learn by doing.

- You use a simple strategy like index fund investing.
- You have time, discipline, and interest in managing money.

When a Pro Might Be Best:

- You're too busy to manage your finances.
- Your income, assets, or taxes have become more complex.
- You're feeling overwhelmed or unsure what to prioritize.
- You're entering retirement and need distribution planning.

Action Steps:

1. Review your investment strategy: Is it working? Are you confident?
2. If you're DIY-ing, schedule a quarterly review with yourself.
3. Interview 2-3 financial advisors, even if you're not ready to hire yet.
4. Ask your network for referrals to fiduciary, fee-only advisors.
5. Revisit your plan annually and update it when life changes.

Bold Encouragement:

You have the power to build wealth. Whether you DIY it or get help, don't delay action waiting for perfection.

Call to Act:

Make one money move before you go to bed tonight. Just one. And then do another next week.

Final Note:

This isn't about proving you're smart enough to do it alone. This is about being wise enough to get the support you need when it matters most. Whether you manage your investments or hire someone to help, the goal is the same: financial confidence, freedom, and peace of mind.

Your future self will thank you.

So will your bank account.

So will your sanity.

Chapter 39: Taxes for Pharmacists – What to Know and How to Prepare

Let's talk about something most pharmacists would rather avoid: taxes. Not the sexiest topic in the world, I know. But if you're serious about building wealth, keeping your financial life clean, and protecting your future—understanding how taxes work isn't optional. It's essential.

This chapter is for the smart, driven pharmacist who's tired of feeling confused every April—or worse, blindsided. Whether you're filing your taxes yourself, working with a CPA, or simply trying to figure out where all your money went this year, this chapter is your plain-language, judgment-free guide to what you need to know.

No shame. No confusion. Just clarity, confidence, and control.

Why Taxes Matter More Than You Think

You may have heard the quote: "It's not about how much you make. It's about how much you keep." Taxes are the number one reason why some high-income professionals—yes, even pharmacists—feel like they're always behind.

If you don't understand taxes, you could be overpaying every year.

If you don't plan for taxes, you could be making money moves that backfire.

If you don't file your taxes properly, you could be missing deductions, paying penalties, or inviting audits.

Let's fix that.

Here's what we're going to cover:

1. Understanding the tax system (federal, state, local)
2. What pharmacists should know about their W-2
3. Deductions, credits, and the most common write-offs
4. Side hustles and self-employment taxes
5. Tax-advantaged accounts (401k, HSA, FSA, 529, IRAs)
6. Common tax traps (and how to avoid them)
7. How to organize your taxes year-round
8. When to hire a tax professional (and how to vet them)
9. Tax planning vs. tax filing (they're not the same!)
10. Rules of thumb for pharmacists

We'll walk through each of these with clear, practical advice—plus stories and scenarios to help make it real.

Understanding the Tax System: Federal, State, and Local

The U.S. tax system can feel like a maze—especially if you were never taught how to navigate it. Here's a breakdown:

Federal Taxes: This is what most people think of when they say "income taxes." Your federal tax rate depends on your income level and filing status (single, married, head of household, etc.). The U.S. uses a progressive tax system, which means different portions of your income are taxed at different rates.

State Taxes: Not every state charges income tax (hello, Texas, Florida, Nevada!). But most do. Your state income tax rate can significantly impact your take-home pay.

Local Taxes: Some cities or counties add their own income taxes on top of state and federal. If you live in places like New York City or certain areas in California, expect a heavier tax burden.

Social Security and Medicare: These are payroll taxes deducted from your paycheck. You pay 6.2% for Social Security and 1.45% for Medicare. If you're self-employed, you're paying the full 12.4% and 2.9% because you are both the employer and the employee.

What Pharmacists Should Know About Their W-2

As a W-2 employee, your employer handles much of the tax withholding process for you—but that doesn't mean you're off the hook. Your W-2 shows:

- Your total taxable wages
- How much was withheld for federal, state, and local income taxes
- How much went to Social Security and Medicare
- Contributions to retirement plans, HSAs, or FSAs

Pay attention to your W-2 box by box. Mistakes happen more than you'd think. And if you worked multiple jobs during the year, each employer will send a separate W-2—make sure they're all included in your return.

Tax Deductions, Credits, and Common Write-Offs

Here's a rule of thumb: Deductions reduce your *taxable income*. Credits reduce your *tax bill* dollar-for-dollar.

Standard vs. Itemized Deduction: Most pharmacists take the standard deduction unless they own a home, give generously to charity, or have significant medical expenses.

Common deductions:

- Student loan interest (up to $2,500, depending on income)
- HSA and FSA contributions
- 401(k) or 403(b) contributions
- IRA contributions (sometimes deductible, depending on income)

Common credits:

- Lifetime Learning Credit (if you're taking courses or certifications)
- Child Tax Credit (if you have kids)
- Saver's Credit (if you contribute to retirement accounts on a lower income)

Side Hustles and Self-Employment Taxes

Pharmacists are increasingly exploring side income—consulting, writing, speaking, tutoring, telepharmacy, or even a wellness business. That's great. But remember: once you're earning outside your W-2, you're responsible for your own taxes.

This includes:

- Income tax on your net profits (income minus expenses)
- Self-employment tax (15.3% total for Social Security and Medicare)

Pro tip: Track every business expense—software, home office, licenses, phone, travel, mileage, etc. You only pay taxes on profit, not revenue.

Tax-Advantaged Accounts Every Pharmacist Should Use

These are your best tax shelters, plain and simple:

401(k) or 403(b): Pre-tax contributions reduce your taxable income today. Some employers match—take that free money!

Roth IRA: Contributions aren't deductible, but your money grows tax-free, and qualified withdrawals are tax-free.

HSA (Health Savings Account): Triple tax-advantaged—contributions are deductible, growth is tax-free, and qualified withdrawals are tax-free.

FSA (Flexible Spending Account): Use-it-or-lose-it for healthcare or dependent care expenses. Great if you have predictable costs.

529 Plans: For education expenses—yours, your kids', or grandkids'. Grows tax-free if used for qualified education costs.

Common Tax Traps for Pharmacists

- Withholding too little and owing a big bill in April
- Failing to report side hustle income
- Ignoring capital gains taxes on investments
- Not adjusting withholdings after marriage, kids, or a major raise
- Not using an HSA or FSA when eligible
- Forgetting about RMDs (Required Minimum Distributions) in retirement accounts once you hit age 73

How to Organize Your Taxes Year-Round

Don't wait until April to care about taxes. Here's how to stay ready:

- Set up a folder (physical or digital) for tax documents
- Keep receipts for business expenses
- Download monthly pay stubs and retirement account contributions
- Use software or a spreadsheet to track side hustle income and expenses
- Check your W-4 annually to make sure your withholding is accurate

When to Hire a Tax Professional

If your tax situation is simple, software may be enough. But if you:

- Have a side hustle
- Own property
- Are married with kids
- Are saving for retirement across multiple accounts
- Received an inheritance

Then it might be worth hiring a CPA or EA (Enrolled Agent). Look for someone who:

- Understands high-income W-2 earners
- Works with other pharmacists or healthcare professionals
- Offers year-round tax planning, not just filing

Tax Planning vs. Tax Filing

Tax filing is what you do in April. Tax planning is what you do all year. Smart pharmacists think ahead:

- Should you contribute to a Roth or traditional IRA?
- Should you sell investments this year or next?
- Should you max out your HSA now or spread contributions?
- Can you prepay next year's property taxes or charitable gifts?

Rules of Thumb for Pharmacists

- Save at least 20–25% of side hustle income for taxes
- Max out your 401(k) if possible, or at least contribute to the match
- Use an HSA if you're eligible—don't leave that tax shelter on the table
- File early to avoid fraud
- Don't ignore mail from the IRS—open it and respond

Call to Action

Make one tax-related money move this week. Maybe it's updating your W-4, opening a Roth IRA, scheduling a meeting with a CPA, or tracking your expenses. One step.

And then another next week.

You've got this.

This chapter wasn't just about forms and deadlines. It was about power. Control. Confidence.

You went to pharmacy school to help others. This is how you help yourself.

Let's make sure your money works as hard as you do.

Your future self will thank you.

So will your bank account.

So will your sanity.

Chapter 40: Side Hustles, Consulting, and Entrepreneurial Opportunities

Let's be honest. You didn't go to school for six or more years to feel stuck, overworked, or underpaid. Yet, for too many pharmacists, that's the reality. Burnout is real. Stagnation is common. But what if your PharmD could be the launchpad for something more? Something bigger? Something that gives you financial freedom and personal fulfillment beyond the four walls of a pharmacy?

This chapter is about unlocking that potential. We're going to talk about how pharmacists—yes, pharmacists—can be entrepreneurs. Whether it's launching a side hustle, building a consulting business, or turning a passion into passive income, you have more options than you think.

This isn't just about making extra money. It's about building a life with more freedom, more flexibility, and more power to say "no" to burnout and "yes" to opportunity.

Why Pharmacists Make Great Entrepreneurs

Let's get this straight: pharmacists have some serious skills.

Attention to detail? Check.

Problem-solving under pressure? Check.

Communication and education? Every single day.

You're already used to translating complex information, working within systems, and managing risk—all of which are foundational to running a successful business. You just haven't applied those skills to your own financial life yet. Until now.

There are thousands of pharmacists across the country who have turned their knowledge into profitable side businesses. Some do it for a few extra bucks. Others scale it into full-time ventures. Either way, the journey starts with a shift in mindset: from employee to entrepreneur.

Mindset Shift: You Are More Than Your Job Title

A side hustle isn't just a hobby. It's a business. And to build one, you have to see yourself not just as a pharmacist—but as a brand. As an expert. As someone who has value to offer outside your employer's payroll system.

That shift can be uncomfortable at first. You've spent years training for a clinical role. You were taught to follow protocol, avoid risk, and stay within the lines. But entrepreneurship is different. It rewards initiative. Creativity. Experimentation. Learning by doing.

So if you're feeling stuck in your 9-to-5, if you've got ideas you can't shake, if you want to build a financial cushion or a complete escape plan, then you're in the right place.

Types of Side Hustles for Pharmacists

Let's break this down by categories, so you can start to see what's possible—and what might be a fit for your interests, skills, and schedule.

1. Health and Wellness Consulting

- Medication therapy management (MTM)
- Nutritional supplement advising
- Functional medicine
- Health coaching
- Diabetes education

1. Writing and Speaking

- Health blogging
- Medical content writing
- Creating CE courses
- Speaking at conferences

- Podcasting or YouTube content

1. Teaching and Tutoring

- Pharmacy student tutoring
- Test prep (NAPLEX, MPJE)
- Adjunct faculty positions
- Precepting or mentoring

1. Product-Based Business

- Skincare lines (especially if you know dermatology)
- Vitamin or supplement companies
- Herbal remedies
- eCommerce stores (Shopify, Etsy)

1. Online Education Platforms

- Build and sell courses
- Create ebooks or guides
- Host webinars or paid workshops
- Private Facebook or subscription communities

1. Real Estate

- Rental property investing
- Short-term vacation rentals (Airbnb)
- REIT investing (more passive)

1. Financial Coaching

- Budget and debt coaching (yes, even without being an advisor)
- Helping other pharmacists with financial literacy

1. Pharmacist-Specific Startups

- Tech tools for pharmacies
- Workflow improvement tools
- Mobile apps for medication adherence

The list goes on. But the key takeaway is this: you are already qualified to get started. You don't need another degree. You don't need permission. You just need a plan.

How to Choose the Right Side Hustle

This is where many pharmacists get stuck. Too many options, too little clarity. Here's a framework to help:

1. Leverage What You Know
2. If you're already an expert in infectious disease, don't start by trying to sell hand-poured candles (unless you really love candles). Build on what you know.
3. Solve a Problem People Will Pay For
4. Ideas are cute. Solutions are profitable. Your side hustle should address a real pain point for a specific group of people.
5. Match It With Your Time and Energy
6. Be honest with yourself. If you're working 12-hour shifts five days a week, don't choose a side hustle that needs 30 hours a week to build.
7. Start Small, Validate Fast
8. You don't need a logo, a website, or an LLC to start. You need a Google Doc, a Stripe account, and a willingness to test.
9. Stay Legal and Compliant
10. If your side hustle involves healthcare advice, prescriptions, or anything that falls into a regulatory gray area—get clarity. Check your state board. Talk to a lawyer. Protect your license.

Part V: Risk Management and Protection – Guarding Your Income, Assets, and Peace of Mind

This part of the book is about defense—not offense. You've worked hard to earn your degree, your license, your paycheck, and your peace of mind. But one lawsuit, one illness, one accident, or one overlooked insurance policy can unravel years of progress. Risk management isn't just about having insurance—it's about building a financial life that can withstand uncertainty, stress, and storms.

In this section, we walk pharmacists through the key areas where protection matters most: malpractice insurance, disability income coverage, life insurance, health insurance, liability shields, estate planning, and more. We break it all down in plain English—no jargon, no scare tactics, just clarity and strategy.

Whether you're a retail pharmacist working full-time, a part-time consultant, a newly self-employed entrepreneur, or planning for the unexpected alongside a partner or children, this section gives you the tools to shield what you've built. Because wealth without protection is like a house without a roof—it might look great on the outside, but it's vulnerable.

Risk management isn't fear-based. It's freedom-based. It's what allows you to say *yes* to the future without worrying about losing everything to one bad break.

This part is your personal firewall. Your safety net. Your Plan B, so your

Plan A can thrive.

Chapter 41: Insurance Essentials – Health, Life, Disability, and Malpractice

Let's talk about protection.

Not the kind that comes in a bottle or behind a counter—the kind that protects your paycheck, your peace of mind, and your future.

If investing is the offense in your financial life, insurance is the defense. It doesn't grow your wealth directly, but it absolutely protects it. And for pharmacists—especially those with high income, high debt, and high responsibility—the right insurance can mean the difference between long-term stability and sudden financial crisis.

This chapter is your plain-English guide to the four essentials: health, life, disability, and malpractice. We're going to walk through what each one does, why you need it (or not), and how to avoid the common traps that even smart professionals fall into.

You don't have to become an insurance expert. You just have to become an informed consumer who knows how to ask the right questions. That's what this is about.

Let's break it down.

HEALTH INSURANCE

Why It Matters:

Health insurance isn't optional. One trip to the ER without coverage can wipe out your savings. And even if you're healthy now, you're one accident or diagnosis away from financial chaos without the right plan.

Key Concepts:

- Premium: What you pay each month just to have coverage
- Deductible: What you pay out of pocket before insurance starts covering costs
- Coinsurance: The percentage you pay after the deductible
- Out-of-pocket maximum: The most you'll pay in a year, period

Types of Plans:

- PPO: More flexibility, higher premiums, bigger networks
- HMO: Lower premiums, less flexibility, referrals required
- HDHP (High-Deductible Health Plan): Often paired with HSAs

Tips for Pharmacists:

- If your employer offers an HSA-eligible plan, run the numbers—the tax savings can be huge.
- Always know your out-of-pocket max. That's your worst-case scenario.
- Don't just pick the lowest premium—look at total expected costs for the year.

LIFE INSURANCE

Why It Matters:

If someone depends on your income—a partner, a child, a parent—you need life insurance. It's not about betting on your death. It's about protecting your people.

Types of Life Insurance:

1. Term Life

- Covers you for a set period (e.g., 20 or 30 years)
- Much cheaper

- No investment component
- What most pharmacists should start with

1. Whole Life / Permanent Life

- Covers you for life (as long as premiums are paid)
- Builds cash value
- More expensive
- Often oversold by commission-based agents

How Much Coverage Do You Need?

A general rule: 10-15x your income. If you make $120,000/year, that's $1.2M to $1.8M in term coverage.

Tips for Pharmacists:

- Get coverage early while you're healthy and it's cheap.
- If you're young and single with no dependents, you might just need enough to cover funeral costs and debts.
- Buy term, invest the rest.

DISABILITY INSURANCE

Why It Matters:

Your most valuable asset as a pharmacist isn't your 401(k) or your house. It's your ability to earn an income. If you can't work, everything else stops. That's why disability insurance might be the most overlooked, but most essential, type of coverage you can get.

Short-Term vs. Long-Term Disability:

- Short-Term: Covers you for a few weeks to a few months
- Long-Term: Kicks in after short-term ends; can last years or until retirement

Key Features to Look For:

- Own-occupation coverage: You get paid if you can't work as a pharmacist, even if you could do another job
- Elimination period: How long you have to wait before benefits kick in
- Benefit period: How long the insurer will pay you
- Non-cancelable and guaranteed renewable: So your policy can't be changed or canceled

Tips for Pharmacists:

- Many employer policies are not true own-occupation. That matters.
- Don't rely solely on group disability—it's often not enough.
- If you're early in your career, lock in a personal policy now while you're healthy.

MALPRACTICE INSURANCE

Why It Matters:

As a licensed healthcare provider, you can be sued. Period. Even if you're a great pharmacist. Even if the error wasn't technically your fault. Malpractice coverage is your legal shield.

Employer-Provided vs. Personal Policies:

- Most pharmacists get coverage through their employer, but it often protects the company first, not you.
- A personal policy ensures you're covered if you work multiple jobs, do consulting, or get blamed personally.

Claims-Made vs. Occurrence-Based:

- Claims-Made: You must have the policy active when the claim is filed (not just when the incident happened)
- Occurrence: You're covered as long as you had the policy when the event occurred

Tips for Pharmacists:

- Know what your employer's policy covers (and doesn't).
- If you do any side work, get your own policy.
- Malpractice lawsuits can be devastating. This is not the place to cut corners.

COMMON INSURANCE MISTAKES TO AVOID

1. Thinking You're Invincible
2. Young pharmacists often skip coverage because they feel healthy. But that's when coverage is cheapest and easiest to get.
3. Overpaying for the Wrong Coverage
4. Permanent life insurance, accident-only policies, or random niche plans are often unnecessary. Keep it simple.
5. Assuming Work Coverage Is Enough
6. Group policies are better than nothing, but they're often limited. Supplement where needed.
7. Failing to Update Coverage
8. Did you get married? Have a baby? Buy a house? Your coverage should evolve with your life.
9. Not Understanding the Policy
10. Don't buy what you don't understand. Ask questions. Read the fine print. Make sure you're protected.

ACTION STEPS FOR PHARMACISTS

1. Review your employer's benefits package line by line. Know what coverage you have and what you need to supplement.
2. Schedule a meeting with an independent insurance broker to review your options for term life, disability, and malpractice coverage.
3. Build an emergency fund to cover deductibles and short-term gaps in coverage.

4. Set calendar reminders to revisit your insurance coverage every year (or after any major life change).
5. Protect your future income like it's your most valuable asset—because it is.

REMEMBER THIS

Insurance isn't sexy. It doesn't have a cool app. It doesn't show up on your Instagram highlight reel. But it is one of the most powerful, strategic, grown-up financial moves you can make.

It's not just about fear. It's about freedom. The freedom to build wealth knowing your foundation is solid. The freedom to take risks knowing your back is covered. The freedom to sleep at night knowing you've done the smart, responsible thing.

Make one money move before you go to bed tonight. Just one. And then do another next week.

You've got this.

This isn't just about protection. It's about power.

It's about taking control of your financial life.

It's about being the kind of pharmacist who doesn't just fill prescriptions—they fill their future with peace of mind.

And that's worth every premium.

Your future self will thank you.

So will your bank account.

So will your sanity.

Chapter 42: Umbrella Insurance – What It Is and Why You Might Need It

Let's talk about protection. Not the kind you dispense behind the counter or counsel patients about. The kind that protects *you* — your career, your savings, your family, and your future. Because if you're earning good money, building wealth, and living a life where you're proud of what you've built, then you also have something to lose.

This chapter is about umbrella insurance. It's not flashy. It won't make you wealthier overnight. But it can quietly protect everything you're working so hard to build. Think of it as the moat around your financial castle. The invisible shield that kicks in when the storm comes.

What Is Umbrella Insurance?

Umbrella insurance is a type of personal liability insurance. It goes above and beyond the limits of your existing home, auto, or renters insurance. If you get sued and your underlying policy maxes out, umbrella insurance is the backup plan that can save your bank account, your assets, and your peace of mind.

It's called "umbrella" because it sits over your existing coverage. It doesn't replace your home or auto policy. It supplements them.

Here's an example:

Let's say you cause a car accident. It's your fault. Someone sues you for $750,000 in damages. But your auto policy only covers $300,000. That leaves a $450,000 gap. Who pays it? If you don't have umbrella insurance, you do. That could mean draining your savings, selling your house, garnished wages, or worse.

But if you had a $1 million umbrella policy, it would cover that gap. Clean. Simple. Game-changing.

Who Needs Umbrella Insurance?

Let's be real: not everyone needs umbrella coverage. But as a pharmacist, there's a good chance you do.

Here's why:

- You have a high income
- You own a home or other valuable assets
- You have kids (who can accidentally cause expensive damage)
- You drive regularly (risk of accidents)
- You host people in your home (risk of injury)
- You have a public presence (risk of defamation claims)
- You have rental property or a side hustle

When you earn more, people are more likely to sue you.

When you have assets, people can take them.

When you think it won't happen to you—that's usually when it does.

Pharmacists are respected professionals. But you're also human. You could be one slip, one accident, one misunderstanding away from a financial nightmare. Umbrella insurance is how you sleep better at night.

What Does Umbrella Insurance Cover?

It covers things like:

- Bodily injury liability (e.g., someone gets hurt in a car accident you caused)
- Property damage liability (e.g., you damage someone's expensive property)
- Personal liability (e.g., libel, slander, defamation lawsuits)
- Landlord liability (if you own rental property)
- Legal fees to defend you in a lawsuit

What It Usually Doesn't Cover:

- Your own injuries
- Damage to your own property
- Business activities (get separate coverage)
- Malpractice or professional liability (also separate)

How Much Coverage Do You Need?

The most common umbrella policies start at $1 million in coverage. That sounds like a lot. But in the world of lawsuits and medical bills, it can go fast.

Rules of thumb:

- If your net worth is over $500,000, consider at least $1 million in coverage.
- If you have kids, real estate, or a high-profile job, add another million.
- If you're a landlord, own multiple vehicles, or have other people financially dependent on you, go even higher.

The good news? Umbrella insurance is *cheap*.

You can often get $1 million in coverage for $150 to $300 per year. That's less than $1 a day. You're protecting hundreds of thousands of dollars—maybe millions—for the cost of a Netflix subscription.

Why Pharmacists Are Often Underinsured

Most pharmacists think, "I'm careful. I'll be fine."

But here's the thing: careful doesn't matter when *other people* make mistakes and blame you.

You could be:

- Driving responsibly, but someone else sues you after a fender bender
- Hosting a backyard barbecue, and someone trips and gets injured
- Owning a rental property where a tenant falls on a broken stair
- Misquoted in a social media post that leads to a defamation suit

The risks are everywhere. And lawsuits don't always come from people who want justice. Sometimes they just want a payday. If you look like you have deep pockets, they'll try to reach in.

How to Get Umbrella Insurance

1. Start With Your Existing Insurer
2. Most home and auto insurers offer umbrella policies. You'll typically need to have both home and auto coverage with them before they add umbrella coverage.
3. Meet the Minimum Requirements
4. Most insurers require:

- $250,000 or more in auto liability coverage
- $300,000 or more in home liability coverage

These ensure your base policies handle smaller claims before the umbrella policy kicks in.

1. Decide How Much Coverage You Need
2. Start with $1 million and increase based on your net worth and risk factors.
3. Shop Around
4. Prices can vary. Compare quotes. Ask about bundling discounts.
5. Ask Questions
6. Understand what's covered. What's excluded. How claims work. Don't just look at price—look at protection.

Real-Life Scenarios

- **Scenario 1:** You're driving to work and accidentally run a red light. You hit another car. The other driver has a traumatic brain injury and sues you for $2 million. Your auto insurance covers $300,000. Your umbrella policy covers the rest.

- **Scenario 2:** Your kid invites a friend over. They slip and fall on your wet tile floor and break their arm. The parents sue you for $600,000 in medical and pain-and-suffering damages. Your homeowner's policy caps at $300,000. Your umbrella policy steps in.
- **Scenario 3:** You post a review online criticizing a health supplement company. They sue you for defamation and demand $1 million. Your umbrella policy includes personal liability protection.

Pros and Cons of Umbrella Insurance

Pros:

- Affordable protection
- Covers legal fees
- Fills liability gaps
- Gives peace of mind
- Protects your future income

Cons:

- Requires higher base policy limits
- Doesn't cover everything
- Not useful for people with no assets

When to Reevaluate Your Coverage

- When your net worth increases significantly
- When you buy property or get married
- When you add a teenage driver
- When you start a business or side hustle

Build Your Financial Fortress

Umbrella insurance isn't about fear. It's about strategy.

You work hard. You save. You invest. You protect your patients every day. Don't forget to protect yourself.

Having the right insurance doesn't mean you expect the worst. It means you're smart enough to prepare for it.

Action Step:

Call your insurance agent this week. Ask about umbrella coverage. Get a quote. Start protecting your legacy.

Because financial freedom isn't just about growing your wealth.

It's about guarding it, too.

Chapter 43: Wills, Trusts, and Basic Estate Planning for Pharmacists

Let's have the kind of conversation that most pharmacists never have until it's too late: estate planning. Not exactly a sexy topic, right? But here's the truth—the most financially powerful people don't skip this. They don't delay it. They handle it early. Confidently. Strategically. And quietly, it becomes one of the most dignified moves they ever make.

This chapter isn't about fear or worst-case scenarios. It's about clarity. Legacy. Love. It's about making sure that what you've built gets where it needs to go, without drama, confusion, or courts getting in the way.

Whether you're 28 with a new job and zero kids, or 58 with a growing estate and grandkids on the way, this chapter is for you. Let's walk through what estate planning is, why it matters, and how you can tackle it with confidence.

What Is Estate Planning, Really?

Estate planning is just a fancy phrase for this: planning what happens to your stuff, your money, and your responsibilities when you're not here.

It's not just for millionaires. It's not just for retirees. And it's not just about death. A good estate plan answers these questions:

- Who gets what?
- Who makes decisions if I can't?
- Who takes care of my kids or pets?

- How do I protect my partner, my parents, my kids?
- How do I keep the government, courts, and chaos out of it?

This is dignity in action.

The Core Documents You Need

Let's start with the must-haves. At a minimum, a complete estate plan should include:

1. **A Will** – This tells the world who gets your assets and who will care for your minor children (if any). It's your official set of instructions.
2. **A Durable Power of Attorney** – This allows someone you trust to handle financial matters if you become incapacitated.
3. **A Healthcare Power of Attorney** – This appoints someone to make medical decisions for you if you can't.
4. **A Living Will (Advance Directive)** – This outlines your wishes regarding life support and end-of-life care.
5. **A Trust (in some cases)** – More on this shortly, but a trust helps avoid probate, manage assets for heirs, and control how/when your money is distributed.

Start with these. Build from there.

Why Wills Aren't Enough

A will is important. But by itself, it won't keep your assets out of probate. Probate is the court process your estate goes through when you die. It can be slow, public, and expensive. If you want privacy, speed, and control, a trust may be worth considering.

Common Types of Trusts

1. **Revocable Living Trust**

- You create it while alive.
- You control the assets.
- You can change or revoke it anytime.

- Assets in the trust avoid probate.

1. **Irrevocable Trust**

- Cannot be changed once set up.
- Offers asset protection and potential tax benefits.

1. **Testamentary Trust**

- Created by your will.
- Goes into effect after death.
- Useful for controlling inheritance (e.g., for minors).

1. **Special Needs Trust**

- Designed for beneficiaries with disabilities.
- Helps them maintain eligibility for government benefits.

Do You Need a Trust?

Not everyone needs a trust. But here are clues you might:

- You own property in multiple states.
- You have children from a previous marriage.
- You want to keep your estate private.
- You want to avoid court involvement.
- You want to control how your heirs receive assets (especially if you have young or financially immature children).

Naming Beneficiaries: The Overlooked Estate Plan

Want to hear a secret? The beneficiary designations on your 401(k), IRA, life insurance, or HSA actually override your will. If you say your daughter gets your IRA in your will but your ex is still listed as the beneficiary on the account paperwork—guess who gets it?

Update your beneficiaries regularly. Check every account. This is estate planning 101.

Guardianship for Children

If you have kids under 18, naming a guardian is one of the most important things you can do. Otherwise, the courts will decide. Even if you think your family will figure it out, don't leave it to chance.

You can name a guardian in your will. You can also name a different person to manage the money (a trustee) if needed. Choose wisely. Choose lovingly. Revisit it over time.

Digital Assets and Passwords

In today's world, your digital footprint matters. Think:

- Online bank accounts
- Email
- Social media
- Cryptocurrency
- Cloud storage

Include a plan for how loved ones can access, manage, or shut down these accounts. There are tools like password managers (1Password, LastPass) that can help. Leave instructions your executor can follow.

Estate Planning Is for the Living

Here's what most people don't realize: estate planning isn't just about what happens when you die. It's about what happens if you live but can't speak, act, or manage your affairs.

What if you have a stroke at 42?

What if you're in a car accident?

What if you're unconscious for weeks?

Who handles your mortgage?

Who manages your pharmacy student loans?

Who updates your business or practice partners?

Having powers of attorney in place means you're prepared.

Taxes, Probate, and the IRS

Let's talk logistics. Most pharmacists don't have to worry about estate taxes—yet. The federal estate tax exemption is over $12 million per person (as of this writing). But that could change.

More common are the *costs of probate*:

- Court fees
- Legal fees
- Delays (sometimes months or years)

You can minimize or eliminate probate by using trusts, joint ownership, and proper beneficiary designations.

What Happens If You Don't Have a Plan?

If you die without a will (called dying intestate), your state decides who gets what based on local laws. Spouse, children, parents, siblings—there's a hierarchy.

That might work. Or it might not. Don't let a judge who never met you decide.

Where to Start

1. **Get organized** – List your accounts, assets, debts, and insurance policies.
2. **Meet with an estate planning attorney** – Many offer flat-fee packages.
3. **Discuss with your partner or family** – Talk through what you want.
4. **Update your documents every few years** or after major life changes.

Real Talk: Why Pharmacists Avoid This

Let's be honest. Estate planning feels overwhelming. It feels expensive. It feels like something for later.

But it's one of the most generous, responsible, and empowering things you can do.

It's the pharmacist version of writing clear, clean instructions on a prescription. You're just doing it for your life.

Call to Action

Don't put this off. Schedule your first estate planning meeting. Make a checklist. Review your beneficiaries. Start with just one document if you must. But start.

Bold Encouragement

You don't have to be wealthy to protect your wealth. You just have to be willing to act.

Your financial life isn't complete without an estate plan. This is how you finish strong.

And when you do? You'll sleep better. Love better. And lead better.

Your future self will thank you.

So will your family.

So will your legacy.

Let's build something worth leaving behind.

Chapter 44: Long-Term Care Insurance – When Should You Think About It?

Let's talk about something you probably weren't taught in pharmacy school: how to protect your future self when life gets real.

And by "real," we mean the years down the road—when you may need care, not because of a broken bone or an illness with a clear cure, but because of the slow, steady challenges that come with aging, chronic illness, or cognitive decline. That's where long-term care (LTC) insurance comes in.

This chapter is about understanding what LTC insurance is, when to think about it, how it fits into your bigger financial picture, and whether or not it makes sense for you. It's a conversation about protecting your dignity, your savings, and your peace of mind.

Because if there's one thing that can derail even the most well-built retirement plan, it's the cost of long-term care.

What Is Long-Term Care?

Long-term care refers to the services and support needed by people who are unable to perform basic activities of daily living (ADLs) on their own. These include:

- Bathing
- Dressing
- Eating
- Toileting

- Transferring (getting in and out of a bed or chair)
- Continence

This isn't medical care in the traditional sense. It's personal care. And it can be provided in a variety of settings:

- At home (with a home health aide)
- In assisted living facilities
- In adult day care centers
- In skilled nursing facilities (nursing homes)

Why It Matters for Pharmacists

You're a high-income earner with a lot of responsibility. You've worked hard to build your savings and retirement plan. But the risk of needing long-term care could threaten everything you've built.

Here's what the numbers say:

- Nearly 70% of people over age 65 will need some form of long-term care during their lifetime.
- The average annual cost of a private room in a nursing home is over $100,000.
- Medicare doesn't cover long-term care beyond short stays in a nursing facility after hospitalization.
- Medicaid covers long-term care only after you spend down most of your assets.

In other words: if you don't have a plan, the cost of care could wipe you out financially—or put enormous pressure on your spouse or children.

What LTC Insurance Covers (and Doesn't)

LTC insurance policies typically cover:

- In-home care services
- Assisted living facilities

- Skilled nursing care
- Memory care units
- Adult day care
- Respite care for caregivers

But they don't cover:

- Care provided by a family member without formal training
- Services not included in the policy's terms
- Medical procedures or acute care (those are for health insurance)

Most policies pay a daily or monthly benefit once you're unable to perform 2 out of 6 ADLs or suffer from severe cognitive impairment. There is usually a waiting (elimination) period before benefits kick in—often 30, 60, or 90 days.

When to Think About Buying LTC Insurance

Here's the tricky part: the best time to buy long-term care insurance is before you think you'll need it.

Why? Because the younger and healthier you are, the cheaper the premiums. Once you have a chronic condition or get older, your chances of being denied coverage increase significantly.

The sweet spot for evaluating long-term care insurance tends to be your mid-to-late 40s through early 60s.

A general rule of thumb:

- Under 40: probably too early unless you have a family history or specific concern.
- 45–55: prime time to consider it.
- 60+: more expensive, but still possible (if healthy).

How to Evaluate Whether You Need It

Not everyone needs LTC insurance. The question is: what are you trying to protect?

If you've built enough assets to self-insure—meaning you could pay $100K per year out of pocket for several years without endangering your spouse's financial future—you may not need a policy.

But if your assets are in that in-between zone where long-term care could severely erode your retirement security, then insurance becomes a powerful tool for:

- Protecting your savings
- Relieving family from caregiver stress
- Ensuring access to quality care
- Preserving your dignity

Key Terms You Need to Know

1. Elimination Period
2. This is like a deductible measured in time. It's the waiting period between when you become eligible for benefits and when the insurer starts paying. Common options: 30, 60, or 90 days.
3. Daily/Monthly Benefit Amount
4. The maximum amount the policy will pay per day or month for care. Make sure it matches costs in your area.
5. Benefit Period
6. How long the policy will pay for care. Options range from 2 years to lifetime coverage.
7. Inflation Protection
8. A must-have for younger buyers. This adjusts your benefit amount over time to keep up with rising care costs.
9. Partnership Policies
10. Some states offer partnership programs that allow you to protect more of your assets if you need to qualify for Medicaid after using your LTC benefits.

Alternatives to Traditional LTC Insurance

Because traditional LTC insurance premiums have risen sharply over the years, newer options have emerged:

1. Hybrid Policies (Life + LTC)
2. These combine permanent life insurance with a long-term care rider. If you don't use the LTC benefits, your heirs get the death benefit.
3. Annuities with LTC Benefits
4. Certain annuities can be structured to pay for long-term care needs.
5. Health Savings Accounts (HSAs)
6. You can use HSA funds tax-free to pay for LTC insurance premiums (within IRS limits).
7. Self-Insurance
8. If your net worth is high enough, you can create your own LTC reserve through investments or a dedicated savings account.

How LTC Insurance Fits Into Your Broader Financial Plan

Here's the thing: LTC insurance isn't just about coverage. It's about strategy. It's about:

- Protecting your 401(k) and IRA from being drained by healthcare expenses
- Giving your spouse the ability to live comfortably even if you need care
- Ensuring you get a choice in the type and quality of care you receive
- Keeping your kids out of the caregiving crosshairs

A good financial plan doesn't just ask, "How much will I need to retire?" It also asks, "What could blow this plan up?" Long-term care is one of those risks. And having a plan—insurance or not—is what puts you back in control.

Real-Life Scenario

Imagine you're 58. You're healthy, married, and have $1.2 million saved for retirement. You plan to retire at 65.

Now imagine you develop Parkinson's disease at 72. Your care needs grow over time. Your spouse tries to keep up but becomes exhausted. Eventually, you need professional care at home.

If that care costs $6,000 per month, that's $72,000 per year—every year—until death.

How long would your savings last? Would your spouse still be able to retire? Travel? Handle their own future healthcare costs?

That's the reality LTC planning prepares you for. Not because it's fun. But because it's possible.

Common Myths That Keep People From Buying

Myth 1: Medicare Will Cover It

Truth: Medicare covers only short-term skilled care, not long-term custodial care.

Myth 2: My Kids Will Take Care of Me

Truth: Maybe. But caregiving is emotionally, physically, and financially demanding. Many adult children aren't equipped—or available.

Myth 3: It's Too Expensive

Truth: LTC policies aren't cheap, but neither is $100K+ per year for care. Options exist for partial coverage.

Myth 4: I'll Just Use My Savings

Truth: You might. But ask yourself: what if you need care for 8 years? What if your spouse needs it too?

Take Action: How to Start Planning Today

1. Run the Numbers
2. Use online calculators to estimate your LTC costs in your state.
3. Talk to an Advisor
4. A fee-only financial planner can help assess whether LTC insurance makes sense for you.
5. Research Policies
6. Compare quotes. Look at financial strength ratings. Ask about premium increases.
7. Don't Wait for the Perfect Policy

8. Some coverage is better than none. Start with what you can afford.
9. Loop in Your Family
10. Let your spouse or adult children know your plans. It will give them peace of mind too.

A Final Word

Thinking about needing care one day isn't easy. But neither is going broke in your 80s, or watching your spouse or kids burn out trying to care for you.

Long-term care insurance isn't a magic solution. But it's a tool. One that, when used wisely, can preserve your savings, protect your family, and give you the dignity you deserve.

This isn't just about money. It's about legacy. It's about choice. It's about peace of mind.

And that's worth planning for.

So tonight, make one money move. Pull up a long-term care cost estimator. Block time to talk to your financial advisor. Ask your HR rep about group LTC options.

Because future you is counting on present you.

And future you deserves peace.

Chapter 45: Asset Protection – Divorce, Lawsuits, and Professional Risks

Let's start with the uncomfortable truth: your income and assets are exposed to more risk than you think.

You've spent years earning a doctorate. You work long shifts. You make solid money. And maybe you've even started to build some real wealth. But the moment you have something to lose, the world starts to notice.

That could mean a contentious divorce.

A surprise lawsuit.

A medical error you never saw coming.

Or a financial predator who sees you as a walking ATM with a license.

This chapter isn't about paranoia. It's about protection. It's about waking up to the fact that building wealth is only one part of the game. Keeping it? That's the other.

As a pharmacist, you are in a unique position. You earn a high income. You often work in high-liability environments. You may be responsible for supervising technicians, handling controlled substances, and managing medication errors. And if you have outside assets—a home, brokerage accounts, a business, or rental property—those could all be exposed in the event of a judgment against you.

The good news? You don't have to be a target. But you do have to be intentional.

Let's walk through how.

Start With the Basics: Know What You Own

Before we dive into asset protection strategies, you need to do something most people avoid: a full financial inventory.

- What's in your bank accounts?
- How much equity do you have in your home?
- Do you own investment properties?
- Do you have a taxable brokerage account?
- Is your 401(k) or IRA fully protected?
- Do you have an LLC for any business or consulting work?

Knowing what you own helps you know what needs protection.

Risk #1: Divorce – Protecting Yourself and Your Future

Let's be real: nobody goes into marriage planning for divorce. But as any pharmacist who's been through one will tell you, the financial fallout is real.

If you're not married yet:

- Consider a prenuptial agreement. It's not unromantic. It's responsible.
- Understand what counts as marital vs. separate property in your state.
- Be honest about debt, student loans, and income before tying the knot.

If you are already married:

- Make sure both partners understand the financial picture.
- Keep good records of what you brought into the marriage.
- Think about estate planning. Who gets what if something happens to you?

If you are divorced or going through one:

- Update beneficiaries on life insurance and retirement accounts.
- Close joint accounts.

- Talk to a CPA about tax implications of alimony or asset transfers.
- Don't skip therapy. Divorce is as emotional as it is financial.

Risk #2: Lawsuits – How to Make Yourself a Smaller Target

America is litigious. And high-income professionals are easy targets. Here's how to legally make yourself less attractive to someone looking to sue:

1. Max Out Legal Protections

- Retirement accounts like 401(k)s and IRAs are often protected from creditors.
- Homestead exemptions in some states protect your primary residence.

1. Use Legal Entities Wisely

- If you do consulting or own rental property, don't keep it in your personal name. Use an LLC.
- Separate business and personal finances.
- Keep good records and insurance.

1. Get Adequate Insurance

- Umbrella insurance: this is a must. It gives you extra liability coverage above and beyond your home and auto policies.
- Malpractice insurance: even if your employer provides it, understand what's covered.
- Renter or landlord insurance if you own property.

1. Titling Matters

- In some states, assets titled as "tenants by the entirety" between spouses may be protected from the other spouse's creditors.

1. Avoid Commingling

- Keep business and personal accounts separate.
- Don't pay personal expenses from your LLC account or vice versa.

Risk #3: Professional Risks – What If You're Named in a Claim?

Whether you work retail, hospital, or independent pharmacy, mistakes can happen.

- Know your malpractice insurance coverage.
- Ask if your employer's policy includes tail coverage.
- If you consult independently or do MTM on the side, get your own policy.
- Document everything. If it's not written down, it didn't happen.

Your reputation and license are invaluable. Protect them the same way you would your money.

Estate Planning As a Shield

Estate planning isn't just for the ultra-wealthy. It's for anyone who wants control over what happens to their assets—and their family—if something happens to them.

- A will dictates who gets what.
- A trust can keep assets out of probate and offer some creditor protection.
- Powers of attorney and healthcare directives let others act on your behalf if you're incapacitated.
- Life insurance can provide liquidity for taxes, debt, or family needs.

Every pharmacist should have an estate plan. Period.

When to Talk to a Pro

Asset protection isn't one-size-fits-all. Depending on your net worth, business structure, family situation, and state laws, you may need a:

- Financial planner
- Estate planning attorney
- Asset protection attorney
- CPA or tax strategist
- Insurance broker who understands high-income professionals

The best time to do this? Before you need it.

Real-Life Scenario: The Pharmacist Landlord

Let's say you own a duplex you rent to tenants. A kid falls off the porch and breaks a leg. The parents sue you for $250,000. If that property is in your personal name, your home, your checking account, your brokerage account—all could be on the line. If that property is in an LLC, the lawsuit is limited to the LLC's assets. Add umbrella insurance on top of that, and you're even better protected.

This is how wealth survives unexpected storms.

Rules of Thumb

- Get umbrella insurance once your net worth exceeds $250K.
- Use LLCs for rental properties or consulting work.
- Max out employer retirement plans—protected and tax-advantaged.
- Revisit your estate plan every 3-5 years or after major life events.
- Don't co-sign loans you can't afford to repay yourself.

Final Encouragement

You don't have to live in fear. But you do have to live with foresight.

You worked too hard for your income, your family, and your future to leave it all exposed. Start where you are. Layer in protection over time. And remember: offense builds wealth, but defense keeps it.

Make one protection move this week. Just one.

Call your insurance agent. Book a consult with an estate attorney. Open a file labeled "Asset Protection Plan."

Then do another next week. And the week after that.

Your financial fortress won't be built overnight.

But brick by brick, it will be unshakable.

Closing Chapter 46: The Financially Free Pharmacist

Let's take a breath.

You've made it to the end of this book—but not the end of your journey. In fact, this is where the real work begins. The good kind of work. The kind that creates freedom, not more burden. The kind that lifts your head, not lowers your shoulders. The kind that gives you options.

You didn't become a pharmacist to feel exhausted, boxed in, or forever behind financially. You did it because you wanted to help. To serve. To heal. But somewhere along the way, the financial system was never explained to you. Debt piled up. Paychecks got stretched thin. You made good money but never felt rich. You were respected, but quietly overwhelmed.

That ends now.

This book was never about turning you into a spreadsheet-obsessed, budget-worshiping, investment-slinging machine. It was about awakening your power. Putting language to the unease you may have felt for years. Giving you a roadmap to build something better—not just in your finances, but in your life.

Let's recap the mindset you need to carry with you:

- You are not behind. You are beginning, boldly, on your terms.
- You are not defined by your debt. You are defined by what you do next.
- You are not just a pharmacist. You are a whole, complex, evolving person who deserves options, rest, and joy.

The chapters you just read were full of strategies. Budgeting tips. Credit tips. Investment breakdowns. Debt payoff plans. Insurance guides. Career pivots. But underneath every strategy was a message: you're in control. Even when it feels like you're not.

The world will tell you that financial success means owning a big house, driving a luxury car, and maxing out your 401(k). But I want to give you a better definition:

Financial success is the ability to make decisions based on joy, not fear.

Financial success is being able to take a break without going broke.

Financial success is knowing your money works as hard for you as you work for it.

Financial success is sleep. Peace. Sanity.

As you leave this book, here are 7 reminders to carry into your next season:

1. Don't try to fix everything in one weekend. Pick one move. Make it. Then another.
2. Money is emotional. That doesn't make you weak. That makes you human.
3. You are allowed to want nice things. Just don't let them own you.
4. Every "yes" you give someone else is a "no" to yourself. Choose wisely.
5. Wealth is built with boring decisions done consistently.
6. A well-rested pharmacist is a dangerous thing. Rest like your future depends on it.
7. You are not alone. Ask for help. Talk to a pro. Build your team.

Your life is more than pharmacy. And your finances are more than formulas. They are the fuel for the legacy you want to leave.

So go. Dream bigger. Spend with intention. Save with purpose. Invest with clarity. And build a life where you don't just survive—you thrive.

You deserve nothing less.

Make one money move before bed tonight.

Then do another next week.

Then another after that.

Your future self—the one who travels freely, retires early, gives generously, and lives joyfully—is waiting.

Let's go meet them.

Disclaimer and Educational Purpose

This book, *Financial Literacy For Pharmacists,* was written with the intention to educate, empower, and encourage pharmacists—from new graduates to seasoned professionals—to take control of their financial lives with clarity and confidence. The information shared throughout these pages reflects the author's personal experiences, professional knowledge, and insights gathered from over two decades in financial services, healthcare planning, and financial literacy education.

That said, it is critical to understand:

This publication is not a substitute for personalized legal, financial, tax, accounting, or investment advice. It is a general educational resource and should not be relied upon in place of professional guidance from licensed experts.

Educational Purpose Only

The content in this book is presented for general educational purposes. Its goal is to provide pharmacists with foundational financial concepts, frameworks for smarter decision-making, and awareness of the challenges and opportunities unique to the pharmacy profession—from student loans and budgeting to investing, insurance, and retirement.

It is not personalized advice. It is not a roadmap tailored to your unique situation. Financial literacy is powerful, but applying that knowledge requires context—your income, your goals, your family, your timeline, your risk tolerance.

What works for one pharmacist might not be right—or even safe—for another.

Before making financial decisions—especially those involving large purchases, investment strategies, legal documents, or business ventures—it is strongly recommended that you consult with a licensed professional: a financial advisor, tax preparer, accountant, or attorney.

No Legal Advice

This book does not provide legal advice and is not intended to serve as a replacement for the insight of an attorney. Whether you're considering forming a business entity for a side hustle, reviewing a pharmacy employment contract, planning your estate, or navigating liability coverage—it is critical that you speak with a qualified legal professional familiar with your specific circumstances and state regulations.

No Financial or Investment Advice

Although this book covers vital financial topics like saving, budgeting, investing, retirement planning, and insurance, it does so from an educational and general perspective. It is not personalized financial advice, and it does not recommend specific investments or products.

You should never take financial action based solely on the content of this book. Speak with a Certified Financial Planner™, licensed investment advisor, or fiduciary professional before committing to any financial plan, especially when it comes to complex areas like portfolio management, tax strategies, or retirement distributions.

Every financial decision should consider your personal timeline, tax bracket, career trajectory, family structure, and goals.

No Accounting or Tax Advice

This book is not written by a CPA or tax attorney. It does not provide formal tax advice. While we discuss high-level topics like student loan interest deductions, business write-offs, retirement contribution limits, and tax-favored investment accounts (such as HSAs, IRAs, and 401(k)s), all content is based on public information and educational interpretation—not formal tax counsel.

Tax law changes frequently, and your filing status, income, location, and business activity all affect how you should file and plan. If you're earning money through side work, owning a business, taking advantage of pre-tax benefits, or navigating multi-state tax concerns, seek guidance from a licensed tax advisor or enrolled agent.

No Guarantees or Promises

Reading this book does not guarantee wealth, financial security, or career satisfaction. Financial success depends on many variables—your habits, income, expenses, timing, decision-making, investment performance, and sometimes just plain luck.

This book is not offering financial certainty. It's offering structure, mindset, and awareness. Any case studies, scenarios, or success stories mentioned are for illustration only.

Limitation of Liability

By reading this book, you agree that the author, Pat Brown, MBA, and all affiliated brands and educational platforms (including but not limited to FinancialLiteracyForPharmacists.com, FinancialLiteracyForDoctors.com, and related sites) are not liable for the results of any financial, legal, or tax decisions you make based on the content in these pages.

Neither the author nor any affiliate mentioned shall be held responsible for losses, penalties, liabilities, or adverse outcomes incurred as a result of actions taken from this book's content.

Encouragement to Seek Professional Guidance

One of the core messages of this book is simple: You deserve a strong financial foundation—and you don't have to build it alone.

If you do not currently have a trusted financial advisor, estate planning attorney, insurance professional, or CPA in your corner, start seeking one out. Ask questions. Get referrals. Interview professionals like you would a job candidate. The sooner you build a team, the sooner you can shift from financial reaction to strategic planning.

Pharmacists are highly skilled, highly educated, and deeply trusted by their communities. You deserve financial advice that matches the standard of excellence you bring to your patients and profession.

This book is here to complement—not replace—that professional support. Use it to guide your questions, clarify your options, and give you the confidence to act with purpose.

Because when you know better, you plan better. And when you plan better, you build a financial life that reflects your values, your goals, and your worth.

Annual Financial Planning Calendar for Pharmacists

A Month-by-Month Guide to Staying Ahead Financially

This calendar isn't just about taxes—it's about staying proactive, organized, and strategic. Whether you're a newly licensed pharmacist navigating your first paycheck, a mid-career professional juggling a family and retirement goals, or an entrepreneur with a side business, timing your financial moves throughout the year can have a major impact.

Here's your month-by-month guide to keep your money working smarter all year long.

January

New Tax Year Begins

- Start tracking income, expenses, and receipts for the new year.
- Set up or refresh a budget for fixed costs, loan payments, savings goals, and lifestyle categories.
- Review your paycheck withholding and adjust your W-4 if your life circumstances have changed (marriage, kids, new job, etc.).
- Rule of Thumb: Save 25%–30% of any 1099/self-employed income for taxes.

Jan 15 – 4th Quarter Estimated Tax Payment Due

- If you earned freelance, PRN, or consulting income last year and didn't withhold taxes, this payment is due now.

- Form to Know: IRS Form 1040-ES

Jan 31 – Deadline for Receiving Tax Documents

- Expect to receive W-2s, 1099s (freelance/contract work), 1098-E (student loan interest), and investment statements.
- Tip: Store all documents in a digital folder labeled "2024 Taxes – Pharmacy"

February

Organize Tax Documents

- Start gathering tax documents, receipts, and reports.
- If you did PRN work, telehealth consulting, or owned rental property, track expenses and income carefully.
- Know Your Forms:
- Schedule C – Self-employment income
- Schedule E – Rental income
- Schedule SE – Self-employment tax

March

March 15 – Business Tax Filing Deadline for S-Corps or Partnerships

- If you've formed a PLLC, LLC, or S-Corp for consulting, speaking, or side income, this is your tax deadline.
- Form to Know: Form 1120S

April

April 15 – Federal Tax Day

- File your tax return.
- Make 1st quarter estimated tax payment for this year.
- Last chance to contribute to a Traditional IRA, Roth IRA, or HSA for

the previous year.

- Forms to Know:
- Form 1040 – Income Tax Return
- Form 4868 – To file an extension

Tax Tip: File even if you can't pay yet. The penalty for not filing is worse than the penalty for not paying.

May

Mid-Year Financial Checkup

- Review budget, debt repayment, and retirement contributions.
- Adjust spending or savings habits based on year-to-date performance.
- Book a meeting with your advisor to check progress on goals.

June

June 15 – 2nd Quarter Estimated Tax Payment Due

- This applies if you're earning freelance income or running a business on the side.
- Reassess how much you're withholding or saving for taxes.

July

Mid-Year Review and Reset

- Are you on pace to hit your savings goals for Roth IRA, HSA, or 401(k)?
- Review insurance coverage (disability, health, malpractice, umbrella).
- Update your estate plan or beneficiary designations if life circumstances have changed.

August

Loan Review and Credit Refresh

- Review student loan balances and repayment plans.

- Consider refinancing if it makes sense.
- Pull your free credit report at AnnualCreditReport.com.

September

September 15 – 3rd Quarter Estimated Tax Payment Due

- If you have consulting or business income, don't miss this deadline.
- Prep early for year-end deductions and income adjustments.

October

October 1 – FAFSA Opens (for those with college-age kids)

- If you're supporting dependents through college, this impacts your financial aid planning.
- Check deadlines and submit early.

October 15 – Extended Tax Return Deadline

- If you filed for an extension in April, this is your final deadline to submit your return.

November

Year-End Planning Season Begins

- Meet with your CPA or advisor to review:
- Retirement contributions
- Business deductions
- Charitable giving strategies
- Income smoothing or Roth conversion opportunities

Tip: Maximize Section 179 deductions if you've made business-related purchases.

December

December 31 – Final Day for Many Tax Moves

- Make final contributions to SEP IRA or Solo 401(k) if self-employed.
- Book any professional development, coaching, marketing, or business travel to count this year.
- Consider tax-loss harvesting in brokerage accounts.

Tax Tip: Meet the IRS safe harbor rule by paying at least 100% of last year's tax liability (or 110% if your AGI was over $150,000) to avoid penalties.

Bonus: Financial Best Practices for Pharmacists

- **Always Save 25%–30% of Contract/Side Hustle Income for Taxes**
- **Keep Business & Personal Accounts Separate**
- **Track All Expenses and Miles if You're Self-Employed**
- **Use Free Tools:** Google Sheets, QuickBooks, MileIQ, or Keeper Tax
- **Review Benefits Annually:** Maximize 401(k), HSA, FSA, and insurance options during open enrollment
- **Build Your Team:** Financial advisor, CPA, attorney, and insurance agent

Definitions and Questions!

Financial Terms

Asset – Anything you own that has value (cash, stocks, property).

Liability – Money you owe (debts, loans).

Net Worth – What you own (assets) minus what you owe (liabilities).

Budget – A plan for how you spend and save your money.

Emergency Fund – Money set aside for unexpected expenses.

Compound Interest – Earning interest on both the money you invest and the interest it earns over time.

Diversification – Spreading your money across different investments to reduce risk.

Roth IRA – A retirement account where your money grows tax-free.

Brokerage Account – An account that lets you buy and sell investments.

ETF (Exchange-Traded Fund) – A type of investment that holds many stocks or bonds in one package.

Inflation – The rising cost of goods and services over time.

Credit Score – A number that shows how trustworthy you are with credit.

Interest Rate – The cost of borrowing money, or what you earn on savings.

Risk Tolerance – How comfortable you are with investment ups and downs.

Stock – A share of ownership in a company.

Bond – A loan you give to a company or government that pays you back with interest.

Capital Gain – Profit made from selling an investment for more than you paid.

Liability Insurance – Insurance that protects you if you're legally responsible for damage or injury.

Term Life Insurance – Life insurance that covers you for a specific time period.

Financial Literacy – Understanding how money works so you can make smart decisions.

Accounting Terms

Income – Money you earn from work, business, or investments.

Expenses – Money you spend on living or business costs.

Profit – What's left after you subtract expenses from income.

Loss – When expenses are more than income.

Cash Flow – Money moving in and out of your account.

Invoice – A bill you send when someone owes you for a product or service.

Receipts – Proof of purchases or expenses.

Write-Off – An expense you subtract from your income to lower your taxes.

Deduction – A legal reduction in taxable income.

Depreciation – The decrease in value of something you own over time.

Revenue – Total money made before subtracting expenses.

Net Income – What you keep after taxes and expenses.

Gross Income – Total money earned before expenses or taxes.

Audit – A review of your financial records, usually by the IRS.

Chart of Accounts – A system for organizing financial transactions.

Bookkeeping – Keeping track of income and expenses.

Taxable Income – The income you pay taxes on after deductions.

Form 1099 – IRS form that reports income from freelance or contract work.

Form W-9 – The form clients may ask you to fill out before paying you.

Schedule C – Tax form used to report business income and expenses.

Questions to Ask a Financial Advisor

Do you work with pharmacists or other healthcare professionals?

Are you a fiduciary, and how do you get paid?

Can you help with both short-term budgeting and long-term retirement planning?

How do you help clients with tax planning, insurance, and investing?

What's your overall philosophy on helping people build wealth?

Questions to Ask a CPA (Certified Public Accountant)

Do you have experience with healthcare professionals or small business owners?

Can you help me organize and track business-related expenses?

Do you offer tax planning throughout the year, not just during filing season?

What documentation should I keep to prepare for tax time or an audit?

Do you represent clients during audits or disputes with the IRS?

Questions to Ask an Attorney

Do you review contracts and business agreements for healthcare professionals?

Can you explain legal risks in simple terms before I sign anything?

Can you help me set up an LLC or business structure for consulting or side income?

Do I need a will or estate plan—and can you help with that?

What legal protections should I have if I create content, courses, or media?

Questions to Ask Potential Business Partners

What are your long-term goals for this project or company?

What do you expect from me, and what are you contributing?

How will we handle disagreements or business challenges?

Are you financially committed to this venture, and prepared for ups and downs?

How will we divide profits, and what happens if one of us wants out?

Bonus: Pharmacist-Specific Terms to Know

Formulary – A list of medications covered by a particular insurance plan.

PBM (Pharmacy Benefit Manager) – A third-party administrator of prescription drug programs.

MTM (Medication Therapy Management) – A service that helps patients get the best results from medications.

Preceptor – A licensed pharmacist who mentors and trains pharmacy students.

White Coat Investor – A term often used to refer to high-earning professionals navigating finance.

Work-Life Balance – The healthy boundary between professional and personal life.

Burnout – Emotional and physical exhaustion caused by prolonged stress—often a risk in healthcare.

CE (Continuing Education) – Required courses to maintain pharmacy licensure.

PRN Work – As-needed pharmacy shifts, often at higher hourly pay.

Residency – Postgraduate training for pharmacists, usually 1–2 years.

Credentialing – The process of verifying qualifications to practice in a specific setting.

Scope of Practice – The legal boundaries of what you can do as a pharmacist.

Pre-Tax Benefit – Employer-provided savings options like FSA or HSA that reduce taxable income.

Out-of-Pocket Maximum – The most you'll pay in a year before insurance covers 100%.

Vesting Schedule – The timeline for when employer retirement contributions become yours to keep.

White Coat Syndrome – A humorous or ironic phrase, but also a real condition involving increased blood pressure during clinical visits—used here to relate to financial "anxiety."

Final Word

This book exists because financial education is a powerful tool. It can open doors, protect your legacy, and give you the confidence to take control of your future. But just like in pharmacy—and in life—long-term success depends on strategy, discipline, planning, and knowing when to bring in the right experts.

Use this book as a guide, not a rule book. Let it inspire action—but don't let it replace the value of professional advice. Be curious. Stay informed. Ask questions before making important decisions.

Need Help? Start Here.

Connect with trusted professionals who understand the financial challenges pharmacists face.

Contact:

Pat Brown, MBA

Financial literacy advocate and advisor to healthcare professionals nationwide

info@financialliteracyforpharmacists.com

www.financialliteracyforpharmacists.com

Subscribe to our newsletter for tools, insights, and pharmacist-specific money tips straight to your inbox.

Final Word: Use This. Don't Shelf It.

These tools weren't meant to gather dust. They were meant to help you make confident, informed decisions. Revisit this book. Share it with colleagues. Annotate it, highlight it, personalize it. Your future self—the one who's stress-free, debt-free, and on a path toward financial peace—will thank you.

30 Questions to Ask a Financial Advisor or CPA as a Pharmacist

Choosing the right financial professionals can make a massive difference in your financial success. Whether you're working with a financial advisor, a CPA, or both, asking the right questions up front can help you avoid costly mistakes and build a stronger plan. Below are 30 questions to help you vet the professionals who may guide your financial life.

Financial Advisor Questions – General Fit and Philosophy

1. Are you a fiduciary 100% of the time—and can you put that in writing?
2. How do you get paid—fee-only, commission-based, or fee-based?
3. Do you work with healthcare professionals or pharmacists regularly?
4. What licenses and certifications do you hold (e.g., CFP®, CFA, MBA, ChFC)?
5. What's your investment philosophy?
6. How do you approach risk management for someone in their 30s or 40s?
7. How will you customize a financial plan based on my goals and pharmacist career path?
8. What types of clients do you typically serve—individuals, couples, business owners?
9. What's your minimum asset requirement, if any?
10. Can you work with clients virtually, or are in-person meetings required?

Financial Advisor Questions – Services and Support

1. What services are included beyond investment management?
2. Will you help me with insurance, tax strategy, estate planning, and college planning?
3. How often do we meet to review or update my plan?
4. What software or tools do you use to help me track progress?
5. Can you review and help me optimize my workplace benefits and 401(k)?
6. Do you offer budgeting and cash flow analysis?
7. Will you help me understand my student loan options and repayment plans?
8. Do you coordinate with my CPA or attorney?
9. How do you evaluate success or progress toward my goals?
10. What happens if I decide to stop working with you—are there penalties or transfer fees?

CPA or Tax Advisor Questions – Tax Planning and Filing

1. Do you have experience working with pharmacists or healthcare professionals?
2. Can you help with both tax preparation and proactive tax planning?
3. How are your fees structured—hourly, flat rate, or ongoing retainer?
4. How do you minimize taxes across W-2, 1099, and investment income?
5. Will you help with estimated quarterly taxes if I have a side hustle or consulting income?
6. Can you advise on tax-efficient charitable giving strategies or donor-advised funds?
7. Do you offer audit support or IRS representation if needed?
8. Can you help with Roth conversions, HSA strategies, and retirement account taxes?
9. Do you assist with tax-efficient investing alongside my financial advisor?
10. How do you stay current on tax law changes relevant to high-income

professionals?

Use these questions to vet professionals before hiring them—and don't be afraid to ask follow-ups. The right advisor or CPA will welcome your questions. After all, it's your money, your future, and your peace of mind on the line.

Made in United States
Orlando, FL
04 November 2026

90201059R00223